HIGHWAYS AND BYWAYS
DISCOVERING CATHOLIC ENGLAND

HIGHWAYS AND BYWAYS

Discovering Catholic England

Nicholas Schofield

GRACEWING

First published in England in 2023
by
Gracewing
2 Southern Avenue
Leominster
Herefordshire HR6 0QF
United Kingdom
www.gracewing.co.uk

All rights reserved.
No part of this publication may be reproduced, stored in a retrieval system, or transmitted in any form or by any means, electronic, mechanical, photocopying, recording or otherwise, without the written permission of the publisher.

The rights of the editor and contributors to be identified as the authors of this work have been asserted in accordance with the Copyright, Designs and Patents Act 1988.

Compilation and editorial material
© 2023 Nicholas Schofield

ISBN 978 085244 720 8

Front cover:
The Slipper Chapel, Walsingham
© Catholic Bishops' Conference of England and Wales
(photograph by Alex Ramsay)

Cover design by Bernardita Peña Hurtado

Typeset by Word and Page, Chester, UK

CONTENTS

The South-West

Tonic for the Soul (Buckfast, Devon)	2
A Chalk Giant (Cerne Abbas, Dorset)	5
Saintly Bishops (Exeter, Devon)	7
The Holy Thorn (Glastonbury, Somerset)	9
Crossing the Tamar: Cornwall and its Saints (Launceston, Cornwall)	11
St Michael's Mount (Mount Bay, Cornwall)	16
A Monastery in the Cotswolds (Prinknash. Gloucestershire)	19
St Levan (St Levan, Cornwall)	22
A Cornish Fishing Village and its Saint (St Mawes, Cornwall)	25
'Like the sun in full orb' (Salisbury, Wiltshire)	27
Catholic Families: The Arundells of Wardour (Tisbury, Wiltshire)	30
In Search of the Bensons (Truro, Cornwall)	33
Dancing Nuns (Wimborne Minster, Dorset)	36

The South-East

The Martyred Earl (Arundel, West Sussex)	40
Home of the Scapular (Aylesford, Kent)	43
A Papal Invasion of England? (Battle, East Sussex)	45
The Holy Rood (Boxley, Kent)	48
In Search of Mrs Fitzherbert (Brighton, West Sussex)	51
A Pilgrimage to Canterbury (Canterbury, Kent)	55
The Devils of Denham (Denham, Buckinghamshire)	61
Saints of the White Cliffs (Dover, Kent)	64
Catholic Families: The Biddulphs (Duncton, West Sussex)	66
Manning Country (East Lavington, West Sussex)	69
An Unlucky King (Eton, Berkshire)	74
'Irreclaimedly French' (Farnborough, Hampshire)	77
Royal Saints (Folkestone, Lyminge and Minster, Kent)	80
Hampshire's Village of Saints (Froyle, Hampshire)	82
Hever's Catholic Past (Hever, Kent)	84
The Head of St Valentine (Hyde Abbey, Hampshire)	87
Two Kentish Holy Wells (Kemsing and Otford, Kent)	90
A Family Pew (Langley Marish, Berkshire)	92
On Mulberry Trees (Loseley Park, Surrey)	95
The 'Jack-in-the-Box' Priest (North Marston, Buckinghamshire)	97
A Buckinghamshire Doom (Penn, Buckinghamshire)	99

St Augustine and the Conversion of England (Ramsgate, Kent)	102
Rochester and St William (Rochester, Kent)	105
The Churches of Romney Marsh (Romney Marsh, Kent)	107
The Protomartyr of his Companions (St Albans, Hertfordshire)	109
Calleva Atrebatum (Silchester, Hampshire)	112
The Boy with the Wooden Cart (Steyning, West Sussex)	114
The Abbey in the Water Meadow (Waverley, Surrey)	117
'The Little Cottage in the Forest' (West Grinstead, West Sussex)	120
The Chapel on the Heath (Weybridge, Surrey)	122
The Treasures of St George's Chapel—and an Apostate Dean (Windsor, Berkshire)	124

London and Middlesex

Entrée: The Catholic Underground	128

CENTRAL LONDON

A Silent Corner of the City (Charterhouse)	131
Secrets of Bucklersbury (Mithraeum)	134
London's Most-Hallowed Space? (St Giles-in-the-Fields)	137
An Apostle of the Sacred Heart (St James's Palace)	140
A Catholic Burial Ground (St Pancras)	144
On the Road to Canterbury (St Thomas à Waterings)	147
Before Wren (St Paul's)	149
Locked in the Tower! (Tower of London)	152
To Tyburn (Tyburn)	156
At the Confessor's Shrine (Westminster Abbey)	159
'Cardinal Vaughan's Railway Station' (Westminster Cathedral)	162

MIDDLESEX

Hampton Court (Hampton)	165
A Martyr's Secret Garden (Harefield)	168
Parish Priest and Martyr (Isleworth)	172
Syon Abbey (Syon Park)	174
Conversation with a Gravedigger (Uxbridge)	177
A Suburban Tudor Mansion (West Drayton)	180
London's Black Madonna (Willesden)	184

The East of England

The Jesuits of Anmer Hall (Anmer, Norfolk)	188
Buckden Towers (Buckden, Cambridgeshire)	192
A Priory Come Back to Life (Clare, Suffolk)	195
The Holy Land of the English (Ely, Cambridgeshire, and the Fens)	198
A Flitch of Bacon (Great Dunmow, Essex)	201
Catholic Families: The Petres (Ingatestone, Essex)	204
Our Lady of Ipswich—and Nettuno (Ipswich, Suffolk)	207

England's Nazareth (Little Walsingham, Norfolk)	209
The Glory of Long Melford (Long Melford, Suffolk)	213
Catholic Families: The Bedingfields (Oxburgh, Norfolk)	216
Between Church and Sea (Southend-on-Sea, Essex)	219
Sutton Hoo (Sutton Hoo, Suffolk)	221
Waltham and its Holy Cross (Waltham, Essex)	224

The Midlands

Catholic Families: The Ferrers (Baddesley Clinton, Warwickshire)	228
St Werburgh and her Goose (Chester, Cheshire)	231
Lully, lulla (Coventry, Warwickshire)	233
Recusant Cardigans (Deene Park, Northamptonshire)	235
St Birinus (Dorchester-on-Thames, Oxfordshire)	238
Evesham and its Abbey (Evesham, Worcestershire)	241
The End of the Queen of Scots (Fotheringhay, Northamptonshire)	243
A Leicestershire Catholic Utopia (Grace Dieu and Mount St Bernards, Leicestershire)	246
The Romance of Kenilworth (Kenilworth, Warwickshire)	249
In Newman's Footsteps (Littlemore, Oxfordshire)	251
England's First Shrine to the Sacred Heart (Maryvale, Birmingham)	255
An Afternoon at the Manor (Milton, Oxfordshire)	257
St Gilbert of Sempringham (Sempringham, Lincolnshire)	260
The Churches of Shrewsbury (Shrewsbury, Shropshire)	263
Shakespeare's Guild Chapel (Stratford-upon-Avon, Warwickshire)	266
Waterperry (Waterperry, Oxfordshire)	269
Abbey Ghosts (Woburn Abbey, Bedfordshire)	272

The North

St Cuthbert's Resting Place (Durham, County Durham, and Lindisfarne, Northumberland)	276
Cumbrian Abbeys (Furness and Shap, Cumbria)	279
Catholic Families: The Vavasours (Hazlewood, North Yorkshire)	283
Howden and its Minster (Howden, East Riding of Yorkshire)	285
A Lakeland Jesuit (Kendal, Cumbria)	288
The Saints of Derwentwater (Keswick, Cumbria)	291
Forgotten Lancashire Shrines (Ladyewell, Lancashire)	293
'Bare Ruined Choirs' (Rievaulx, North Yorkshire)	296
Treasures on the Moors (Ushaw, County Durham)	298
The Skull of Wardley Hall (Wardley Hall, Lancashire)	301
St Hilda and her Abbey (Whitby, North Yorkshire)	304
The Many Pearls of York (York, North Yorkshire)	307

Epilogue

Our Final Pilgrimage	311

INTRODUCTION

As I sit writing these words, I can see a set of handsome blue volumes sitting on my bookshelves which I have collected over the years. The gold lettering on the spine always starts with the words 'Highways and Byways in . . '.. Published by Macmillan between 1898 and 1948, each book covers a different county or region, and is more an 'appreciation' than a guide in the strict sense, mixing history and architecture with folklore and topography.

This volume contains a similar collection of highways and byways, focusing on the Catholic heritage of England. Some are well-known highways—Canterbury, for example, the Tower of London, or Walsingham—but there are plenty of byways off the beaten track that, after a little digging, reveal interesting sidelights on our history.

The pieces are mostly based on articles written for my weekly 'Nova et Vetera' column in the *Catholic Times* between 2010 and 2020. They would usually be facilitated by days off and holidays, as well as important anniversaries. This book does not claim to be a comprehensive guide to religious 'sites', more an 'appreciation' and celebration of them, and it is probably best dipped into rather than read from cover to cover. There will, of course, be some similarities between successive tales of dissolution and martyrdom, of foundation and revival, but each place has its own unique colour and its own lessons to teach us. I have unashamedly included venerable traditions and folk memories that may seem of dubious merit – not only because they are interesting in themselves but can often deepen our understanding. Although the focus is largely Catholic, many of the places covered are now in the care of the Church of England and relate to our wider Christian story.

There are, of course, numerous omissions, and every reader will immediately spot some major ones as they scan the table of contents. This is very much a personal selection. I am more than aware, also, that, since I live on the edge of west London, places within a day's drive tend to predominate. Nevertheless, I hope that these reflections encourage the reader to explore the highways and byways in their locality and see how our Faith is embedded in the very soil of this land.

Thanks are due to those who journeyed with me: Mikey Atkins, the late Frances Atkins, the late Fr Jerome Bertram (who encouraged me to publish these columns), Fra' Richard Berkley-Matthews, Fliss,

Grahame and Marcus Davenport, Kevin Flaherty, Christian Holden, Fr Marcus Holden, Dr James Kelly, Peter and Dawn Kent, Judi McGinley, Bill, Maria and Gabriella Michell, Fred and Marion Michell, the late Tess and Harry Montgomery, Bob, Tina, Dan and Jade Nunn, Suzanne von Pflugl, Professor Michael Questier, Susannah Rayner, Dr Samuel Seddon, Joanna Simpson, Fr Paul Smyth, Canon Peter Vellacott, Fr Mark Vickers, Fr Richard Whinder, and Dr Christopher Wright.

I have been accompanied and supported on so many of these journeys—as for much of the last decade—by Angela Atkins. I affectionately dedicate this book to her, in the hope of many more adventures!

Nicholas Schofield

THE SOUTH-WEST

BUCKFAST, DEVON

Tonic for the Soul

'The longer one stays here, the more does the spirit of the moor sink into one's soul, its vastness, and, also, its grim charm. When you are once out upon its bosom you have left all traces of modern England behind you'. Dartmoor is a wild, sometimes desolate place. No wonder Arthur Conan-Doyle used it as a setting for his *Hound of the Baskervilles*. Yet, on its south-eastern edge, is a place of safety and spiritual succour: Buckfast Abbey.

The name means 'stag's fastness', for long before monks settled here deer would come from the moors to drink from the Dart. Appropriately enough, a stag can still be found on the coat of arms. The origins of the first monastery are lost in the mists of time; some have claimed that St Petroc founded a cell here around 550, while written records give 1018 as the date of foundation. The community passed from Savignac to Cistercian Rule; the centuries passed and then, in the poetic language of Dom Ernest Graf, 'were the voices of God's minstrels hushed and the sanctuary lamp quenched in this valley'. Buckfast was dissolved—and it is intriguing that the agent of Thomas Cromwell responsible for this was William Petre, a man of personal Catholic sympathies who later acted as a supporter of the composer William Byrd and whose house at Ingatestone is one of our great recusant centres.

Buckfast passed into secular hands but was eventually put on the market in 1882. An advert was providentially placed in *The Tablet*, as a result of which a purchase was made by a group of French monks, exiled from their abbey of La Pierre-qui-Vire due to the latest anti-clerical laws. The early days were full of hardship; packing-cases were used as tables and chairs, the grounds had to be cultivated, and a temporary church erected. A committee was formed so that the monastery could properly be rebuilt, under the leadership of Lord Clifford of Chudleigh and with the expertise of the architect Frederick Walters (also responsible for the abbey at Ealing). Such designs were assisted by the discovery in the vegetable garden of medieval foundations.

Vocations were also an issue. The monks were largely French, with the exception of one Scotsman and two Germans, from Swabia in the kingdom of Württemberg. Since there were no active monasteries in that region, a recruitment drive was begun with great effect.

Buckfast became a largely German rather than French community, though firmly rooted in its Devon setting. Its first abbot was one of the original German monks, Dom Boniface Natter, blessed on St Matthias' Day 1902—the anniversary of the abbey's surrender to Henry VIII. The preacher referred to this ceremony as a 'landmark in the history of Catholic England and signal evidence of the indestructability of the Catholic Church', despite 'Tudor tyranny, Stuart bigotry, Orange malice... and Hanoverian oppression'. Yes, 'Glastonbury, Fountains, Furness and Rievaulx still lie in desolation, but Buckfast was dead and risen again'.

Natter had previously worked in Rome with the Abbot General and in 1904 was elected as Abbot Visitor, which involved making occasional trips to monastic communities around the world. In June 1906 he set out with his fellow Buckfast monk (and German), Dom Anscar Vonier, to Barcelona, to board the *SS Sirio*. This would take him across the Atlantic, where a visit would be made of the Argentinian community of Niño Dios, the first Benedictine foundation in Hispanic America. Unfortunately, the ship sank after striking rocks off Cape Palos, in sight of the Spanish coast. Both monks prepared for death and helped their fellow passengers as much as they could. Dom Anscar somehow survived: 'as soon as I felt the water, I made an effort to get out, and succeeded, but how I cannot tell. The only thing I remember is that I clutched something, which I determined not to let go'. He described the sea as being 'alive' with bodies: 'wherever I looked, a ghastly sight met my eyes, heads, legs everywhere'. The abbot was last seen clutching a plank and making the sign of the cross. His body was never found. The Brazilian Archbishop of São Paulo also drowned in the disaster.

Dom Anscar was duly elected second abbot of Buckfast. Given his recent trauma, he might have been forgiven for concentrating on the basics of monastic leadership and keeping his head down, but he quickly made a surprise announcement: the abbey church was to be built and, given the limited means at his disposal, it would be completed by the monks themselves. It would be a labour of love that took thirty-two years. The stones were cut and dressed by a team of up to six monks, led by a brother who had studied masonry in France. The work continued through the dark days of the First World War, when the German members of the community were regarded as 'enemy aliens' and could only leave Buckfast with a special licence. Donations were received from various benefactors, including Lady Seaton, last descendant of Sir Francis Drake and owner of Buckland Abbey. She considered her gift as a way of making amends for Buckland's spoliation. Meanwhile, Abbot Vonier combined such all-consuming building works with the writing of erudite theological volumes, which in some cases prefigured the teachings of the Second Vatican Council.

The celebrations surrounding the church's opening in 1922 began with the translation of Our Lady of Buckfast to its new shrine chapel—the fourteenth-century statue had been found hidden in a wall, still with traces of its original paint. The following day, Cardinal Bourne preached on the text, 'Shall these dry bones live?' The church was finally consecrated in 1932 and the tower completed five years later. It seemed, says Dom Ernest Graf, that the 'Second Spring' was passing into a 'Second Summer'.

Buckfast today, like its medieval predecessor, is a spiritual hub for the area, and a popular destination for tourists on their way to the 'English Riviera'. There is plenty to do: eating at San Benedetto's Pizzeria, visiting exhibitions, walking in the grounds, or enjoying the shops. Buckfast is famous for its produce: the tonic wine, which originated from a recipe brought over by the French monks, and the honey made by the Buckfast Bee variety, as developed by Brother Adam Kehrle, perhaps the twentieth century's greatest beekeeper. The church itself has had further additions, including the stunning glass in the Blessed Sacrament. A timeless place on the edge of Dartmoor, and yet contemporary in its outreach and legacy.

CERNE ABBAS, DORSET

A Chalk Giant

Cerne Abbas, located between Dorchester and Sherborne, has been described as England's most desirable village. It has it all—a beautiful location, charming streets, the remains of a once great abbey, plenty of water and, of course, a well-endowed giant carved into the chalk hillside.

The name of the Dorset village calls to mind the great abbey of Cerne. Founded (or possibly re-founded) in 987, this Benedictine house dominated the village for five and a half centuries, its daily round of prayer and work interrupted by at least one Danish raid and occasional royal visits. In its early days it boasted the presence of Ælfric of Eynsham, who wrote his famous series of English homilies there. 'Then came the Reformation, like a devastating cyclone', wrote one local historian, 'and now the town shields in its bosom the few poor relics of the long dead Abbey', including a magnificent gatehouse. The final days of Cerne were marred by controversy, its last abbot being accused of mismanagement, immorality and 'wasting the goods of the house on his mistresses and natural children'. It is impossible to know how well-founded these charges were, but they were convenient to the reformers, who closed the monastery in 1539.

The monks of Cerne claimed a connection with St Augustine of Canterbury; some said that he had even founded the abbey. This reminds us that the 'Apostle to the English' did not merely convert the kingdom of Kent but travelled across southern England preaching the Gospel. We know that he met representatives of the British Church at 'St Augustine's Oak', somewhere around the borders of Somerset and Gloucestershire, and there is no reason to doubt that he included modern-day Dorset in his travels.

According to legend, he visited Cerne Abbas and spoke to some shepherds grazing their flocks on the rolling hills. He offered them refreshment, asking if they would prefer beer or water. They went for the latter and the saint struck the staff against a rock, exclaiming *Cerno El* ('I perceive God') as the water gurgled out. This was either the origin of the old name of the village, Cernel, or perhaps a pun on an existing place name.

William of Malmesbury told another story of how the locals made fun of the Roman missionaries by fastening tails on their backs. St

Augustine told his brethren, *Cerno Deum qui et nobis retribuet gratiam et furentibus illis emendationem infundet animae* ('I see God who shall give us grace and impart to these deluded people a change of heart'). Their hearts were soon changed, and they were baptised in the spring at Cerne Abbas. One tradition holds that, as a punishment, several generations of villagers were born with tails, though this deformity seems to have since disappeared.

Such legends may have been embellished (or even invented) by the monks of Cerne. There may have been a merging of traditions, since there was also a local cult of St Edwold, a Mercian prince who became a hermit and lived beside a spring that had been identified to him in a vision.

The link with St Augustine was certainly believed, since before the Reformation a chapel dedicated to the saint stood there. 'St Augustine's Well' became the subject of much local folklore and even to this day there are ribbons tied to the branches of the surrounding lime trees (known as the 'Twelve Apostles'). It is believed, for example, that on Easter morning you can see the faces of those who will die that year reflected in the water, that the waters (full of iron) cured infertility, and that a laurel leaf dipped in the water could heal disorders of the eyes. New-born babies were placed into the spring (perhaps an allusion to the baptisms celebrated here by St Augustine) and girls would make wishes to help them find husbands.

Whatever the well's origins, it is a rather mysterious place. The same could be said for the most famous resident of Cerne Abbas, the 180-foot-long giant carved into the chalk of a nearby hill. No-one knows for sure his age or identity: a Celtic or Saxon deity, perhaps, or the Roman god Hercules, or even a seventeenth-century royalist caricature of Oliver Cromwell. Some even say that there is a real giant buried there. One wonders if St Augustine saw it on his travels and decided to make a special effort to bring the light of the Gospel to this beautiful area.

EXETER, DEVON
Saintly Bishops

Exeter Cathedral sits majestically in the heart of the city, once the Roman base for the south-west. It is an understated cathedral but full of interest, boasting one of the oldest clocks in the world, a minstrel's gallery, some fascinating monuments and even a medieval flap for the (salaried) cathedral cat. As a cathedral, though, it faced one distinct disadvantage in the Middle Ages: no great shrine, no major relic that could draw pilgrims.

That is not to say that Exeter is lacking in saints. There is the shadowy St Sidwell, a young girl who possibly lived in the eighth century. According to legend, her evil stepmother hired a reaper to murder her. He duly cut off her head with his scythe, which became her artistic symbol. Very little is known about her, though a well is supposed to have sprung up at the place her head fell and became a popular place of pilgrimage. To this day one of the city's main thoroughfares is called 'Sidwell Street'.

Then there is St Boniface, born nearby in Crediton and educated at the monastery of Exeter under Abbot Wolfhard until the age of sixteen. Thus, he grew in holiness and eloquence and went on to become the great Apostle of Germany and the Netherlands.

Yet Exeter Cathedral still lacked its major relic. To counter this there were attempts in the later Middle Ages at developing cults around several bishops of Exeter. The first of these concerned James Berkeley, appointed bishop in 1326. He was consecrated the following year but before he got settled into the post died unexpectedly at his manor of Peterhayes. There is hardly any evidence of what he intended to do as a bishop, but he was considered to be a saint and by the end of September 1327 over £3 worth of candles had been sold at his tomb. It is hard to know whether his cult was a result of the holiness of his life or the suddenness of his death at a time of political upheaval. The authorities never encouraged pilgrimages to his tomb and his successor even publicly discredited a miracle that was attributed to his intercession. Still, income was received from pilgrims until the end of the fourteenth century and partially paid for the cathedral's on-going building projects.

If there was going to be a bishop venerated as a saint a more likely candidate was Berkeley's predecessor, Walter de Stapeldon, the first

English bishop to die violently since St Thomas Becket. Stapledon made some notable achievements: he was responsible for much of the rebuilding of Exeter Cathedral, including the enormous episcopal throne which rises sixty feet above the floor and was made of oak taken from his estates. His other great monument was a college at Oxford—named after the city—founded in 1314 in order to educate priests for his diocese and to provide funds for poor scholars. As a bishop and Treasurer of England, however, Stapledon became heavily involved in the unpopular regime of Edward II, which made him a wealthy man and led to his violent death at the hands of a mob in 1326, shortly after the king lost power to his wife, Isabella, and her lover, Roger Mortimer. Stapledon was violently assaulted and beheaded with a bread knife. One cannot help but think that had he been on a different side he might have been venerated, at least unofficially, as a martyr; only a few decades later the Archbishop of Canterbury, Simon Sudbury, was killed in the Peasants' Revolt and regarded by many as such. But not so for Stapledon.

A more resilient cult was that of Edmund Lacy, bishop between 1417 and 1455. He had been close to Henry V and present on the field of Agincourt. As bishop he was conscientious in visiting the diocese, despite suffering from weak health, and promoted the cults of Our Lady and St Raphael, for whom he composed a liturgy which won papal approval. He wrote a book on the four senses of Scripture and by the time he died in 1455 already had a reputation as a living saint. It was no surprise, then, that pilgrims gathered at his tomb, which was (perhaps not coincidentally) opposite that of 'St' James Berkeley.

Following the devastating 1942 air raid that damaged part of the cathedral, repair work revealed a collection of wax votive offerings that had been placed around the tomb by devotees. They depicted parts of the human body, horned cattle, pigs, horses, even a foot in a pointed shoe. Together with these 'ex votos' were bits of stone, oyster shells, slaked lime and glass which may also been mementoes left by long forgotten pilgrims. Bishop Lacy was obviously seen as a heavenly healer and miracles were attributed to his intercession.

In the end, none of these medieval bishops were officially canonised and what was left of their cults was finally suppressed at the Reformation. Yet the lack of a major shrine does not affect the modern visitor to Exeter; the very stones, which could tell of so many graces received and prayers muttered down the ages, are surely just as sacred.

GLASTONBURY, SOMERSET

The Holy Thorn

On 14 December a simple service takes place each year at the church of St John the Baptist in Glastonbury. The oldest child from the local infant school, aided by the mayor, cuts a sprig from a hawthorn tree that stands in the churchyard. This is then sent to the adorn the Sovereign's Christmas table—a custom that originated during the reign of James I and was revived in 1922.

As you might imagine, this is no ordinary tree. As the children sing:

> There is a very special tree
> We call the Holy Thorn,
> That flowers in December
> The month that Christ was born.

Indeed, of all the trees associated with Christmas—of which there are many—Glastonbury's 'Holy Thorn' is one of the most celebrated because it flowers twice a year: once around Easter (like other hawthorns) and also around Christmas. This was deemed to be miraculous and a sure sign of its holy origins.

According to legend, St Joseph of Arimathea came to Glastonbury and planted his staff on Wearyall Hill before taking a rest—the hill's name is supposed to derive from the saint's exclamation that 'we are weary all'. On waking the next morning he found that his staff—which some say was made from the same hawthorn tree that produced the crown of thorns—had rooted into the ground. St Joseph is, of course, remembered as the founder of the church in Glastonbury. He reputedly brought the Child Jesus with him on business trips as he traded for tin and iron in the West Country (not completely implausible) and then returned after the Ascension with a group of companions and (some say) the Holy Grail. He built a little wooden chapel dedicated to Our Lady and, according to the Glastonbury tradition, established the British Church.

The 'Holy Thorn' is first mentioned just before the Reformation in a verse *Lyfe of Joseph of Aramathia*, and grew hugely in significance because, unlike the abbey and its many relics, it survived the dissolution. The story of its connection with Joseph of Arimathea was first mentioned in the seventeenth century and used to support different agendas of the times. For Protestants it was a link to the 'non-papal' origins of British Christianity; for Catholics the 'Holy Thorn' was a symbol of continuity. Lacking churches in which to worship, persecuted Catholics put added emphasis on trees, rocks and other natural places. Perhaps they also found comfort in the fact that the venerable tree at Glastonbury flowered in the midst of winter, thus promising hope in their desperate situation.

The tree in St John's churchyard is not the original 'Holy Thorn'. In the sixteenth century there were three thorns growing on Wearyall Hill and the last surviving one was destroyed by the Puritans in the 1640s—though the godly man who felled the tree is said to have been blinded by a flying splinter of wood. However, new trees were grown from cuttings that had been carefully preserved. They could be found not only on Wearyall Hill but in the grounds of the ruined Glastonbury Abbey, St John's church and elsewhere. In the 1720s one local is reported to have had a nursery of cuttings from the Holy Thorn and sold them for a crown a piece, like the relic and indulgence sellers so criticised by the Protestant reformers.

When Britain belatedly adopted the Gregorian calendar in 1752 and eleven days were struck off from that year many were curious to see which calendar the 'Holy Thorn' would follow. According to the *Gentleman's Magazine* 'a vast concourse of people attended the noted thorn on Christmas-day, new style; but, to their great disappointment, there was no appearance of its blowing, which made them watch it narrowly the 5th of January, the Christmas-day, old style, when it blowed as usual'.

Saplings have since been sent all over the world, even as far afield as Australia and New Zealand. The Wearyall Hill specimen that was planted in the 1950s had a dramatic recent history: it was vandalised in 2010 and its replacement was irretrievably damaged in another attack in 2012. Nevertheless the 'Holy Thorn' remains an important part of Glastonbury's claim to be the 'cradle of English Christianity'. At Christmas the flowers point towards our Saviour, a branch of the Tree of Jesse, whose feet 'in ancient time' may well have walked 'upon England's mountains green'.

LAUNCESTON, CORNWALL

Crossing the Tamar: Cornwall and its Saints

Once we crossed the Tamar into Cornwall, a Londoner quickly became a 'foreigner'. Not that the river is very broad as the A30 crosses it; in fact, without the sign on the side of the motorway it would hardly be noticed. Yet were it not for the fact that its source is less than four miles from the northern coastline, this river nearly makes the county—or should I say duchy—into an island.

Across the Tamar the road signs begin to look different. Often, they are both in English and Cornish, and there are many places named after saints—not just well-known ones but holy men and women with peculiarly Celtic names: Brioc, Kew, Petroc, Tudy. As the saying goes, there are more saints in Cornwall than in Heaven, and many of them came to Cornwall from Wales and Ireland in the centuries following the collapse of Roman rule in order to spread the Gospel. Many have links, also, with Brittany ('little Britain'), where they are widely venerated.

The Cornish have always been open to the transcendent, not surprising given the natural beauty that surrounds them. This can be seen in the 'age of the saints', the holy wells and standing stones, the many legends and traditions that have been passed down, and the vibrancy of the medieval Church. In more recent times, a religious revival left Methodist chapels in most settlements. As John Betjemin wrote, 'John Wesley inspired the Cornish in Georgian times rather as the Celtic saints had inspired them a thousand years before. What shoutings of glory must have been heard from those windows; what soul-converting sermons and full-throated Hallelujahs must have sounded from here.'

The Cornish flag, a white cross on a black background, is proudly flown everywhere. It is known as 'St Piran's Flag' and the white cross symbolises the light of the Gospel dispelling the darkness—or, alternatively, the white tin coming out of the black ore. St Piran is supposed to have been a pioneer in the art of tin smelting, which had for so long been a Cornish speciality. Indeed, before the birth of Christ Cornish tin was being transported across the Mediterranean; some think it may have been used in the construction of the Temple in Jerusalem. St Piran's rediscovery of this ancient art occurred when he built a fire on a black hearthstone and a white liquid appeared, forming a cross. Less picturesquely, historians believe that the flag may have originated in the arms of the earls of Cornwall or those of the Saint-Peran family. Interestingly, it is the reverse of the Breton flag, which is a black cross on a white background.

St Piran is fairly typical of so many Cornish saints; indeed, little is known about him for sure. It is thought that he came from Ireland, and many have identified him with the St Ciaran who is the patron of Ossory in Leinster; a 'c' in Irish becomes a 'p' in Cornish. Others say he came from Wales and popular tradition depicts him being thrown out of his home country by pagans with a millstone round his neck. Instead of acting as the instrument of his death, however, the millstone became a makeshift raft, bringing him providentially to the north coast of Cornwall. Here he built a chapel in the sands, lived as a hermit and worked many miracles.

His name can be found in several placenames on the north coast: Perranporth, Perrancombe, Perranzabuloe. The saint's chapel can be found near the latter, at one time claimed to be 'the oldest place of Christian worship in England with parts of it four walls still standing'. Historians now think it dates from after 800, though on the site of a much older structure which may have direct links to the saint. Formerly one of the chief pilgrimage destinations in Cornwall, the original oratory was for many centuries lost, until shifting sands at the beginning of the nineteenth century revealed it once again.

Near Perranporth there is an intriguing open-air medieval theatre or *plain-an-gwarry* ('playing place'), known as the 'Perran Round'. This circular enclosure, which may have originated as an Iron Age earthwork, was used for the performance of mystery plays in the Cornish language, teaching salvation history and the lives of the saints to the largely illiterate population. Though it looks unimposing, a circular mound in a field, it takes only a little imagination to picture a crowd of hundreds sitting on the terraces, waiting excitedly for the play to begin. A hollow pit known as the 'devil's spoon' was used for the representation of hell and to facilitate the appearance of demons from 'below'.

Many of the surviving plays were produced by the clergy of Glasney College, near Penryn, including the three plays (performed over three days) of the *Ordinalia*, dating from the late fourteenth century. These religious dramas make up much of the surviving Cornish literature of the period. The Reformation, interestingly, had a disastrous effect on this cultural world and the tradition of mystery plays gradually died out, until their modern revival. The introduction of the English *Book of Common Prayer* in 1549 also accelerated the demise of Cornish. This was not without controversy; not only were the faithful attached to the old ways, but they resented the imposition of an English liturgy on a population that was only partially English-speaking. The result was the so-called 'Prayer Book Rebellion', in which a petition was sent to Edward VI declaring the new liturgy to be 'like a Christmas game' and demanding 'the old service of Matins, Mass, Evensong and Procession in Latin as it was before. And so we the Cornish men (whereof certain of us understand no English) utterly refuse this new English'.

Launceston is known as 'the gateway to Cornwall'. This charming town, situated two miles west of the Tamar, was an important thoroughfare and base of power. Dominated by the imposing Norman castle (now in ruins), it has been the location of a mint and was, until 1835, the county town. Its name is a shortened version of 'Lan-Stephan', deriving from a Saxon ecclesial foundation staffed by secular canons and dedicated to the first Christian martyr. From 1127 the town was the site of a prestigious Augustinian priory, dissolved in 1539, by which time the community only numbered eight. Little remains of the buildings above ground.

The town is perhaps best known for one of the most astonishing of Cornish churches, St Mary Magdalen, just by the market square. At a distance it does not look particularly imposing but the outside walls of granite—one of the hardest of rocks—is intricately carved. John Betjemin thought it 'looks, at first glance, almost like a Hindu temple in the elaboration of its decoration'. On the south porch St George can be found killing the dragon, as well as St Martin giving away his cloak and floral patterns based on spikenard and pomegranate, which were thought to have been used to make Magdalen's costly ointment, mentioned in the Gospel. Most striking is her recumbent figure on the east end, on the other side of the wall of the old high altar. She is surrounded by kneeling choristers and the words of a Latin prayer, and it is apparently a local custom for children to turn their backs and throw a stone over their shoulder towards the image. If the stone lodges on the saint, then they will receive a set of new clothes.

The church was built between 1511 and 1524, just before the Reformation. Within the lifetime of its builders and masons, society would be torn apart by religious changes. Those who differed from the status quo found themselves the victims of persecution and the dungeons of Launceston Castle were inhabited by several notable religious prisoners. They covered the whole spectrum of belief. In 1555, during the reign of Mary I, Agnes Prest was incarcerated here for a time; she was found guilty of denying the Real Presence and taken to Exeter to be burnt at the stake. Exactly a century later it was the turn of

George Fox, the Quaker founder. When he refused to pay a fine for not removing his hat in the presence of the judge, he was taken to the small cell at Launceston known as 'Doomsdale'. He later wrote that this was 'a nasty stinking place where they said few people came out alive; where they used to put witches and murderers before their execution; where the prisoner's excrements had not been carried out for scores of years'.

It was here that the Catholic St Cuthbert Mayne, 'protomartyr of Douai college and all the seminaries', was kept before his execution in 1577. Mayne was a West Countryman, born at Youlston near Barnstaple (Devon) in 1544, the son of a farmer. He was educated at the local grammar school and then in Oxford, at St Alban's Hall and St John's College. Ordained as an Anglican minister, he served the living of Huntshaw (Devon), and then returned to his college of St John's as chaplain, where he was highly regarded by Catholics and Protestants alike. Here he was influenced by Catholic-minded fellows, in particular St Edmund Campion and Gregory Martin (one of the translators of the Douai Bible). Mayne eventually embraced the Catholic faith, fled Oxford and boarded a boat that would take him to the newly founded English College, Douai. He was ordained a Catholic priest on 7 February 1575.

Like so many of the English Martyrs, his priestly ministry in England was tragically short. Employed as chaplain by Sir Francis Tregian, the nephew of Sir John Arundell (the leading Cornish Catholic), he lived at Golden Manor near Probus, five miles east of Truro. He celebrated Mass here and at Lanherne, the home of the Arundells, and visited the scattered Catholics in the area.

In 1577 the Archbishop of Canterbury, Edmund Grindal, was asked by the queen to suppress Puritan religious exercises known as 'prophesyings', which were seen as politically subversive. Grindal had evangelical leanings and refused to follow the royal order, which eventually resulted in his house arrest. Instead, he commissioned a survey of recusants to show the queen that the real danger lay with Catholics who refused to attend church. It listed one and a half thousand names, including future martyrs such as St John Paine and St Margaret Clitherow, and it was around this time, as attitudes towards recusants hardened, that Mayne was arrested at Golden.

The raid on this remote manor was an elaborate affair, involving at least eight JPs and a hundred-armed men, but it was not primarily aimed at 'papists'. The new sheriff of the county was Sir Richard Grenville, described by historian A. L. Rowse as 'hot-tempered, determined, energetic, harsh', though often remembered as a swashbuckling seafarer and privateer, the captain of *The Revenge*. Grenville was searching for a fugitive, one Anthony Bourne, but was only too happy to have the opportunity to strike at Arundell and Tregian, both of whom had threatened his business interests by serving on a piracy commission. Rowse depicts this as a struggle of 'men of inland interests against those of the sea', religious faith being used as an extra means of attack.

Mayne was discovered in a locked room and arrested, along with his employer and several others. On his person was found a waxen *Agnus Dei*, a devotional item that had been blessed by the pope, and among his papers a papal bull—a rather inoffensive one which, since it announced the indulgences of the Holy Year of 1575, had long expired. Nevertheless, it was a prohibited document in the eyes of English law.

Mayne was held in chains at Launceston Castle for five months and charged with obtaining and publishing a papal bull, denying the queen's supremacy, possessing a 'vain sign and superstitious thing called an *Agnus Dei*' and celebrating Mass at Golden. He was condemned to death at the Michaelmas Assizes and on St Andrew's Day 1577 dragged to the town square on market day, not far from the church of St Mary Magdalen. A modern plaque on the pavement stands on the site of the unusually high gallows, erected as a 'terror to the papists'. When he was cut down to be quartered, he fell heavily onto the scaffold, causing (according to one account) one of his eyes to be dislodged, and thus was mercifully insensible to the torture of being disembowelled. His quarters were displayed at Barnstaple, Bodmin, Wadebridge and Tregony (near Golden), and his head impaled over the castle gate. This was retrieved by sympathisers and kept as one of the great treasures of the Arundell family; it is now at Lanherne.

St Cuthbert Mayne was the first of the seminary priests to be martyred. A few weeks later, in early 1578, he would be followed by two other alumni of Douai: Blessed John Nelson and Blessed Thomas Sherwood (the nephew of Tregian). Mayne is remembered in the Catholic church at Launceston, founded in 1886 and for many years served by the Canons Regular of the Lateran (who, like their medieval predecessors at Launceston, followed the Rule of St Augustine). In 1921 the first pilgrimage in his honour was organised, with an impressive procession with the saint's relic through the streets of Launceston to the place of his martyrdom. More recently this has been organised every three years, often with the involvement of other churches, but still known locally as 'Catholic Sunday'. As St Cuthbert Mayne prayed beside the gallows, he must have hoped that the religious violence would end, and that people's hearts would be converted. The blood of the martyrs is the seed of the Church.

MOUNT'S BAY, CORNWALL

St Michael's Mount

An interesting map occasionally surfaces called the 'Sword of St Michael', demonstrating how a straight line can be drawn between seven of the chief sanctuaries dedicated to the archangel. The line begins in the west with Skellig Michael, just off the coast of County Kerry (Ireland) and ends with the Stella Maris monastery at Mount Carmel (Israel), passing through Mont St Michel (France), the Italian shrines of Sacra di San Michele and Monte Gargano, and the Greek monastery of Symi.

The only English sanctuary on the map is St Michael's Mount. Quite apart from its religious connotations, this is one of the most iconic and enchanting of places. A small island connected to the mainland by a causeway at low tide, it is surmounted by a castle and chapel, which look down on a small village, beautifully terraced gardens and a harbour. The wide arc of coastline around the Mount includes the distant town of Penzance, often glittering in the sunshine; beyond the island is the open ocean.

The day of my visit was sunny and calm, and it was easy to forget that this can be a place of violent storms and shipwrecks, of earthquakes and even tsunamis (three-metre waves struck this coast in the aftermath of the great Lisbon earthquake of 1755). The inhabitants of the island must develop a deep awe for the beauty and power of Mother Nature, never taken for granted.

The Mount has long been a place of importance. A Mesolithic arrowhead found on the island points to the presence of hunter gatherers around 8,000 years ago, while during the Bronze and Iron Ages the island was a centre of trade, not just for locals but for those from further afield. Diodorus Siculus, writing in the first century BC and referring to an older authority, wrote of a tidal island called 'Ictis' where merchants would buy British tin and then transport it to the continent. Many claim that St Michael's Mount is the most likely location for such a place, revealing the sophisticated and cosmopolitan nature of pre-Roman Britain.

Christianity had presumably reached the Mount by the sixth century, when a meeting supposedly took place there between the Welsh missionary St Cadoc and the holy virgin St Keyne. There may have been a religious community from an early stage; certainly after the

Norman Conquest William I's half-brother, Robert of Mortain, Earl of Cornwell, granted St Michael's Mount to Mont St Michel, the equally iconic island abbey off the coast of southern Normandy. It is unclear whether this confirmed what already existed or was a generous gift, establishing ecclesiastical links between the two sides of the Channel.

St Michael has long been considered a patron of Cornwall. The archangel has many churches dedicated to him, including the atmospheric hermit's chapel (now ruined) on Roche Rock in the centre of the duchy, but St Michael's Mount is the pre-eminent Cornish sanctuary. Legend speaks of the heavenly warrior appearing to fisherman around 495, warning them of danger. The spot of the apparition is said to be on the west side of the Mount, where there is a split between two cliffs, now known as 'Cromwell's Passage' — where Parliamentarian troops tried to capture the castle during the Civil War. On that occasion they were unsuccessful. Was St Michael protecting the Mount once again, I wonder?!

Another legend has a connection with the triumph of good over evil. In the mists of time, a giant called Cormoran lived on the Mount and terrorised the local population. He stole hens, lamps, pigs and even little children and took them to his liar to feed upon. One night, a farmer's son called Jack crept onto the island, dug a deep hole and covered it with branches as a trap. He then woke the giant, who, angrily chasing the young lad, promptly fell into the hole. From that moment on, he became known as 'Jack the Giant-Killer'.

St Michael's Mount was for many centuries a place of pilgrimage. At the entrance to the causeway on the mainland you can climb onto Chapel Rock — a good vantage point for photos. A chapel once stood there, where prayers were said before boats set off for the island at high tide. Some pilgrims went on from the Mount to Santiago de Compostela. The island received various privileges and indulgences, including in 1070 independence from the local bishop (a much sort after exemption!).

The priory was a daughter house of Mont St Michel. Some have suggested it acted as a novitiate, testing the will of junior monks in the hope that if they could survive several Cornish winters and the sometimes-harsh conditions, they would be fit for life at the mother house across the Channel. Certainly, the architecture is very similar and the connection between the two places doubtlessly strengthened devotion to St Michael.

The various wars with France made the relationship between the two houses increasingly strained. Revenues were sometimes confiscated and orders given for French monks to return home. Finally, in 1414, Henry V gave the Mount to his new Bridgettine abbey at Syon (Isleworth, Middlesex) and so it remained until the Dissolution of the Monasteries, except for a brief period under King's College, Cambridge.

In this final century of Catholic activity, pilgrimages continued and the religious life of the Mount prospered. There were several moments of political crisis: in 1473 the Mount was captured by the Lancastrians during the Wars of the Roses, while in 1497 it was caught up in the rebellion led by Perkin Warbeck, who claimed to be one of the 'princes in the Tower' and therefore the rightful king of England. After the Dissolution, the Mount entered private ownership. From the mid-seventeenth century it has been the home of the St Aubyn family, who still run the island along with the National Trust.

I doubt many of my fellow visitors regarded themselves as pilgrims in the strict religious sense. As we walked in a long line across the causeway, almost as if we were in procession, I could imagine a festal day centuries ago. In my mind Mount's Bay became filled with chants, muttered prayers, excited conversations and sellers displaying their trinkets and pilgrim badges. Their destination was the chapel at the Mount's summit, near the place where St Michael had once appeared. That world is largely lost now but perhaps after the last tourists have gone and the waters cover the causeway, a peace descends upon the island and the Mount becomes a sanctuary once again.

PRINKNASH, GLOUCESTERSHIRE

A Monastery in the Cotswolds

At first glance, Prinknash (pronounced Prinnage) does not look like a monastery. The monks reside in St Peter's Grange, the sort of old manor house one expects to see in *Downton Abbey*. Before the Reformation it was used as a country residence of the abbot of Gloucester and much of the current building dates from the 1520s. There are some fascinating historical connections: Henry VIII and Anne Boleyn visited Prinknash while hunting in the area in August 1535 and during the Siege of Gloucester (1643) Prince Rupert used the house as his headquarters.

The community was founded by Aelred Carlyle in 1896 as a group of like-minded men who wanted to live the Benedictine life within the Church of England. It moved between locations, starting with the Isle of Dogs and eventually settling on the remote island of Caldey, near the Pembrokeshire town of Tenby.

This picturesque spot had associations with a host of Celtic saints, including St David and St Samson, and during the Middle Ages was attached to St Dogmaels by Cardigan Bay, a monastery belonging to the obscure Order of St Benedict of Tiron. Carlyle thought that these medieval monks dressed in white habits and so he got his men to do the same. Caldey soon attracted vocations and many curious visitors, including Ronald Knox (while still an Anglican). Many years later he described the island as having 'a faint-air of make-believe' with its 'untenanted sandy beaches, the rocks, and surf over the rocks, the timeless, stone-built remains of antiquity' and 'all the consolations of the Catholic religion, the Latin Office, and Benediction, and the Salve Regina, and all the rest of it, without being called upon to assert your belief in the hard facts of Catholic dogma'.

Caldey was indeed an anomaly. Carlyle claimed that it did not fall within any diocese and that he could do more or less what he wanted. However, in order to regularise his position in the Church of England he invited the Bishop of Oxford, Charles Gore, to carry out a visitation in 1913. Before doing this Gore laid down a number of conditions, including the removal of references to the Immaculate Conception and Assumption in the liturgy and the abandonment of Exposition and Benediction of the Blessed Sacrament. This led to a crisis meeting within the community; the result was that Carlyle led nineteen of his brethren into the Catholic Church, an unprecedented event in monastic history.

Carlyle then undertook a Catholic novitiate at Maredsous Abbey in Belgium and returned to Caldey in 1914, just as war was breaking out. He was given the status of abbot although financial difficulties and poor health led to his resignation in 1920. He spent most of his remaining years as a missionary in Canada.

The community that he had founded continued, although as they settled into the Catholic Church and dealt with financial uncertainties, professions and ordinations were suspended for several years up until 1926. Soon afterwards, a much-needed boost was given when a recent convert, Thomas Dyer-Edwardes, offered his property of Prinknash Park as their new home. He had long hoped it would one day serve as a religious house. Meanwhile, with the help of Pius XI, a Cistercian community was found to buy Caldey. And so the monks moved to Gloucestershire in 1928, though the process of transition was not an easy one. At Prinknash rooms had to be divided to make cells, others had to be expanded to make the communal spaces like the refectory or chapel. At Caldey all sorts of things had to be packed, including the large library, printing press and kiln. Even the hives were transported, although the bees woke up with the jolting of the lorry as it was speeding through Wales and most of them escaped, with the exception of those that chose to sting the poor driver.

In 1937 Prinknash formally became an abbey and subsequent years saw a massive expansion. Such was the number of monks that for a time there was an overflow community in a house in the Wye valley and then in Shropshire. Daughter houses were eventually founded at Pluscarden, near Elgin (where the monks still wear the distinctive white habit) and Farnborough (replacing the French monks from Solesmes).

At Prinknash plans were drawn up for new buildings by the well-known architect H. S. Goodhart-Rendel, designed to be 'a powerhouse of prayer for the Conversion of England, and a centre of contemplative life'. Cardinal Hinsley laid the foundation stone on 3 May 1939 but work was delayed by war and the ambitious plans soon had to be simplified. In fact, the amended plans were only agreed in 1963 and the modern monastery was finally ready by 1972. By this time Goodheart-Rendel had died and was buried in the crypt, the sole part of his church to be built. He had also donated a valuable painting of *The Flight into Egypt* by Jacobo Bassano and the sale of this in auction added substantially to the building fund.

While excavations were made for the new buildings a large amount of clay was found which led to the development of a thriving pottery industry, which was for many years a household name. This tied in with the abbey's artistic tradition—vestment-making, weaving, painting and wood-carving. As the years rolled on, the size of the community decreased and in 2005 the decision was made to move back to St Peter's Grange, their original home.

Despite the many changes in location, the timeless Benedictine life continues in the beautiful Cotswold countryside. The monks meet in the sixteenth-century chapel six or seven times a day to chant the Divine Office (in English and Latin) as well as for community Mass and times of silent prayer. These regular 'hours' punctuate the various types of manual work: jobs around the house and grounds, administration, even the production of incense for liturgical use—the monks do this work themselves and the abbey is the oldest major incense blender in Europe. Staying in the monastery guesthouse, the days pass by effortlessly and the rhythm of prayer and work helps us live each moment in the presence of God, surrounded by His love and peace.

ST LEVAN, CORNWALL

St Levan

Serendipity plays an important part in all holidays and can sometimes lead to the most amazing of discoveries. On being turned out of the famous Minack Theatre, where a matinee was about to begin, it was decided to head towards Land's End. This is a stunning part of the country. As John Betjemin described it, 'the granite coast with its rocky islands and deep fissures has white sands which turn the shallow sea emerald on a fine day fading to purple over seaweed and lapis in the deep water'. Within a few minutes signs to the car park of St Levan were spotted. Most people were using this for the theatre or the coastal path. But we decided instead to visit the ancient church.

Levan is a shortened version of 'Selevan', which is the Cornish and Welsh way of saying 'Solomon'. 'Sullivan' comes from the same root. Though we often associate the Celtic saints with exotic-sounding names, they were also fond of Biblical ones. Thus, the patron of Wales was 'David', a Breton missionary bore the name 'Samson' and Britain's second smallest city is 'St Asaph', recalling one of its founding bishops who was named after a psalmist.

Little is known about St Levan. It seems he lived in this isolated spot as a hermit and gave his name to a nearby holy well, the waters of which were recommended for those with eye problems or toothache. William Borlase, the eighteenth-century antiquary, recorded that 'the path along which the saint was accustomed to walk' from his hermitage to 'St Levan's Rocks' could still be seen since 'the grass grows greener wherever the good priest trod'. Like so many Cornish saints, he was said to have been of noble birth and various pedigrees were drawn up.

Living on the coast, it is little surprise that fish formed an important part of his diet and these appear in the colourful stories passed down in local tradition. There is the tale of the saint fishing on a Sunday and being reprimanded for doing so by a local lady, Johanna, who was tending her garden near what is now the Minack Theatre. He quickly retorted that fishing was no worse than gardening on the Sabbath. The pair argued over the point, until St Levan called the woman a fool and declared that in future any child of the parish bearing her name would be even more stupid than she. According to the well-researched church guidebook, 'a search of the St Levan baptism register (which begins in 1694) reveals only one Johanna and one Joanna'.

On another occasion, the saint caught two chad (or bream) on the same hook. Only wanting the one fish that formed his daily sustenance he threw them both back into the sea, but a second and a third time the two were caught again. St Levan eventually took this as a sign and returned to his hermitage with the two fish. Here he found that his sister (St Breaca) had paid an unexpected visit, along with his two nephews. The fish were duly cooked but the hungry children were careless and both choked to death—a rather depressing story that reminded generations of children to beware of fish bones and graciously accept the gifts sent them by God. Locally bream is known as *chuck-cheels* or 'Choke-childs'.

In the churchyard there is an intriguing looking rock, split in two. According to tradition, St Levan used the stone as a resting place and a platform for preaching. One wonders how many people were around to receive his message; even today the church is isolated and does not form part of a village. Shortly before his death, the saint struck the stone with his fist and it split in half. The saint said:

> When, with panniers astride,
> A pack-horse, one can ride,
> Through St Levan's stone,
> The World will be done.

The great scholar of Cornish saints, Canon Gilbert Doble, recorded in 1928 that 'it was more than fifty years since I first made acquaintance, as a child, with the St Levan Stone, and it may be a satisfaction to many to know that the progress of separation is an exceedingly slow one'.

The more likely truth behind the St Levan Stone is just as compelling as these charming legends. The split stone may be the remnants of a pagan holy site, Christianised in the sixth or seventh century and now bearing the name of the founder of the church. The fact that the light of the Gospel had triumphed over the darkness of the past is underlined by the presence of an Anglo-Saxon stone cross standing a few feet away, beside the path leading to the church.

The subsequent history of St Levan is full of interest. The medieval church building boasts stunning fifteenth-century pew-end carvings, featuring (among others) a Santiago pilgrim and both a 'grim' and 'jolly' fool. There are remnants, too, of the rood screen that once divided the chancel from the nave. Here the visitor can spot the Instruments of the Passion, plants and mythical beasts, such as the unicorn and the wyvern. The transept of the little church is charmingly known as 'The Diary', for it was used as such for many years.

During the turmoil of the Reformation, William Alsa, who may have been a priest serving St Levan, was hanged for his part in the Prayer Book Rebellion of 1549, protesting against the liturgical changes of Edward VI. Until the nineteenth century the church was, along with its sister church of St Buryan, a Royal Peculiar, meaning that (like Westminster Abbey and the Chapels Royal) it came directly under the Crown.

A few miles away, Porthcurno, which is part of the parish, is an early centre of international communications, with telegraph cables stretching to Bombay. It is perhaps appropriate since the legacy of St Levan extended across the sea to Brittany, where the name 'Selevan' or 'Selawen' can be found in several places. The Celtic saints constituted a web of sanctity and mission that joined together Ireland, Wales, Cornwall, Brittany and beyond. Of course, the exact details of St Levan's life have long been forgotten. Canon Doble commented on the 'decided comic element' in his legends which 'sometimes scandalises humourless people who forget that the countryman has frequently a very strong sense of humour'. Yet, 'we must not conclude from the childish stories which popular imagination has woven around them that the men who gave their names to Cornish parishes were idiots or eccentrics. They were saints and heroes'.

ST MAWES, CORNWALL

A Cornish Fishing Village and its Saint

The Cornish village of St Mawes, situated at the end of the Roseland peninsula, is a favourite with tourists. According to one survey, it is also one of the country's most 'hip' places, whatever that means. Dominated by one of a pair of castles built by Henry VIII to protect nearby Falmouth from the aggressions of Catholic Europe, it is well known for its charming fisherman's cottages, narrow streets, calm waters and extraordinarily fine pasties available from the local bakery.

If today it is frequented by visitors intent on leisure, in the past the village was an important fishing and trading port. Rather than navigate round the treacherous waters of Land's End, goods would be taken overland between the northern port of Tregony and Roseland in the south. Moreover, the village is located on what is said to be the world's third largest natural harbour. Its size is apparent when you consider that a regular ferry connects it to Falmouth, less than a mile away but some thirty miles by car!

Cornwall was especially famous for its tin. Indeed, an ingot of tin weighing 1581 lbs was found at St Mawes by fishermen in 1812; although it is most likely medieval, some have suggested that it is Iron Age or Roman. It is astonishing to think that Cornish tin could be found across the civilised world—in Rome, Egypt, even (it is said) on the Temple at Jerusalem.

The village of St Mawes developed around a spring or holy well, which now stands beside the steep road leading down to the centre. In 1433 the Bishop of Exeter granted an indulgence of forty days to raise funds for 'repair of the culvert adjoining the chapel of St Madyt'.

Nearby is the church of St Mawes, which, compared to many Cornish churches, is relatively modern: built in 1882 and the latest in a series of churches to have stood on the spot. One of the most attractive aspects of the church are its stained-glass windows, depicting the story of St Mawes. This is useful, since, like so many of the Cornish saints, little is known for sure about him and he remains elusive. It is likely that he lived in the sixth or seventh centuries and he may have originated in Ireland. When John Leland, the antiquary, visited an earlier chapel here, in the sixteenth century, he described St Mawes, or 'St Mat', to be a Breton 'bishop', often 'painted as a scholemaster'.

Not only did the Cornish village have his well and chapel, but, 'a little without', 'his chaire of stone'.

In these windows the saint is depicted as teacher, abbot and missionary. We see him seated on his stone chair under a whitethorn tree, instructing his disciples SS Bothmael and Tudy. It seems that the saint left a more visible 'footprint' in France, where he ended his days and is known variously as 'Maudez', 'Maudé' or 'Modez'. He is remembered as the founder of a monastery on the Ile Modez, off the coast of Brittany, after having driven away the snakes. The whitethorn refers to one on the island under which he often preached and which, if cut, is said to bleed profusely.

In the middle window St Mawes is depicted as an abbot, in full pontificals, blessing those who make a pilgrimage to his church, and in the final panel he is crossing the sea in a boat, with yellow and red striped sails. In the background there is a round tower known as 'Forn Modez' on the Ile Modez and his stone cross on the nearby Ile de Brehat.

There is also reference to a popular legend linked to the saint. His first life was written six centuries after his death and contains many generic stories and miracles that can be found in many other lives. Yet, there may be traces of an oral tradition going back to an earlier date. One day, the saint was disturbed in his prayer and study by a demon. He was driven away and turned into a rock. Although this tradition is normally linked to Brittany, locals in St Mawes will point towards the Lugo (or seal) rock just by the castle as the petrified evil spirit.

The enigmatic saint seems to have only stayed in Cornwall briefly, giving his name to the village, chapel and holy well. Across the Channel over 130 sites bear his name or image; in Brittany there are over sixty churches and chapels dedicated to him alone. His cult was spread across France largely because of the dispersion of his relics. His relics were taken to Bourges and Sainte-Mandé (near Paris) to safeguard them from the raids of the Norsemen. His head was eventually returned to Brittany and kept at an abbey near Lanmodez. The saint's intercession was regarded as powerful: 'wherever there is a chapel or statue of St Maudez a pinch of earth or dust is taken and mixed with water to be drunk by the sick, and particularly by children suffering from worms'.

If you find yourself in St Mawes, perhaps kayaking, paddling or gorging yourself on a pasty, spare a thought for its patron. He may appear to be a figure of legend but, whatever the exact details of his life, he found God in this stretch of the Cornish coast and brought Christ's light and mercy a millennium and a half ago.

SALISBURY, WILTSHIRE

'Like the sun in full orb'

The crypt of St Peter's, Rome, is usually crammed full of pilgrims and tourists—some paying their respects to the mortal remains of past popes, others eager to find a good photo opportunity or simply escape the repressive heat of the Roman day. Few notice the tomb of a largely forgotten fifteenth-century pontiff, Callistus III (1455–8), and the adjacent images of two saints that he raised to the altars of the Church. One of these was half-English, though he was brought up in Valencia: St Vincent Ferrer (c. 1350–1419), a noted Dominican preacher and miracle worker. The other was a member of the Norman aristocracy who made England his adopted home: St Osmund (c. 1040–99), Bishop of Sarum. Canonised in 1457, he was the last Englishman to be so honoured before St Thomas More and St John Fisher in 1935 and one of the few English saints to be depicted in the command-centre of the Church.

Traditionally it was claimed that St Osmund was the son of Henry, Count of Séez and Isabella, the sister of William the Conqueror. There is little evidence for this; all that we can safely say was that he was born of a noble family in Normandy around 1040 and was probably educated at one of the great monastic centres, such as Bec. He came over to England in the aftermath of the Norman invasions and served as a chaplain in William's household. Here, the king soon spotted him and by 1070 he was serving as chancellor. It was perhaps this close relationship with William that led future writers to identify him as the king's nephew—a claim that undoubtedly looked impressive in the canonisation process and gave Salisbury added prestige.

As chancellor, St Osmund grew wealthy and was given various grants of land, including several holdings in Dorset, and in 1078 he was consecrated Bishop of Sarum. His predecessor, Herman, had become the first bishop after the dioceses of Ramsbury (Wiltshire) and Sherborne (Dorset) were united (1058). The bishop's seat was transferred to the royal centre of Old Sarum in 1075. The elevation of St Osmund to the episcopate demonstrated the growing tendency of Normans to be appointed to the major ecclesiastical offices as they fell vacant, thereby consolidating the new regime.

St Osmund was very much the Norman bishop: full of *Normanitas*, and zealous in administrative reform and the building of great churches, potent symbols of Norman power. St Osmund helped prepare the *Domesday Book*, arranged the great Council of Sarum (1086), reorganised his diocese and administered justice.

But he was also a man of great sanctity. William of Malmesbury speaks of his purity and learning, his strictness both with himself and with others, and a notable absence of greed or ambition. William—himself a monk of Malmesbury—also praised his promotion of the cult of St Aldhelm, Abbot of Malmesbury, first Bishop of Sherborne and an influential scholar. Thus, St Osmund's approach to the heritage of the English church was far more sympathetic than many of his Norman *confreres*, like Abbot Paul of St Alban's, who had broken up the tombs of the Saxon abbots since they had been 'uncultured idiots', or the abbot of Abingdon who had tried to eliminate the memory of that "English rustic", St Æthelwold.

St Osmund took his duties as bishop seriously. He completed the cathedral at Sarum, situated in the same enclosure as the castle—the foundations can still be seen today—although the tower was struck by lightning just five days after the consecration ceremony. At the cathedral, St Osmund established a community of canons, living under a rule like that of St Chrodegang of Metz. Much evidence abounds of the liveliness of intellectual life among these canons. Like St Aldhelm, St Osmund encouraged scholarship and built up a valuable library, much of which still survives. Perhaps the most appealing image of St Osmund that has come down to us is that of a godly bishop who was never happier than when copying and binding his books in the Sarum *scriptorium*. It is no wonder that he was said to suffer from constant pains in his neck and shoulders!

Most importantly, the canons of Sarum became widely respected for the care they showed over divine worship—a concern that laid the foundations of what later became known as the 'Use of Sarum'. This was the 'usage', a sort of liturgical 'dialect' within the Roman Rite, followed in Sarum and later in the 'new town' of Salisbury. Noted for its colourful splendour, love of processions and elaborate ritual (on great feasts there might be as many as three cross-bearers, two thurifers and seven deacons and subdeacons), the Usage soon spread far beyond the diocese to most of England south of the Humber and even to parts of Ireland and Portugal. In 1256 Giles de Bridport reported: 'among the churches of the whole world, the church of Salisbury shines like the sun in full orb, in respect of divine service and ministries, shedding her beams on every side so as to make up the deficiencies of other churches'.

Even the papacy recognised Sarum's unique liturgical status. According to an English *Martyrology* of 1608, 'the bishops of Salisbury obtained the titles of the Pope's Master of Ceremonies at Rome, according to that dignity'. Many writers have seen St Osmund as the author of the Use of Sarum and consequently as the 'Father of English Liturgy' but, in reality, Bishop Richard Poore codified the Use at the beginning of the thirteenth century. This was at the same time as the growing cult of 'St Osmund' and so it was perfectly understandable if Poore, in an attempt to get approval for the cult from Rome, exaggerated the use's origins by attributing later developments to his saintly predecessor. Poore's pioneering work clearly codified many uses that had existed before, some of which probably dated back to the time of St Osmund, but it was largely a more recent creation.

St Osmund died on 3 December 1099 and was buried in his cathedral the following day. 121 years later a new cathedral was started in the meadows below Old Sarum as part of a spacious 'new town', a masterpiece of medieval town planning. St Osmund's body was transferred there on 14 June 1226. Though St Osmund had long been venerated as a holy man, the cause for his canonisation was begun in 1228 and became one of the longest and most expensive in medieval England. It was closely linked to the need for a heavenly protector for the new town and cathedral. Proceedings dragged on and by 1416 the chapter were even allocating a tenth of their income for seven years for this very purpose.

Bishop Osmund was finally canonised on 1 January 1457, backed by nineteen miracles, and this was followed by the translation of his body to a new shrine in the Lady Chapel on 16 July 1457. His cult continued to grow up until the Reformation, the saint's intercession being particularly invoked against toothache, paralysis, rupture and madness.

Meanwhile, the Sarum liturgy remained triumphant until the Reformation and was revived under Mary I—indeed many of the martyrs would have used the Sarum Missal when they lacked access to the more recent Tridentine books. At the time of the Restoration of the Hierarchy (1850) there was, apparently, talk of reviving the Sarum Use, but the prevalent Ultramontane mood prevented this and so the ancient liturgy of Salisbury remained the preserve of antiquarians, liturgists and occasional 'reconstructions', like those organised by the Oxford University Newman Society at Merton College in the late 1990s.

St Osmund was one of the great Norman bishops, combining the more temporal aspects of his episcopate with tremendous learning, high liturgical standards and personal holiness.

TISBURY, WILTSHIRE

Catholic Families: The Arundells of Wardour

At first glance St John's church in Tisbury (Wiltshire) looks like hundreds of other English medieval churches—Norman arches, a hammerbeam roof and, in the churchyard, a particularly ancient yew. A distinctive feature, however, can be found in the Arundell Chapel, where many members of this venerable family await the Day of Resurrection. Not only were they staunchly Catholic but they boasted a title not often found in this country: 'Count of the Holy Roman Empire'.

High up on the wall of the chapel is a helmet, the 'Arundell Helm', which once belonged to Thomas, first Baron Arundell of Wardour. Unlike most funerary helms it was actually used in battle, its owner having fought for the Emperor Rudolf II against the Turks in 1595. He won fame at Gran (modern-day Esztergom), where 'breaking from the line Sir Thomas scaled the walls of the citadel, cut down six Turks with his sabre, wrested from a seventh Turk the standard of the Prophet' and brought it back in triumph.

Arundell had been given permission to fight for the Imperial Army as part of an Elizabethan charm offensive. The Queen had secretly negotiated with the Sultan since they shared a common enemy (Spain); Turkish campaigns in the east acted as a useful distraction that reduced the threat of another Armada in the west. However, quite understandably, some accused Elizabeth of being a traitor to Christendom. A gallant English soldier capturing the Turkish standard did her reputation no harm.

When the grateful Emperor created Arundell 'Count of the Holy Roman Empire' (a hereditary title), the queen was furious. 'I will not have my sheep branded with a foreign mark or have them following the piping of a foreign shepherd', she said, or according to another version: 'as chaste wives should have no glances but for their own spouses, so should faithful subjects keep their eyes at home and not gaze on foreign crowns'. Shortly afterwards an Act was passed making it illegal to accept foreign titles; however, under James I, Arundell was created a Baron.

The Arundell family originally hailed from Lanherne (Cornwall) and purchased Wardour Castle (just outside Tisbury) in 1547. It seemed a sensible move since they already possessed lands in the area that had once belonged to the powerful Shaftesbury Abbey. Catholic families were not afraid to obtain former monastic properties in the aftermath of the Dissolution, though there is some speculation that Sir Thomas Arundell (grandfather of the hero of Gran) intended to save the land for the nuns eventual return. He had already (unsuccessfully) pleaded their cause before Henry VIII. Visitors to Tisbury can still visit Place Farm, an impressive grange once belonging to the abbey with what claims to be the largest tithe barn in the country.

The Arundells made Old Wardour Castle their home and the Catholic Faith flourished there during penal times. The original castle was destroyed during the Civil Wars — seized by the Parliamentarians in 1643, after a heroic defence mounted by Lady Blanche, it was then besieged by Lord Arundell himself, who made the painful decision to mine his own home. Ruined beyond repair it may have been, but at least it was out of the Roundheads' grasp.

The family began to restore their fortunes, thanks largely to a series of advantageous marriages, and by 1770 the eighth Lord Arundell was able to build a new Wardour Castle, designed by James Paine in the neo-classical, Palladian style. Paine seems to have been particularly favoured by the great Catholic families, also designing Thorndon Hall for the Petres and Worksop Manor for the Duke of Norfolk. Although conditions were improving for English Catholics, discretion was still crucial and this made the neo-classical style ideal for a Catholic house. Fashionable elegance proclaimed to the world the family's status, while the lack of iconography prevented any anti-Catholic sensibilities from being offended.

The chapel of All Saints, designed by Paine along with Giacomo Quarenghi (who went on to work for Catherine the Great) and Sir John Soane, is situated in the West Wing; splendid inside but the model of discretion from without. It was opened by Bishop Walmsley, Vicar Apostolic of the Western District, in 1776 — giving the opportunity for a splendid ceremony rarely seen in those times. The chapel was not only for the use of the family but for the local Catholic population, which was one of the largest outside of London.

Times may have been changing but within a few years of its opening the chapel was threatened by an angry mob. The passing of Catholic Relief led to the Gordon Riots (1780); in London Catholic homes were pillaged and the chapels of the Sardinian and Bavarian Embassies damaged. In Bath the newly opened Catholic chapel was set alight. Lord Arundell feared a mob would arrive at Wardour and posted notices declaring that trouble-makers 'will be punished with the utmost Severity'. He further arranged for a keeper of the peace to be stationed at the back of the chapel during Masses; his box pew can still be seen beside the main entrance.

Wardour Castle is no longer the residence of the Arundell family. The sixteenth and last Lord Arundell died in 1944, having served with the Wiltshire Regiment and spending four years as a prisoner of war (including a spell at Colditz). When news reached Wardour that he was coming home, there was much jubilation and a triumphal arch was quickly erected. Then a communication arrived stating that he was critically ill with tuberculosis. He died shortly afterwards in a Liverpool hospital.

Although the house is now divided into flats, ownership of the chapel was transferred to a trust in the 1890s and is still used for Mass. It boasts a magnificent collection of vestments, some of which date back to before the Reformation. On my visit I had the privilege of wearing the famous 'Westminster Chasuble' — which once belonged to Margaret of York (sister of Edward IV). Before processing out of the sacristy, the server mentioned that Cardinal Wolsey (whose secretary was Thomas Arundell) may have worn the vestment at the Field of the Cloth of Gold! It was certainly very heavy and never have I been so careful of my movements during a Mass, in case I caused irreparable damage.

TRURO, CORNWALL

In Search of the Bensons

Epiphany House, on the outskirts of Truro, has a long and colourful history. In recent years it has been a school, Anglican convent and ecumenical retreat centre, but it was originally a vicarage, situated next to the parish church of Kenwyn, the mother-church of Truro. The church bears the dedication of St Keyne, a Welsh virgin who lived for many years as a hermit in Cornwall and belonged to a large family of saints; the great St Cadoc was her nephew.

Kenwyn vicarage would once have been at the heart of the local community. In 1787 it was visited by John Wesley, who left such a deep mark on the region; it is said that during his stay he stood on the churchyard wall and preached to 3,000 people.

In 1876, after many years of campaigning, an Anglican diocese was re-established in Cornwall. A millennium previously such a diocese had existed, based at St Germans (near Saltash) and eventually merged with that of Exeter. This proved to be a rather large and unwieldly diocese, especially given the poor road network in Cornwall and the number of isolated parishes. Moreover, in the eighteenth century the Church of England was challenged by the preaching of Wesley, so that as many as two-thirds of the Cornish population considered themselves Methodist. The established Church came to realise the necessity of renewal and reform and the need for an independent Cornish diocese. It was finally decided that Truro would be the site of a new cathedral and the vicarage at Kenwyn promoted to bishop's residence.

Edward White Benson was chosen as the first bishop. Born in 1829, he not only had great organising skills but a strong romantic imagination. As a child he built his own oratory, complete with cross, prie-dieu, decorative brasses and cunning traps devised for any nosey sisters. Here the canonical hours would be recited with his friends. Educated at King Edward's Grammar School, Birmingham, and Trinity College, Cambridge, he won a name for himself by founding the Cambridge University Ghost Story, dedicated to psychical research. In adulthood his talents were quickly recognised, as can be seen in his impressive *curriculum vitae*: Master at Rugby, Fellow of Trinity (his *alma mater*), Anglican priest, Headmaster of the newly created Wellington College and Chancellor of Lincoln Cathedral.

During these years of great industry, he married Mary Sidgwick, later called by Gladstone the cleverest woman in Europe, and together they brought into the world a remarkable dynasty: Edward Frederic (author of the *Mapp and Lucia* stories), Arthur Christopher (who produced the words for *Land of Hope and Glory*), Margaret (an Egyptologist) and Robert Hugh (Catholic convert and priest of the archdiocese of Westminster). Their supposedly brightest offspring, Martin, died while a schoolboy at Winchester. It was a talented family, though marked by the black dog of depression and a definite eccentric twist. Relations within the family could be intense; indeed, Arthur wrote a two-volume biography of his often-overbearing father and Edward produced a memoir simply entitled *Mother*. It was a clan that wrote its own history.

The family duly moved to the vicarage at Kenwyn, which was renamed Lys Escop (Cornish for 'Bishop's Court'). It remained strongly in the imagination of the children. E. F. Benson set his charming ghost story 'Pirates' at the house, in which the main character returns to his deserted childhood home after the death of his siblings and remembers how 'Lescop had been so noisy and alert and full of laughter with its garden resounding with games, and the house with charades and hide-and-seek and multitudinous plans'. For A. C. Benson, 'no sweeter place could be imagined': 'in the soft air trees and shrubs grew with great luxuriance' and 'the windows commanded a wide view down the green valley in which Truro lies'. In his *Confessions of a Convert*, Robert Hugh remembered the 'beautiful minute chapel', opened on his birthday, and the solemn Sunday afternoon family walks, often with an improving book. He recalled 'with real delight' the occasion when his father read aloud for half an hour the account of the martyrdom of St Perpetua and her companions, realising with 'irrepressible awe' that he had been translating at sight from the Latin *Acta*.

There was much work to be done. The new bishop travelled round his diocese, visiting remote churches and 'out-of-the-world places', bringing back colourful stories of saints, local customs and Cornish eccentrics. There was, for example, the parish where 'the curate-in-charge had been chained to the altar-rails, while he read the service, as he had a harmless mania which made him suddenly flee from the church if his own activities were for an instant suspended, as, for example, by a response'.

Bishop Benson only stayed in Truro for five years, before being appointed Archbishop of Canterbury. He left a deep impression on the diocese and, on his departure, wrote a *Farewell to Cornwall* in which he admitted: 'I have learnt to love every home and church and school'. Perhaps his most enduring legacy was the Service of Nine Lessons and Carols, first held at Truro at Christmas 1880 and now popular all over the world (especially at King's College, Cambridge). That is not to mention the magnificent cathedral, only completed in 1910 and designed by John Loughborough Pearson so that it would send the worshipper instantly to his or her knees. It was built onto a pre-existing church, dedicated to St Mary, which formed a side aisle

In the garden at Epiphany House, there is a prayer labyrinth. One evening a group of us decided to follow it, tracing the winding paths and reflecting on the journey through life, with its many unexpected changes of direction. At one point the centre seems a few steps away until the path takes you in a seemingly backwards direction, but with perseverance the middle is finally reached.

As I followed the labyrinth, I thought of the Benson family, and particularly of Robert Hugh. His life was full of twists and turns. His father died suddenly in 1896. After being ordained an Anglican priest and joining the Community of the Resurrection, he became a Catholic (causing quite a stir) and won some fame as a preacher and apologist. Continuing the family tradition, he wrote ghost stories as well as historical novels and science fiction, notably the futuristic *Lord of the World* (1907) which Pope Francis referred to on several occasions. Mgr Benson, as he became, set up home at Hare Street (Hertfordshire). Amid all this work, at his very peak, he was struck down by pneumonia while preaching in Salford and died at the Bishop's House in October 1914, aged 42. It is likely that overwork had taken its toll.

It was now getting dark, so we left the labyrinth and returned to the lounge, where we played charades. I wondered whether the Bensons looked down on us approvingly.

WIMBORNE MINSTER, DORSET

Dancing Nuns

Driving on the road to Bournemouth, intriguing signs began to appear to 'Wimborne Minster'. What was unusual was that this was not simply the name of a historic church but of the town that took its name from it. My friend and I decided it was worth a detour.

The church itself is full of interest. The exterior is rather rough and ready, with two towers and stone in different shades; according to Simon Jenkins, it produces an effect of 'a quilt of coloured rags'. It also gives a sense of antiquity—as well it should, for there has been a church here since the early eighth century.

Step inside and there are many indications that this is no ordinary parish church. There are the usual curiosities, such as the coffin of Anthony Ettricke, who died in 1703 and refused burial 'neither below the ground nor above it'. There is a famous chained library, founded in 1686 and containing over 400 volumes. There are royal tombs: a Saxon king (Ethelred the Unready, memorialised by a fifteenth-century brass) and the grandparents of Henry VIII on the Beaufort side. Little wonder that for many centuries the church was a 'Royal Peculiar': exempt from the jurisdiction of the local bishop and coming directly under the Crown.

It is the church's early history, though, which is particularly interesting. The first clue is in the unusual dedication to St Cuthburga, sister of King Ine of Wessex and former queen of Northumbria. It was she who founded a double monastery here around 705. According to Rudolf of Fulda, writing a century or so later and our main source on the subject, there was a house 'for men, the other for women, both surrounded by strong and lofty walls and provided with all necessities that prudence could devise'. Separation was thus complete; priests from the male section celebrating Mass for the nuns and the superior of both communities (the abbess) giving directions from the safety of a window. The lack of interaction between the sexes seems to have been a particular concern of Rudolf, who was pushing forward a particular model of monastic reform.

A prominent early abbess was St Tetta, herself of royal blood, who is said to have ruled over some 500 nuns. One of the most colourful (and human) stories from her reign concerned the 'dancing nuns of Wimborne'. There was a novice mistress who was noted for 'her zeal for discipline and strict observance' but 'as she was too incautious and indiscreet in enforcing discipline over those under her care, she aroused their resentment, particularly among the younger members of the community'. Thus far, anyone who has been through formation in a seminary or novitiate will feel a certain amount of sympathy.

The novice mistress eventually died, still inflexible and stubborn in her ways, and the younger nuns drew a sigh of relief. Their reaction, however, became somewhat extreme. Before the earth had even settled, they 'climbed on to her tomb, as if to stamp upon her corpse, uttering bitter curses over her dead body to assuage their outraged feelings'. Such was the frenzy of their 'dance' that the earth subsided and sunk six inches below the surrounding ground. St Tetta was less than satisfied by the conduct of the younger members of the community and decided that the deceased nun had been punished enough. She gave them a stern lecture about forgiveness and ordered three days of fasting and prayer. On the third day, the nuns processed around the cemetery singing psalms and litanies, while the abbess prostrated herself upon the ground. As she did so, 'the hole in the grave, which previously had appeared to be empty, suddenly began to fill in and the ground rose, so that the moment she got up from her knees the grave became level with the surface of the ground'. It was clear that the poor nun had, at last, entered into the joy of God's presence.

Even more miraculous, though, was the contribution made by Wimborne to the Anglo-Saxon mission to Germany. Such were the number of nuns that the house was able to contribute to these apostolic labours, though St Tetta was reluctant to lose some of her most gifted sisters. St Boniface was familiar with the community — he came originally from nearby Devon and seems to have been related to St Lioba, a woman of great ability and learning, who was promptly sent across the seas to act as abbess of the monastery at Tauberbischofsheim. In later years, she was a figure of some influence at the court of Charlemagne. Then there was St Walburga, possibly also a kinswoman of St Boniface, who led the community at Heidenheim and, after her death and the translation of her body to Eichstatt, became one of the most popular of German saints, partly due to the miraculous oil produced at her tomb. Another Wimborne nun, St Thecla, became abbess at Kitzingen and Ochsenfurt.

Wimborne, then, was no ordinary monastery. Founded by a queen and led by a series of strong-willed women, it made a valuable contribution to the conversion of Germany and the establishment of monasticism there. Though there is little trace of these glory days in the modern town, one gets a sense that the nuns are still dancing in their graves.

THE SOUTH-EAST

ARUNDEL, WEST SUSSEX

The Martyred Earl

Walk into Arundel Cathedral and you soon notice the statue of a noble-looking man wearing an impressive ruff and accompanied by his faithful old dog. This is St Philip Howard, one of the most unusual of the English Martyrs, whose body was brought to the cathedral shortly after his canonisation in 1970.

When we think of the martyrs, we normally picture the many heroic priests who wore clever disguises, celebrated secret Masses and jumped into hiding holes as soon as the pursuivants appeared. St Philip Howard was different. Not only was he a layman but the son and heir of the Duke of Norfolk. His baptism in 1557 was no ordinary one: it took place in the Chapel Royal at Whitehall and his godparents included Philip II of Spain (after whom he was named).

The saint was born into a violent world—his mother died only a few weeks after his birth and, when the boy was fourteen, his father was executed as a result of his treasonable plans to marry Mary, Queen of Scots. The dukedom of Norfolk was suspended (temporarily, as it turned out) and St Philip came to be known, in time, as Earl of Arundel, a title he received through his mother's lineage.

St Philip was no plaster statue saint. He had married Anne Dacre at the age of twelve and, as a young man, abandoned her for the pleasures of the royal court. He soon found himself in debt. A key moment of conversion, in 1580, was provided by a public debate in the Tower of London between learned Protestant divines and the Jesuit, St Edmund Campion. This led him to consider his relationship with God and, after pacing up and down the long gallery at Arundel Castle one day, he decided to embrace Catholicism. In doing so he must have been spurred on by the Catholic influences in his childhood and family, including his wife, with whom he was now reconciled.

Although he did not inform the queen of his conversion, it became increasingly obvious where his sympathies lay and, such was the pressure of his situation, he resolved to leave the country. One of the advantages of Arundel Castle was that it was near the sea. And so he secretly hired a ship from Littlehampton in April 1585 and, after a brief delay, sailed out into the Channel. One can only imagine his sense of relief and freedom as he left English soil and could see the Catholic coastline on the horizon; one can only imagine his horror when his boat was suddenly raided by what seemed like pirates but were in reality government agents, who had been tipped off; one can only imagine his sense of despair as he was taken to the Tower.

At first, he was charged with being reconciled to the Catholic faith, communicating with priests and leaving England without royal permission—if these were crimes, then there was no doubt of his guilt, especially since he had written a letter to the queen explaining the reasons for his departure. Several years later, in 1588, two fellow Catholics in the Tower confessed that Howard had arranged for a Mass to be said for the success of the Spanish Armada, mounted by his godfather. As a result, St Philip was deprived of his titles and condemned to death, thus following in the footsteps not only of his father (the 4th Duke) but his grandfather (the Earl of Surrey) and great-grandfather (the 3rd duke—who only escaped the block because of the timely death of Henry VIII). One historian has written that St Philip's was 'the only case in English legal history where somebody has been condemned as a traitor for *praying* for something to come about'. As the saying goes, be careful what you pray for!

Like a modern death row inmate, he lived in perpetual anticipation of his demise: 'not a bell that sounded, but it might be his knell; not a footstep was heard, but it might be the messenger of death. Each morning, as he rose, he knew not that, before night, he might be a headless corpse; each night, as he lay his head upon his pillow, he was uncertain whether the morning might not summon him to another world'. Though he avoided death on a scaffold, this mental torment continued for six long years and constituted a long martyrdom.

The conditions of his imprisonment were harsh: his room was small and smelly, and there was little chance of exercise. But his faith remained strong. On the walls of his cell he wrote: 'The more suffering for Christ in this world, so much the more glory with Christ in the next'. He prayed, almost as if he were a monk, using a breviary that had been smuggled to him; his biographer informs us that his knees were damaged and blackened because of the length of time he knelt on the hard floor. He also wrote spiritual treatises and composed poems. Though his visitors were few, he enjoyed the company of his faithful dog and it has been suggested that the dog, who enjoyed more freedom than his master, carried messages to other inmates in the Tower (such as another future martyr, St Robert Southwell).

His health weakened and in August 1595 he was taken ill with dysentery; some speculated that he was poisoned. He died on 19 October; even at the last he was denied permission to see his family.

Originally buried within the Tower, his body was later moved to the Fitzalan Chapel at Arundel Castle.

It is interesting to note that St Philip Howard's grandson is also venerated as a martyr, Blessed William Howard (Viscount Stafford), beheaded in the aftermath of the Popish Plot, and his great-grandson was the Dominican Cardinal Philip Howard, a major benefactor of the Venerable English College, Rome. The current duke still plays a major role in the nation's life as Earl Marshal (which means he is responsible for coronations and state funerals) and as the premier Catholic layman.

St Philip himself gives us a wonderful model of holiness in the world and of detachment from wealth and privilege; indeed, when he was condemned to death he merely said *Sic voluntas Dei*, God's will be done.

AYLESFORD, KENT

Home of the Scapular

It was good to revisit Aylesford, so familiar to Catholics in the southeast and, in former times, pilgrims crossing the Medway on the way to Canterbury. Today's Carmelite friary is a re-foundation of an earlier house, established in 1242 by a group of hermits from Mount Carmel using land given them by Richard de Grey, a veteran of the crusades.

The first Carmelites were solitaries gathered around Mount Carmel, made famous in the Book of Kings by the prophet Elijah. The hermits who reached Aylesford were part of a wider migration of Carmelites as a result of the crusades. England would play a vital part in the history of the Order, with early houses not only at Aylesford but at Hulne (Northumberland) and a General Chapter held at Aylesford in 1247. The participants recognised that life in England and other parts of Europe was somewhat different from that in Palestine. While keeping true to their contemplative tradition they decided to adopt the mendicant way of life, influenced no doubt by St Francis and St Dominic. The Carmelite Friars would live in the midst of the community, preaching the Gospel by word and deed, begging for alms and promoting learning. As a result of this momentous chapter meeting, Aylesford became known as the 'second Carmel'.

With its new identity, the Carmelites spread quickly. By the end of the thirteenth century over thirty houses had been opened in England alone, making it the largest of the medieval provinces. It is significant that one of the early Priors General of the Order was St Simon of England, better known as St Simon Stock. He led the friars at a decisive moment in their history and may have contributed two well-known Latin hymns to the Church's liturgy: *Flos Carmeli* and *Ave Stella Matutina*.

Various traditions have grown up around him: that he lived for a time in the trunk of a great tree; that he died at the advanced age of 101; and that he received the Brown Scapular from Our Lady. She told him: 'this shall be the privilege for you and for all the Carmelites, that anyone dying in this habit shall be saved'. This vision happened either at Cambridge or Aylesford.

There has been a certain reluctance in recent years in making too much of this tradition, which perhaps accounts for the understated nature of the Aylesford shrine. The historical facts are uncertain and the first accounts of the vision date from the late fourteenth century. It is undoubtable, though, that the Carmelite Brown Scapular has been a much-loved devotion down the centuries. Friends and benefactors of monasteries were often given the scapular of the habit and, with it, a share in the Order's privileges. Later this grew into a Third Order and the small Brown Scapular that is worn today. The wearing of a scapular is not only a prayer in itself, asking for Our Lady's protection, but the expression of a life centred on and clothed with Christ.

The Carmelite house at Aylesford was dissolved in 1538 and passed into secular ownership. Sir Samuel Pepys wrote on 24 March 1669 that he passed the 'old abbey', by now the seat of Sir John Banks, and noted that 'he keeps the grounds about it and the walls and house very handsome'. The friars were not forgotten either, as can be seen in local folklore: it was said that there was buried treasure, hidden from the greedy hands of Henry VIII, or that a secret tunnel led from Aylesford to Boxley Abbey, fourteen miles away, or that a white friar haunted the so-called 'Monks' Walk' in the garden.

Then in 1949 the friars returned and two years later they were joined by the cranium of St Simon Stock, donated by the Archbishop of Bordeaux. Thus, the 'Second Carmel' continues to welcome pilgrims to this day and assure them of Mary's protection.

BATTLE, EAST SUSSEX

The Papal Invasion of England?

In the summer of 1981, I dressed up as William the Conqueror in the fancy-dress competition at my school's summer fete. The costume was simple: a crown made of card, a plastic sword and an old curtain thrown over my shoulders—a juvenile homage to one of our most famous monarchs and the most iconic date in our history. Even at the age of five I did not find William a particularly attractive figure. Who cannot feel at least some sympathy for Harold Godwinson and admire his decisive defeat of the Danes at Stamford Bridge on 25 September 1066 before rushing down to the south coast, with his exhausted troops, to meet the Normans and, it must be said, very nearly defeat them?

William may not be a much-loved monarch but we acknowledge that he succeeded, against the odds, in conquering England, and in so doing he was elevated from being a mere duke to an anointed king. Of course, as far as William was concerned, he was not so much 'the Conqueror' as the rightful heir to the English throne, which had been promised him by the half-Norman St Edward the Confessor (whose feast, curiously, is celebrated the day before the Hastings anniversary).

Despite his assurances of legitimacy and continuity, William's succession has been described as 'the swiftest, most brutal, and most far-reaching transformation in English history'. This can be seen clearly in the Church: every English cathedral was taken down and rebuilt in the Norman style, diocesan boundaries were re-drawn and many Saxon saints demoted; at Malmesbury the relics of local saints were piled up 'like a heap of rubbish, or the remains of worthless hirelings'. Westminster Abbey was the only major pre-Conquest church to survive unscathed and St Wulfstan of Worcester the only 'English' bishop to keep his *cathedra*.

William was, undeniably, a strong ruler and his reign was marred by acts that appeared both to contemporaries and to us as particularly brutal. The 'Harrying of the North' (1069–70) was aimed at defeating the rebels, though, according to the chronicler Orderic Vitalis, 'to his shame, William made no effort to control his fury, punishing the innocent with the guilty. He ordered that crops and herds, tools and food be burned to ashes. More than 100,000 people perished of starvation ... I can say nothing good about this brutal slaughter. God will punish him'. Sixteen years later, many estates in Yorkshire are still described in the *Domesday Book* as *wasta est* (it is waste).

One thing that could be said in William's defence was that he was a man of considerable piety. He built churches and monasteries, supported the work of church reform and surrounded himself with able and conscientious churchmen, such as Lanfranc (Archbishop of Canterbury, 1070–89), a famed scholar from the monastery of Bec. William of Malmesbury tells us that the Conqueror attended Mass every day and liked to hear Matins and Vespers. Unusually for monarchs and aristocrats of the time, he was faithful to his wife, Matilda of Flanders, and had no illegitimate children.

The Conqueror also had a close relationship with the papacy and this can be seen in the campaign of 1066. Invading England was a high-risk strategy but, as far as William was concerned, he had the support of God against the usurper Harold. The Archbishop of Canterbury, Stigand, was also regarded as uncanonical and added to this was William's willingness to reform the English Church, especially to enforce the celibacy of its priests and attack pluralism.

William gained the backing of Pope Alexander II for his plans. The main contemporary authority for this is William of Poitiers' *Gesta Guillelmi*, though many other sources (including the Bayeux Tapestry) are silent on the matter. According to the *Gesta*, William was able to show off the banner of St Peter at Hastings, along with papal blessings and relics. After the battle, the standard of Harold was sent to Rome 'as an equal return for the gift sent to him by apostolic generosity'. With papal support, William was assured of the rightness of his cause and divine protection, though the Norman invasion was never seen as a 'crusade' as such and offered no spiritual rewards to its participants.

William continued his close links with Rome. In 1070 papal legates arrived in England and crowned William for the second time in Winchester—a unique episode in English history, giving William further legitimacy. A series of ecclesiastical synods were held to push forward church reform and replace the Saxon bishops with Norman 'upgrades'.

There was also the matter of atonement for the spilling of so much English blood. As early as 1067 the bishops of Normandy set a series of appropriate penances for all those involved in the Conquest: the so-called 'Penitential Ordinance', which was confirmed by the legates. These included stipulations that 'anyone who knows that he killed a man in the great battle must do one year's penance for each man he killed'. For the wealthy, sin could be redeemed by the endowing or building of a church. This was the path chosen by William.

The battlefield of Hastings today bears little evidence of bloodshed and reflects its more recent use as a park and farmland. On the hillside where Harold's men made their last stand are the ruins of the once mighty Battle Abbey. This was founded not only as a memorial to the fallen but as an act of reparation. Indeed, the high altar was said to stand on the very spot where Harold was slain—though we will never know whether the cause of death really was that arrow in his eye. By 1076 the choir was ready to be consecrated and the whole church was completed during the reign of the Conqueror's son, William Rufus. By founding the abbey, William not only made his peace with God but asserted his authority on the battlefield where England was changed forever.

BOXLEY, KENT

The Holy Rood

Little now remains of Boxley Abbey, situated near Maidstone, one of the first Cistercian houses to be founded in England. There are still remnants of its gateway and a large barn, which once provided pilgrims to Canterbury with accommodation. Most of the buildings, though, have disappeared without trace, seemingly swallowed up by the well-cultivated land which bears testament to the farming skill of the medieval monks.

The abbey was founded by William of Ypres, Earl of Kent, in 1146. The rationale for the foundation was a desire to atone for his sins, which were apparently manifold. It was never a large house (there were only ten in the community at the Dissolution) but certain events in its history suggest its importance. One of its abbots was involved in the burial of the recently martyred St Thomas Becket (1171); just over twenty years later another abbot was involved in an expedition to southern Germany to locate the captured Richard 'the Lionheart'; Edward II held court there in 1321 and, just before its closure, Cardinal Campeggio adjudicated at the abbey on the great question of Henry VIII's divorce. A small religious house, then, but not without significance in the nation's history.

According to Archbishop Warham, Cranmer's predecessor at Canterbury, the abbey was much frequented by pilgrims and was 'so holy a place where so many miracles be showed'. It was known for its two celebrated images. The first was a stone statue of the obscure St Rumbold. He was a prince of the Saxon kingdom of Northumbria, born around 650 while his parents were travelling through Northamptonshire. On the day of his birth he stated three times 'I am a Christian' and demanded baptism; the next day he expounded on the mystery of the Trinity and preached about the virtues; on the third day he announced his imminent death and quickly passed to his heavenly reward. He was buried in Buckingham. In his 1917 book, *Canterbury Pilgrims and their Ways,* Francis Pott rather unkindly calls him 'the most atrocious specimen of the infant prig ever presented to the attention of the world'.

Pilgrims to Boxley were invited to lift the statue of St Rumbold — easy enough if they were in a state of grace but impossible if they were burdened by grave sin. This was no miracle; the monk on duty had some mechanism which could either hold the statue to the floor or release it, perhaps depending (it is said) on whether they had given a suitable offering.

If they managed to lift the image, the relieved pilgrim would then move on to the great treasure of Boxley: the 'Rood of Grace'. This was a crucifix, which according to tradition had been carved by an English carpenter during his captivity as a 'prisoner of war' in France. He was given liberty to return to his homeland to sell his masterpiece and thus raise enough money for his ransom. As he journeyed around, he apparently stopped at an inn in Rochester, where his horse escaped, along with the crucifix tied to its back. The beast deviated from his master's route and ended up at Boxley Abbey, 'where he so beat and bounced with his heels that divers of the monks heard the noise, came to the place to know the cause, and marvelling at the strangeness of the thing, called the abbot and his convent to behold it'. The carpenter eventually caught up but the horse, with its precious cargo, refused to budge, and so the cross ended up in the monastery church—a quaint story, echoing that of the more famous *Santo Volto* of Lucca, which arrived on a cart driven by oxen but without a driver.

The Boxley rood was unusual in that it was mechanical. Since the earliest descriptions of the crucifix date from the time of its destruction by Protestant reformers and were often exaggerated by anti-Catholic hostility, it is unclear how elaborate its movements were. It is likely that the eyes and mouth moved, affirming the devout pilgrim and reprimanding the sinner. One Protestant writer, John Finch, reported that 'by means of some person pulling a cord, most artfully contrived and ingeniously inserted at the back, the image rolled about its eyes just like a living creature; and on the pulling of other cords it gave a nod of assent or dissent according to the occasion... Then again, by some other contrivance unknown to me, it opened and shut its mouth'.

Since the nineteenth century, historians have debated the nature of the rood. Was it a deliberate deception, conning 'simple-minded' members of the faithful into believing that the wooden crucifix was miraculously communicating with them? Or was it widely understood as a mechanical device, a 'religious attraction' that could both delight and edify? As one of Boxley's Victorian apologists, the Redemptorist Fr Thomas Bridgett, put it: 'either Catholics had been gulled or Protestants have been bamboozled'.

It is easy to see how the story of the rood was a gift for Protestant propagandists, who presented its seizure as a triumph of truth over falsehood. In 1538 the cross was taken to Maidstone on market day by Thomas Cromwell's men and then to St Paul's Cross in London. Here it was exhibited publicly—the corruption of the monks seemingly exposed to the light of day—while the Bishop of Rochester preached a strongly worded sermon. It was then thrown on a large fire.

It seems, though, that the true state of affairs was rather different. When the commissioners arrived at the abbey, the monastic community professed ignorance of the rood's mechanics. Moreover, the controls were not in working order, consisting of 'old wire, old rotten sticks'. It is clear, though, that these devices had once been used but even then the indications are that the rood was understood as a machine. Our medieval forebears were not that stupid.

Fr Bridgett wrote in 1888 that the rood was 'analogous to many bits of fun not unknown in our own days. The visitors to Ripon will remember the underground remains of the ancient abbey still shown in the crypt, and how ladies were invited to go through a small window, called, if I remember rightly, St Wilfrid's needle, as a proof of their chastity, or to obtain good luck in marriage. The verger certainly affirmed to the present writer that an Anglican archbishop's wife had recently done the feat'. Likewise, I have visited the beautiful Peterskirche in Munich several times and always put a coin in the machine at the back, prompting a little statue of the Child Jesus to pop out of the model chapel behind a glass window and give a blessing. At no time have I felt duped into thinking this was a true miracle!

The Church has always used strikingly visual and inventive means to help communicate the good news. Rather than being a corrupt forgery, the Boxley rood was part of the 'new evangelisation' of the Middle Ages, using ingenious mechanics and the carnival atmosphere of a pilgrimage to bring people closer to the mystery of the Cross. If there were miracles at Boxley, it was not because of the movement of statues but because of the offering of pilgrim's prayers.

BRIGHTON, WEST SUSSEX

In Search of Mrs Fitzherbert

Brighton is often called 'London-by-the-Sea', and this is certainly reflected in the extortionate parking charges. Nevertheless, there is much of interest, and, on a fine day, it is hard not to believe Dr Russell, who argued in the eighteenth century that the Brighton air and waters could transform one's health.

Brighton—or, more properly, Brightholmstone—was originally a small fishing port. The old church of St Nicholas on the hill would have been a familiar landmark for boats approaching the coast. Let not the jolly scenes of the modern pier and pebble beach mislead you; the sea has been as much an enemy as a friend to the people of Brighton over the years. French ships raided the town in 1514 and burnt many of the buildings, while storms in 1703 and 1705 caused widespread damage. Daniel Defoe thought the first of these was divine punishment for recent losses against Catholic armies in the War of the Spanish Succession. He wrote that the winds 'stript a great many houses, turn'd up the lead of the church, overthrew two wind-mills, and laid them flat on the ground, the town in general (at the approach of daylight) looking as though it had been bombarded'.

The most fascinating and unusual building in Brighton is surely the Royal Pavilion. As Brighton became an increasingly fashionable resort, it attracted the attention of royalty and, in particular, the future George IV, who first visited in 1783. He bought a farmhouse on the Steine and rebuilt it, firstly in the neo-classical style but then, from 1815, according to John Nash's wildly exotic 'Indo-Islamic' designs, with numerous domes and minarets.

As one walks around the interior, admiring the bamboo fretwork, the palm tree columns, and the huge chandelier in the Banqueting Room, which weighs a ton and is hung from the ceiling by a silver dragon, a note of melancholy strikes the Catholic visitor. At the French Revolution, the Catholic colleges and convents overseas had to be evacuated and the communities found shelter back in England. The English bishops campaigned for years to safeguard their property in France and claim compensation payments. The French government finally handed over nearly £3 million in 1818 to cover all claims made against it. However, those brought by the Catholic institutions were never awarded, because the British authorities felt they could not give money for 'superstitious' purposes. The Catholic community was poverty-stricken and struggled to maintain the institutions brought over from France, including the new colleges at Old Hall Green and Ushaw. Such a large compensation payment would have been invaluable but the rumour persists that the money was used instead to pay off the debt on the Pavilion. Magnificent though the building is, one wonders how the beleaguered Catholics might have spent the money at this critical time in their history.

There is another Catholic connection that springs to mind as one roams around the Pavilion—and one that is no less tragic. In 1785 George secretly married a Catholic widow, Mrs Fitzherbert, who remained, if he is to be believed, his one true love, even though he entered an 'official' and deeply unhappy marriage with Caroline of Brunswick and had a string of affairs.

Maria Fitzherbert belonged to the Smythe family, whose principal seat of Acton Burnell (Shropshire) would later shelter the Benedictine monks from Douai during the French Revolution. She was educated with the 'Blue Nuns' in Paris and in 1775 married Edward Weld, a member of the famous Catholic family based at Lulworth Castle (Dorset). He died within a few months and, three years later, she married Thomas Fitzherbert. She found herself a widow once again in 1781 and moved to Richmond (Surrey).

Despite having been married twice, she was still considered eminently eligible, being beautiful in appearance, attractive in character and aged only twenty-six. She had briefly met the Prince of Wales in 1780 but, after a chance meeting at the opera four years later, George realised he was smitten. She was at first reluctant to return his affections, realising that they were unlikely to lead anywhere. Indeed, there were three main legal obstacles to any possible marriage. The 1701 Act of Settlement excluded members of the royal family who either had married Catholics or professed 'the popish religion' from the succession. The 1772 Royal Marriage Act required the explicit permission of the monarch before a royal marriage was contracted and was introduced after two of the king's brothers married brides who were deemed 'unsuitable'. Finally, the 1753 Marriage Act required marriages to take place before a clergyman inside an Anglican church, unless explicit permission had been granted; Jews and Quakers were the only groups exempted.

Nevertheless, the prince continued his pursuit and, when Mrs Fitzherbert announced she was about to travel to Europe in July 1784, he stabbed himself and threatened to pull off his bandages and bleed to death unless she consented to visit him. This she did and the couple eventually married privately in Mrs Fitzherbert's drawing room in Mayfair the following year, on 15 December 1785. Her uncle, Henry Errington, and her brother, Jack Smythe, were the witnesses, although their names were later cut out of the handwritten marriage certificate for their own protection. The ceremony was performed by Reverend Robert Burt, an Anglican clergyman whose debts, it is said, had been paid by the prince in order to release him from the Fleet Prison!

The marriage remained secret, though rumours about it abounded and Mrs Fitzherbert became a favourite subject of the caricaturists. She was looked down upon, also, by many of her co-religionists, who thought her marriage would lead to anti-Catholic feelings and delay the granting of further relief from the penal laws. Interestingly, although the marriage was illegal in the eyes of the English law, it was valid in the eyes of the Catholic Church—and the Holy See confirmed this to be the case in 1799. The decrees of Trent had not yet been promulgated in England, due to the circumstances of the Reformation, meaning that a marriage, even between two Catholics, celebrated in the Church of England was considered valid. A Catholic priest did not have to be present. Whenever possible, the Anglican service was followed by a Catholic ceremony, as Mrs Fitzherbert had done with her previous two marriages, but this must have seemed inappropriate in the case of her third marriage. Whether or not George knew that his wedding was null and void legally, it soothed the conscience of Mrs Fitzherbert; as far as she was concerned, she was canonically the wife of a prince.

The couple lived separately, though Mrs Fitzherbert was given properties close to Carlton House in London and the Royal Pavilion. For a time the prince seemed a reformed character, avoiding excessive drinking and gambling, and according to one biographer 'the two years after the marriage—together with the few years after their reconciliation in 1800—were probably the happiest of his life'. However, 'a quiet domestic existence with the woman he loved was ill-suited to his temperament and could not satisfy him for long'. Their relationship blew hot and cold and, at times, she was treated contemptuously, especially with his unpredictable moods and his roving eye. There were periods of separation, culminating in a final break in 1811. When he died in 1830 he was buried with a locket containing a picture of Mrs Fitzherbert around his neck and the letter she had written him on his death-bed was placed under his pillow, though, due to his poor health, it was left unanswered.

Mrs Fitzherbert remained 'Mrs Fitzherbert' for the rest of her life. There was a suggestion that William IV offered her the title of duchess, which she refused. After George's death she wore widow's weeds and her servants were dressed in royal livery. She continued to live in Brighton and was treated with respect by the locals, who regarded her home at Steine House as second in importance only to the Pavilion. She was a devout Catholic, giving £1,000 to the new church of St John the Baptist in Kemp Town, to the east of the town centre. The poor remembered her for her generosity, which makes it appropriate that the YMCA is now based in her former home. When a char girl asked the parish priest at St John's why she had to curtesy whenever Mrs Fitzherbert entered, he enigmatically replied 'Well, she maybe she is the Queen of England, and maybe she isn't'.

Mrs Fitzherbert died in Brighton on 27 March 1837 and was buried at St John's. She appears on her monument kneeling at a *prie-dieu*, an open book showing a verse from the twentieth chapter of Acts: 'It is a more blessed thing to give than to receive'. Whatever the arguments about the validity of her marriage to George IV, her tomb tries to have the last word: for on it she proudly wears three wedding rings.

CANTERBURY, KENT

A Pilgrimage to Canterbury

People go on pilgrimage for many different reasons. They may be searching for God, asking for a saint's intercession, pleading for healing, fulfilling a vow or doing penance for past sin. Mixed into the equation are all sorts of worldly motives: the adventure of travel, the escape from the daily grind, the joy of making new friends and the fun of travelling with old ones. There is often an opportunity for sightseeing, feasting and shopping; pleasure and piety have always been a pilgrim's bedfellows. If that is the case in this age of relatively easy travel and disposable incomes, so it was the case in the past.

Perhaps the most famous medieval English pilgrimage was that to St Thomas at Canterbury. Although there is evidence that the popularity of Canterbury was being challenged by new shrines and devotions on the eve of the Reformation, thousands still went every year—especially round the feast of the translation of his relics (7 July) and the two feasts in December of his return from exile (2 December) and the martyrdom itself (29 December). Added to this were the jubilees every fifty years, with special indulgences granted by the pope, the last one taking place in 1470.

Geoffrey Chaucer says very little about the spiritual side of a medieval pilgrimage in his famous *Canterbury Tales*. St Thomas, 'the holy blissful martyr', is only mentioned in passing. However, Chaucer vividly captured the reality of a pilgrimage to Canterbury. His pilgrims display different motivations. The Knight has just returned safely from his campaigns against the Moors; the Wife of Bath is a pilgrimage enthusiast (a type we still see in our midst today).

There is a mixture of seriousness and frivolity in the tales told by the pilgrims—some are rather vulgar; others, like the Second Nun, resorts to the life of a saint while the Parson attempts a serious sermon on the Seven Deadly Sins.

The backgrounds of Canterbury pilgrims were also mixed, from the lowest sections of society to the highest. Quite apart from English royalty, the shrine was visited by Louis VII of France in 1179, who gave a magnificent ruby known as the *Regale*, and the Holy Roman Emperor Charles V in 1520. An early pilgrim was the future Innocent III, who as pope once told the English bishops that they must have over-indulged in drinking beer since their arguments were rather confused. One wonders whether he thought back to what he had observed in the taverns of Canterbury.

The martyr's fame was therefore not just an English phenomenon. Churches were dedicated to him across Europe; he was the subject of an Icelandic poem and a hill was named after him in Esztergom (Hungary).

Then as now, pilgrims liked to take souvenirs home with them and the most popular of these were the cheap, mass-produced badges, normally pinned to the pilgrim's broad-brimmed hat. As the anonymous continuation of Chaucer's work, *The Tale of Beryn*, puts it:

> Then, as the usual custom is, pilgrim signs they bought
> For men at home should know what saint the pilgrims
>   here had sought.

For the shrine, a badge not only raised revenue but provided free advertising. For the pilgrim, it was a way of proving that a pilgrimage had been successfully completed. The badge itself was not only a memento that could be proudly shown off but regarded as a holy object, infused with the grace of the shrine—a sort of sacramental. As well as being treasured possessions, there also seems to have been a custom of throwing badges into a river on the pilgrim's return as a thanks offering, one reason why so many have been found on the banks of the Thames.

The universal sign of a pilgrim was the scallop shell of St James; pilgrims to Compostela collected these from the French and Spanish coast and reflected on the story of St James saving a man from the waters covered in shells. The grooves on the shell coming together at a single point representing the different pilgrim routes taken.

There were more specific symbols for the Canterbury pilgrimage, relating to the life and cult of St Thomas. Pilgrims might wear badges showing the martyr's triumphant return to England shortly before his death, after six years of exile (an event compared to Christ's entry into Jerusalem) or the figure of the archbishop standing on a peacock, which probably referred to the custom of swearing vows on a noble bird such as this. Other badges were linked to the different pilgrimage 'stations' in Canterbury Cathedral—the martyrdom itself, the murder weapon, the magnificent shrine and the reliquary containing part of Becket's head kept in the Corona chapel.

A very common souvenir was an ampulla to contain St Thomas's Water, taken from a well at the cathedral which the saint had used in his lifetime and in which his body had been washed after death.

The monks sometimes coloured it with red dye to recall the martyr's blood and this was seen as particularly efficacious.

Then there were the Canterbury Bells, worn around the neck. As one Lollard critic of St Thomas's cult complained in 1407, the pilgrims had become quite a nuisance 'what with the noise of their singing, and with the sound of their piping and with the jangling of their Canterbury bells'.

Badges helped identify pilgrims and became part of their standard attire. A ceremony of blessing pilgrims developed in the Middle Ages, resembling the taking of a religious habit or the dubbing of a knight. The different parts of the pilgrim's costume gained a deeper significance. The staff, which not only aided walking long distances but could be used as a weapon against wild animals and thieves, was the sign of spiritual combat. The scrip or knapsack in which key provisions were kept was a symbol of the pilgrim's poverty and trust in God. The long tunic, or sclavein, which covered much of the body by day and by night represented God's love for mankind.

It is little wonder that Canterbury's motto is *Ave Mater Angliae*, 'Hail, Mother of England'. There is so much that could be said about the city— how it is the home of England's oldest diocese, founded by St Augustine of Canterbury; how the city was designed as a Kentish version of Rome, complete with a cathedral dedicated to the Saviour, like the Lateran; how its archbishops have shaped England's history— including among them sixteen saints, seven cardinals, two martyrs and a Doctor of the Church.

The cathedral boasts (or boasted) a charming little curiosity that speaks of its antiquity: the cathedral bug, *Argas Reflexus*, a species of tick with 'a pear-shaped, tortoise-shell tinted back' that exists nowhere else in England and is said to have been brought back by crusaders. According to one writer, 'it seems that he lingers here like the monster of Loch Ness, emerging occasionally and (possibly not liking what he finds) retreating once more into the dark and devious crannies where he leads his secret life'.

The crucial decade in Canterbury's story is surely the 1170s. It opened ominously on 29 December 1170, when Archbishop Thomas Becket was murdered in his own cathedral. It is a moment that rocked the whole of Christendom and eight centuries later was still able to inspire stage and screen. The facts, though, are not as well known as they should be.

Born in London of Norman parents, St Thomas was trained in law and became a close friend of Henry II, that remarkable monarch whose territory stretched from Scotland to the Pyrenees. Becket became his

Lord Chancellor. These two strong characters worked hard and played hard together, as comes across in the 1964 film *Becket*. However, the king then had a clever idea. Wanting to extend his control over the Church, he decided to appoint his friend as Archbishop of Canterbury in 1162. The Church was, after all, a major landowner, providing him with troops and money for his Exchequer and acting as a major influence on the lives of his subjects.

The problem was that St Thomas was not content to simply do the king's will. He took his new office seriously, spending much time in prayer and fasting and defending the rights and freedoms of the Church. The poet Tennyson has the saint say:

> I served King Henry well as Chancellor:
> I am his no more, and I must serve the Church.

Reform was in the air; the Church was becoming better organised; its canon law was codified and bishops became increasingly confident in stressing their spiritual authority in the face of the secular power. St Thomas was particularly concerned with the issue of 'benefit of clergy', arguing that a cleric accused of a criminal offence should be tried by an ecclesiastical court. St Thomas eventually fled to the continent and spent six years in exile. He finally returned to England in December 1170, a few weeks before his death. There were signs of an uneasy peace with the king but there was a final controversy. Henry had crowned his son as an associate king and, since St Thomas was in France, asked the Archbishop of York to preside at the ceremony. Crowning a king was the jealously guarded privilege of the Archbishop of Canterbury (as it still is) and St Thomas saw this as a direct attack on his authority and, though it might seem petty to our ears, the thin end of a worrying wedge. His consequent excommunication of most of England's bishops and his refusal to back down led to Henry's famous words: 'what miserable drones and traitors have I nourished and promoted in my household, who let their lord be treated with such shameful contempt by a low-born clerk!'

Four knights took the king literally and set out to confront the archbishop: Reginald fitzUrse, Hugh de Morville, William de Tracy and Richard le Breton. They did not act alone but brought their own men with them, making their entry into the cathedral precincts a small military operation. After a brief confrontation at his palace, St Thomas hurried into his cathedral, where Vespers was being sung by the monks. He ordered the doors of the cathedral to be kept open, saying it was a church not a castle. The knights came in, shouting

'Where is the traitor?' to which St Thomas answered, 'Here I am. No traitor to the king, but a priest of God. What do you want?' They tried to seize him and, in the midst of a scuffle, a blow cut off the crown of his head with such force that the sword broke on the ground. His body lay before the high altar that night and was hurriedly buried in the crypt the next day. In preparing the body for burial the monks were edified to find a monastic habit underneath his robes and a hair shirt, covered with worms and lice.

News of the murder shocked the Christian world. Canterbury Cathedral itself lay desolate for nearly a year, with its crosses veiled, its bells silenced and its liturgy celebrated in the chapter house. Although the monks tried to prevent a cult from developing, it grew spontaneously among the sick and the poor. Since the cathedral was largely inaccessible, it emerged 'off site' through relics of the martyr's blood — cloths that had touched it and, in time, the 'Water of St Thomas'. Events moved quickly. St Thomas was canonised by Alexander III at Segni in 1173; the following year King Henry made a penitential pilgrimage — he walked barefoot from St Dunstan's church beyond the city's West Gate, his feet bleeding copiously, and was scourged by monks at his friend's tomb. The following day his army defeated the Scots at Alnwick and captured King William the Lion — it seemed that he had indeed made his peace with God.

Shortly afterwards, much of the cathedral was destroyed by fire — the second conflagration in just over a century. It proved to be a blessing in disguise, for the monks were able to rebuild a cathedral that was also a magnificent shrine. Unusually, it boasted not only a saint's tomb but also the place of his death. Pilgrims followed a fixed itinerary. First, there was the martyrdom, with the Altar of the Sword's Point. Devotees would then see where St Thomas was initially buried in the crypt and where his body had lain before the high altar. Then there was the magnificent shrine in the apse, where (according to Erasmus) the meanest material was gold and where the faithful could have direct contact with the saint by crawling into arched recesses. They hoped for his intercession and could admire previously granted favours in the magnificent Miracle Windows. Finally there was the relic of the crown of his head in the Corona Chapel. Moreover, there were other sainted archbishops to venerate here, all of them significant in their own way: St Dunstan, St Alphege, St Anselm.

At the Reformation there were attempts to obliterate his memory and churches dedicated to him became churches of 'St Thomas the Apostle'. Since then, there has been a revival of devotion; the English Catholic Church declared him to be patron of the secular clergy.

Despite this, St Thomas is not the most accessible of saints. There is no doubt that he was a difficult character and his behaviour at times appears brash, arrogant and stubborn. He was criticised by his contemporaries just as much as by recent historians. Yet, as his biographer Frank Barlow wrote, 'Thomas' behaviour reanimated the tradition of bellicosity in the church, a truculence which not only protected the church's own rights but also helped to defend the rights of other men against tyrannical rulers'. He fearlessly stood up to the pretentions of a regime that tried to compromise the Church's freedom. He spoke truth to power. Every generation needs a Thomas Becket.

DENHAM, BUCKINGHAMSHIRE

The Devils of Denham

Only a few miles out of Greater London, the village of Denham is full of rural charm and its main street boasts an impressive number of pubs serving real ale. A plaque indicates the former home of the actor, Sir John Mills. There is little indication that in the mid-1580s this sleepy village was the epicentre of a series of Catholic exorcisms that caught the country's attention.

At the time, the Catholic Peckham family lived at Denham Court, a manor which had once belonged to Westminster Abbey and is now an elegant golf club. The monument of one of their number, Sir Robert Peckham, in the local church states that he travelled to Rome, officially for reasons of health, where he died in September 1569 and 'lyethe entombed in the churche of Sainte Gregorie'. He sent his heart back to Denham, however, to be buried 'in the vaulte of his auncestors'.

The family was friendly with Fr William Weston, the Superior of the English Jesuits, who became convinced that 'many people, including Catholics, were tormented by evil spirits who would cause fearful disturbance in those in whom they dwelt'. It was difficult dealing with these cases without attracting attention, since 'usually they let out violent and raucous shrieks during the ceremonies', but Weston believed that 'something had to be attempted'. The result was a veritable campaign of exorcisms, with the patronage of the Peckhams.

Though Weston alludes to these in his *Autobiography*, most of the details come from an anti-Catholic source: Samuel Harsnett's *A Declaration of Egregious Popish Impostures*, written nearly twenty years later by order of the Privy Council. Harsnett, a future Archbishop of York, was not only concerned to condemn Catholic exorcisms, which he thought superstitious and fraudulent, but by doing so attacked extremists within the Church of England, often on the 'puritan' fringe, who promoted similar practices. Much of his information was alleged to come from a Catholic document, now lost, found in the possession of one Robert Barnes.

Weston's astonishing series of exorcisms took place not only in Denham, Uxbridge and the surrounding area but in Hackney and central London. He was assisted by twelve other priests, including two future martyrs: Blessed Robert Dibdale and Blessed John Cornelius. Another, Anthony Tyrrell, who later apostasised, was used as a source by Harsnett. Dibdale was 'hanged, bowelled and quartered' at Tyburn shortly afterwards, in October 1586. Bishop Challoner preserves a testimony that at Denham 'there were three persons bewitched and possessed—two maids and one man. Out of one of the maids he [Dibdale] brought forth a needle at her cheek, and two rusty nails and pieces of lead'. Harsnett recalls that he also spent 'two or three nights' at Uxbridge and lay his hands on a possessed woman who 'felt herself to burn'.

Other strategies were used. After a Mass celebrated by Dibdale, one of the Peckham's servants, Friswood Williams, was bound to a chair with towels and urged to drink 'a pint of Sack and Salad Oil, being hallowed and mingled with some kind of spices'; finally her head was held over a dish of burning brimstone until her face turned black. This was in accordance with a popular work of demonology, *Flagellum Daemonum* ('The Scourge of Demons', 1577), by the Italian Franciscan Girolamo Menghi. The demons also reacted to priestly vestments: another Denham servant, Sara Williams, is described by Harsnett as becoming 'puffed' at the appearance of an amice and the devil within her being 'rent, battered and torn' by the priest's stole.

News of these exorcisms even reached the ears of Philip II's confessor, Diego de Yepez, who added that the devils 'told what relics of the saints each one had privately brought with him, and obeyed the prayers and exorcisms of the Church, confessing and declaring to their own confusion the virtue which the sign of the cross, holy water, and relics (as well of the ancient saints as of those that suffer in these days in England for the Catholic faith) have against them'.

Weston did not only want to defeat evil and help those possibly affected by possession. As he would tell an interrogator in prison, 'I was certain that there were many people who, given an opportunity of observing the power of the Church over evil spirits and monsters, would see and acknowledge at once the difference between the two religions and award the victory to the Catholic faith'. Yepez states that many Protestants 'were convinced by the evidence of what they saw' and were converted.

The house at Denham was eventually raided by pursuivants in June 1586. Weston later recalled: 'They chose what they thought was the most likely time for Mass and for the exorcisms; but, fortunately, they spent a long time knocking at the gate—it was a large house encircled by a high wall—otherwise they would have burst in at all the entrances at once and surprised us'. They eventually gained admittance but met one of the 'possessed' in the entrance hall:

as soon as she saw them, she glared and ground her teeth and said that one of the searchers had a thousand devils hanging on to the buttons of his coat. This scared them. All the mad fury of their first entry was forgotten. Indeed, in their extreme terror they seemed half-dead and became most amenable... Not a thing in the entire house was touched... In point of fact several priests were in the house at the time, some actually saying Mass when the men arrived; but everything was finished and the priests put away in various hiding places before the rogues were let in.

The case of the 'Devils of Denham' proves that Elizabethan priests could be bold in their pastoral strategy. With no episcopal oversight, they showed surprising creativity and pushed their authority to the limits. Moreover, if evil spirits were seen as 'obedient' to the Catholic rites of exorcism, then ultimate sanction was given to the authority and authenticity of the Catholic Church and an unparalleled opportunity given for conversion. For those on the other side of the spectrum, popish exorcists were seen as providing additional proof of their corruption and Harsnett frequently suggests the scandalous behaviour of the priests and their connections with plotters and conspirators.

Harsnett's book and the various names given by him to the evil spirits are said to have inspired Shakespeare for a scene in *King Lear*, where Edgar says: 'Five fiends have been in poor Tom at once; of lust, as Obidicut; Hobbididance, prince of dumbness; Mahu, of stealing; Modo, of murder; Flibbertigibbet, of mobbing and mowing; who since possesses chambermaids and waiting-women'. The 'Devils of Denham' still live on in one of our greatest literary works.

DOVER, KENT

Saints of the White Cliffs

Dover is one of England's most famous coastal towns; 'a unique place', tourists are proudly told, 'where coast meets country, beauty meets history, and England meets the Continent'. The White Cliffs, of course, have become an emotive symbol of England and her dogged resistance in the face of invasion over the years. On a clear day, France can be seen just over twenty miles in the distance—so close and yet so far, though when I had lunch beside the White Cliffs, my mobile told me very definitively that I was in France and subject to special charges!

Dover Castle, 'the Key to England', goes back to the beginnings of recorded history. There was an Iron Age fort here and the Romans built an octagonal lighthouse or *pharos*. This can still be seen today, standing next to the ancient church of 'St Mary in Castro'. This has been rebuilt and restored several times; experts date the current walls to around the year 1000. However, it is quite possibly a much older foundation.

King Eadbald of Kent founded a minster in Dover, staffed by a community of twenty-two secular canons, which seems to have been located within the castle. Others date the church to the time of St Lucius, the semi-mythical second-century ruler, who was perhaps one of the client kings active in Roman Britain. He is said to have requested baptism from Pope St Eleutherius, who sent missionaries across the Channel, guided no doubt by the Dover lighthouse. This tradition would make St Mary in Castro one of the oldest churches in the country.

Eadbald's minster eventually adopted the Augustinian Rule and transferred to a site in the town: the priory of St Mary the Virgin and St Martin. It was re-founded as a Benedictine house in the twelfth century and became a 'cell' of Christ Church, Canterbury.

In early August 1295 Dover was attacked by the French—one of many such small operations during the period. All the monks fled the priory for safety, except Thomas of Hales, who seems to have remained in the dormitory on account of his old age. Some sources say he was also rigorously following the monastic timetable, which suggested a siesta in the afternoon. He was asked to show the French raiders the whereabouts of the house's plate and other treasures. On refusing, he was slain; according to Bishop Challoner, he 'with a Christian liberty upbraided them with their sacrileges, and other wickedness: upon which in a rage they killed him with their swords'.

Thomas was quickly venerated as a martyr, especially after miracles were reported at his tomb. Richard II asked the pope to consider his canonisation and although the process was begun in 1382 it did not proceed very far, probably because of a lack of money. Local devotion continued, however, and as late as 1500 the vicar of Buckland left money for the altar of 'Blessed Thomas de Halys' at Dover Priory. He was also included in the frescoes of English martyrs, past and present, at the Venerable English College in Rome.

A few decades before St Thomas's death, Dover received a visit from another holy man: St Richard, a former Chancellor of Oxford University who went on to become Bishop of Chichester. He came to Dover in late March 1253 to preach the pope's latest crusade. During his stay he dedicated a chapel in honour of St Edmund of Abingdon, his former mentor, but was taken ill the next morning and died shortly afterwards at the *Maison Dieu*. Before his body was taken back to Chichester, his internal organs were removed (as was the custom) and placed in the chapel he had just consecrated. This became a shrine in its own right, often visited by pilgrims on their way to Canterbury.

Dover was and still is a major port and the point of entry for many of the missionary priests returning to England during the sixteenth and seventeenth centuries. Reaching home soil was often a cause for rejoicing. When Blessed Edward Bamber landed at Dover, he knelt down and 'gave God thanks for his passage over the seas and safe arrival in his native country'. However, the authorities detained him, suspecting him to be a priest, and banished him overseas. He later returned and was martyred at Lancaster in 1646. Similarly, Blessed Thomas Cottam arrived at Dover just after his ordination in 1580 and was immediately searched and arrested. He was sent to London and, despite the best efforts of his friends, was confined at the Marshalsea prison, where he probably celebrated his first Mass. Later transferred to the Tower and tortured, he was executed at Tyburn on 30 May 1582.

St Edmund Campion himself came through Dover on 25 June 1580 and was 'by God's great goodness, delivered out of the searchers' and officers' hands, who detained him with them upon suspicion for several hours, upon deliberation to have sent him to the Council'. It was the day after the Nativity of St John the Baptist, the patron of his Oxford college, and Campion considered that his deliverance was due to the saint's intercession.

I wonder how many people passing through the port or using Dover Priory station think of all these sacred connections and ask the intercession of St Richard of Chichester, 'St Thomas of Dover' or their fellow travellers, the English Martyrs?

DUNCTON, WEST SUSSEX

Catholic Families: The Biddulphs

Days off for me normally involve a pub lunch and a historic site. After a satisfying meal at *The Cricketeers* in Duncton—mentioned by Hilaire Belloc in *The Four Men*, an account of a walk/pub crawl through Sussex—we drove a short distance and turned through open gates that denoted a private property. We continued through some woodland before finding ourselves in an open park with an impressive view of a country house: Burton Park.

An Edwardian visitor, E. V. Lucas, wrote that Burton Park was 'a modest sandy pleasaunce, with some beautiful deer, an ugly house, and a church for the waistcoat pocket, which some American relic hunter will assuredly carry off unless it is properly chained'. The house replaced an eighteenth-century mansion that burnt down in 1826 and is now a set of exclusive apartments, with such amenities as tennis courts and a croquet lawn. The tiny church of St Richard is happily still there, at its side, yet to be snapped up by a millionaire across the Atlantic.

There is, apparently, an old Sussex joke that no one had heard of Burton church until a hunting party accidentally stumbled across it. It is indeed remote, next to the local 'great house' but separated from any other habitation by some 140 acres of parkland. On our visit, the church was unlocked and in the compact space there was much of antiquarian interest: a fifteenth-century screen, old oak pews, a Norman font and a fine collection of brasses and monuments in memory of the owners of the house—the Gorings, the Biddulphs and (finally) the Wright-Biddulphs.

Beside one window is the painting of a virgin martyr being crucified. This is thought to be the obscure St Wilgefortis, popular during the Middle Ages, whose name derived from *virgo fortis* (strong woman). In some places she was known as 'Liberata' or 'Uncumber'; women would often pray to her to be 'liberated' or 'unencumbered' from abusive husbands. Her legend stated that she had dedicated herself to God and, in order to avoid potential suitors, was given a miraculous growth of beard on her face. She was eventually crucified for her staunch faith and tenacity. Interestingly, though, the image in Burton Park shows her not only clean shaven but hanging from the cross upside-down, like St Andrew.

Just within the screen that marks off the sanctuary, there is a black slab to Sir William Goring Bart, one of the owners of Burton Park, who died in February 1723, and his brother Henry. This may not seem particularly remarkable, until one notices the words *Requiescant in Pace* and the Jesuit emblem of the letters 'IHS' with a cross and three nails. There is a hint here, within the little Anglican church, of the secret that was hidden within the house for many years; that its owners were Catholic and that Mass was regularly celebrated there.

Sir William Goring himself had, it seems, been briefly imprisoned as a young man during the fictitious Popish Plot of 1678 and was later fined £600 for declining to take the Oath of Supremacy to George I on his accession in 1714. The Gorings had Jacobite sympathies: a letter from Lady Goring in 1711 reveals that she had ordered portraits of the Catholic Stuart claimants to the throne, 'James III' and his wife Maria Clementina. In 1719 Sir William declined to sign a statement recognising the Hanoverian regime in return for the removal of some of the financial burdens faced by English Catholics. However, his approach was perhaps more flexible than some, for he was anxious that no decision should be made without consulting the bishops. After his death, his widow retired to Liège and was a generous benefactress to the English religious houses in the Low Countries.

Soon after Sir William's death, the estate passed to the Biddulphs, also staunchly Catholic, and connected by marriage to the Arundells, Bedingfields and Plowdens. The Catholic chapel at Burton Park, dedicated to Our Lady, was served largely by English Jesuits. After the fire destroyed the Georgian mansion in 1826, a new chapel dedicated to St John the Baptist may have stood in the grounds—there are references to Bishop Bramston, Vicar Apostolic of the London District, blessing it in 1831 and a path in the park is sometimes referred to as 'St John's Walk'. These chapels allowed the Faith to survive and flourish in this corner of the Sussex Downs.

According to Bishop Challoner, the congregation numbered as many as ninety in 1741. As a result, the small Anglican church beside the house was hardly used. In 1778 William Burrell visited the area and wrote: 'there being no Protestant in the parish, divine service is not performed here, the church is shut up and though not in ruins is most shamefully neglected, and full of dirt', being used as 'a receptacle for the cattle to ye great scandal of religion and ruin of two very ancient monuments of the Gorings'.

Conditions gradually improved for Catholics and in the 1860s the then owner of Burton Park, Anthony Wright Biddulph, built a church dedicated to St Anthony and St George on the edge of the estate, designed in the thirteenth-century gothic style by Gilbert Blount. It was consecrated by the Archbishop of Westminster, Henry Edward Manning, who as an Anglican had ministered at nearby Lavington. One wonders whether he ever had cause to visit Burton Park on his journeys around the area as parson.

One of the daughters of the house, Katherine Mary, lived for a time in Rome. She had separated from her husband, Captain Stone, but found a new direction as a correspondent for the *Tablet*, a poet and great friend of the English members of the Papal Zouaves—that glamourous unit comprised of Catholic volunteers from across the world, seeking to defend the pope and his temporal power at the time of the wars of Italian Unification. Mrs Stone was present on the battlefield of Mentana (1867) and during the Italian assault on papal Rome (1870), tending the wounded in the midst of bullets.

The consecration of the church in 1869 had its homely details: Mr and Mrs Wright Biddulph themselves sang the Offertory, a reminder of the 'domestic' nature of Masses at their home in former days. A luncheon followed and, we read in a report from a local newspaper, 'the party then rose and amused themselves by strolling through the beautiful grounds surrounding Burton House, but previous to their going out the generous host rushed out of the room and returned with a double handful of cigars, which he handed round, much to the delight of many of his guests'. It is not recorded whether the archbishop was given one.

Around the church there is now a charming little cemetery, which not only has a row of Jesuit graves but those of the notable Benedictine historian, David Knowles, and a nephew of Blessed Columba Marmion. Had it not been for the Biddulphs, though, it is unlikely that a church would have been built in such a quiet spot; indeed, a quarter of a century later a fine church was built at the more populous Petworth, a few miles away, by another generous benefactor, Charles Willock Dawes, who (it seems) had fallen out with Mr Wright Biddulph.

Such tensions, though, are now a distant memory. The little church at Duncton, overlooking the manor house where Mass was once discreetly said, is testament to the heroism of the few to preserve the Faith for the many.

EAST LAVINGTON, WEST SUSSEX

Manning Country

It is always fascinating looking at old census records. It is as if the past is frozen in time. The details of every man, woman and child living in the UK on a particular day were carefully recorded each decade. If they were away from home they were registered at the address where they were found by the census officials. One of my ancestors, for example, a customs official at Gravesend in Kent, was twice documented by the census as residing on board a ship where he was inspecting goods.

The other day I was looking at the 1891 census records for Cardinal Manning. His entry appears among the list of residents of Carlisle Mansions, just round the corner from the present-day Archbishop's House, although the census taker made a point of calling number 282 'Cardinal Manning's Palace'. It provides a snapshot of his household on 5 April 1891, Easter Saturday. Visiting the cardinal that day were his eventual successor, Bishop Herbert Vaughan, and his brother Kenelm, also a Catholic priest. It is interesting to see the names of Manning's household: his secretary William Johnson, who later became an auxiliary bishop in Westminster, and his 'butler' and 'domestic servant', William Newman. His presence in Manning's home led to a malicious rumour that 'he had been chosen for this name of his because Manning liked to order about a person called Newman—but', added Manning's friend, J. E. C. Bodley, 'this was pure legend'. Then there were the rest of the domestic staff, now long forgotten but essential to this eminent Victorian's well-being: James Coombs, the butler's assistant; Catherine Harnett, 'cook and housekeeper', and (presumably) her daughter, also called Catherine, who was the 'kitchen maid'; and finally Margaret Crankan, 'house maid'.

There is one detail that stands out, however. The occupation of eighty-two-year-old Henry Edward Manning is given, as one might expect, as 'Cardinal Archbishop' but his 'condition as to marriage' is that of a 'widower'. This is not a term that is often associated with a Roman cardinal and raises the question: who was Mrs Manning?

Manning was actually one of two nineteenth-century English cardinals who had formerly been married. The first was Thomas Weld, who in 1796 married Lucy Clifford, by whom he had a daughter, Mary Lucy. His wife died in 1815 and, once his daughter married, he began preparation for Holy Orders. When he was eventually made a cardinal, Mary Lucy watched the consistory from behind a curtain and he attracted much attention in Rome by riding in his carriage with his assembled grandchildren. He was known as the 'Cardinal of the Seven Sacraments'.

Henry Edward Manning, on the other hand, was born in Totteridge, Hertfordshire in 1808 and studied at Harrow and Oxford. His father was a wealthy West Indian sugar merchant but when the family business collapsed the young Manning experienced something of a conversion and prepared himself for Holy Orders in the Church of England. He was ordained in 1832 and took up a seemingly obscure curacy at Lavington and Graffham, not far from the great houses of Petworth and Goodwood in Sussex. The biographies of Manning often talk in bucolic terms about this Downland parish but it takes a little time to locate. First, there is a problem of nomenclature. Now known as 'East Lavington', some still use the village's traditional name of 'Woolavington' and, to add to the confusion, there is also a 'West Lavington' on the outskirts of nearby Midhurst. Then, once you arrive in 'East Lavington', you realise that the place is dominated by an independent school, Seaford College, and that Manning's church serves as its chapel. It is not generally open to the public but the kindly receptionist accompanied us as we paid our respects, giving her shaggy white dog, Coco, a chance to sniff for rats in the churchyard. Perhaps he was also searching for the 'White Lady', the wife of a former squire, who is said to haunt the spot.

'I loved . . . the little church under a green hill-side', Manning later wrote as cardinal, 'where the morning and evening prayers and the music of the English Bible for seventeen years became a part of my soul. Nothing is more beautiful in the natural order, and if there were no eternal world I could have made it my home'. A short distance away, beyond the school grounds, is the old rectory, now called 'Beechwood House', where Manning lived for seventeen years. It was hard to see it properly from the little muddy road but, peering through the hedge, I could spot a majestic oak tree in the gardens and, gazing at the stately Georgian windows, wondered which room Manning had used as a study.

Much has changed since Manning's time but some elements remain constant, such as the close connection between the great house and the parish church in its grounds. The college uses the magnificent buildings that Manning would have known as Lavington Park; its occupants originally had the advowson of the parish, meaning they could choose the incumbent. Originally an Elizabethan mansion, the house was rebuilt at the end of the eighteenth century by the politician John Sargent, whose wife had inherited the property. He died in 1831 and was succeeded by his son, also called John, who was rector of Lavington and Graffham. This dual role of being squire and parson is often referred to as 'squarson', a not unusual occurrence at the time.

Manning married one of his five famously beautiful daughters. Caroline, in 1833, after a three-month courtship. Thomas Mozley met them at a breakfast party in 1829 and looked at them 'with a strong mixture of curiosity and admiration'. He noted that they had a 'peach bloom' on their cheeks, which added to their beauty. It also acted as a harbinger of tragedy, for the Sargents had a weak constitution, with a tubercular strain, and only one of the seven siblings outlived their mother.

The marriage ceremony was performed by the bride's brother-in-law, Samuel Wilberforce, who later became bishop first of Oxford and then Winchester. Caroline's family would later prove influential in her husband's conversion to Rome: two sister-in-laws would eventually be received into the Church with their husbands and children, and a nephew, Fr Ignatius Dudley Ryder, would succeed Newman as Provost of the Birmingham Oratory. The details of the couple's relationship is shrouded in mystery, though it seems to have been generally happy. Some claim that Manning proposed marriage by telling the young lady, 'Caroline, I have spoken to your mother' but, as his biographer Robert Gray suggests, 'the tale was invented to suit the austere Catholic dignitary. All the same; it is difficult to imagine even young Mr Manning on his knees before Caroline'. There are hints that Caroline had some initial reservations about the marriage. On honeymoon, Manning wrote to Mrs Sargent that his bride was now 'more like herself' and 'it really seems as if a weight of uncertainty and depression had been removed'.

John Sargent had been a model shepherd of souls and Manning continued his example. A member of his flock later recalled that 'he counted to call on every house in his Parish once a fortnight—most of his visiting was done by walking—clad in cassock'. Although he was strict and rather sober in his manner, he had a great affection for the local children and 'looked like an archangel when he prayed'. He took his pastoral responsibilities seriously, introducing daily morning and evening prayer. 'It was a picturesque sight', recalled one inhabitant of Lavington, 'to watch the zealous and stately rector, vested in surplice, himself tolling the bell, whilst in the grey of a winter's morning the straggling villagers hurried to morning prayer before going out to their daily toil in the fields'.

The village stands in the shadow of the summits of Graffham Down and Woolavington Down and the forest of Charlton, all now traversed by the South Downs Way. The region has long been associated with sheep, kept by farmers not only for their own sake but also to fertilise the light Sussex soil and so ensure a good harvest of corn. The little church in Lavington, dating from the thirteenth century but still including many of Manning's improvements, was very much a shepherd's church. Being a shepherd had its commitments and it was often impossible to leave the flock to attend church, especially during the lambing season. For this reason there was a charming Sussex custom, following the death of a shepherd, of nailing a tuft of wool on the coffin lid to explain to the recording angel why the deceased had so often missed his Sunday duties! Shane Leslie describes the typical scene on a Sunday:

> in their broidered smocks they offered their prayers in the Sussex dialect in the presence of the Lion and the Unicorn, or snuffed branches of southern-wood [wormwood] during the sermon, while their wives gossiped lightly in red cloaks and black bonnets in the shadow of the green-baized pews—when hymns were delivered upon the pitch-pipe, and the parish clerk, like some fossilized acolyte, answered the Psalms from the lower tier of the 'three-decker' [pulpit].

Despite the beauty of the Downs, this was no idyll. Though on one occasion Manning told his friend Gladstone, the future prime minister, that almost all his parishioners were communicant, there were still those who stayed away from church and showed little interest in the faith. Here, also, he first came face-to-face with widespread poverty and the aftermath of the Captain Swing riots. His concern for the underdog would mark the rest of his life.

Tragedy was soon to strike. In 1837, the same year that Cardinal Weld died, Caroline fell ill. She died of consumption on 24 July, aged only twenty-five, leaving her husband a childless widower. On her deathbed, she told her mother, 'look after Henry', and this she did for a number of years, keeping house for him and acting as a companion. In his *Eminent Victorians* Lytton Strachey claimed that 'in after years, the memory of his wife seemed to be blotted from his mind' and that he saw her death as opening up his career possibilities, numbering it among 'God's special mercies'. Strachey portrayed Manning in a negative light, seeing him as proud and ambitious. In reality, nothing could have been further from the truth. Manning was clearly heart-broken and spent many hours beside his wife's grave, where he would often compose his sermons. He wrote to Newman, 'I try to leave all in God's hands — but it is very, very difficult... No man knows what it is to watch the desire of his eyes fading away'. He confessed to Samuel Wilberforce that he felt 'the absolute need of full employment, and to the best of my powers I maintain a habit of fixed attention, and suffer as few intervals of disengaged time as I can'. If he seldom spoke of Caroline in subsequent years, it may be that he found it too painful, that part of him had died that July day in 1837.

He later erected a stained glass window in Chichester Cathedral in her memory and treasured all her letters. To his great grief, these were stolen while travelling to Rome in 1851, shortly after his conversion. One of his travelling companions remembered that 'at the first moment after the discovery of his loss the expression of grief in his face and voice was such as I have seldom witnessed. He spoke little; and when I was beginning to speak, he laid his hand upon my arm, and said, "Say nothing! I can just endure it when I keep perfectly silent"'. He gradually learnt to accept the loss, reflecting that 'the loss was probably necessary—necessary to sever all bonds to earth' as he began a new chapter in his life as a Catholic priest.

Caroline would not be forgotten; despite his austere appearance, Cardinal Manning clearly had a very human heart. Years later, a flower from her grave would each year be taken to the aged cardinal in Westminster, who regarded it with great emotion. As he lay dying in 1892, he entrusted a volume of his wife's prayers and reflections to Herbert Vaughan, saying: 'not a day has passed since her death on which I have not prayed and meditated from that book. All the good I may have done, all the good I may have been, I owe to her'. The precious volume was kept under his pillow and presumably buried with him.

It is an astonishing thought. Caroline's gravestone at Lavington is now in a rather poor state, covered in lichen and difficult to read, but her personal book of prayers lies with her beloved in the crypt of Westminster Cathedral.

ETON, BERKSHIRE

An Unlucky King

Henry VI was one of the most unfortunate of our medieval kings. He lost his throne twice during the Wars of the Roses and was murdered at the Tower of London on 21 May 1471. Among his more positive contributions, however, was the foundation of 'The King's College of Our Ladye of Eton beside Wyndesore' in 1440. Since then, of course, it has become inextricably linked with numerous prime ministers and the battle of Waterloo (apparently won on its playing fields). Yet its original purpose was to provide education for seventy poor boys, who would then progress to King's College, Cambridge (its sister foundation); it was staffed by a college of clergy and built upon the school linked to the chantry of St Nicholas in the original parish church of Eton (now replaced by the college). It would also be a spiritual centre: pilgrims flocked to venerate the collection of relics gathered by the king and the image of 'Our Lady of Eton'. A special indulgence was also granted for the feast of the Assumption, when a fair was also held at Eton.

Henry is still remembered fondly at Eton. His statue stands majestically in the School Yard and when I repaired to a local hostelry for lunch, I could not resist trying the local speciality: a 'Henry VI burger'. This might seem rather disrespectful but perhaps there is a faint echo of the popular devotion that surrounded the monarch in the decades after his violent death. Indeed, it is likely that he would have been canonised had the Reformation not intervened.

Born at Windsor on 6 December 1421, Henry succeeded to the throne just nine months later on the unexpected death of his father Henry V, the victor of Agincourt. The new king's reign was a troubled one and he is often dismissed as a weak leader, even as a madman. Indeed, not only did he see his kingdom divided between Yorkist and Lancastrian rivals but he lost all English possessions in France, with the exception of Calais, and lacked the worldly wisdom of his celebrated father.

Henry was a gentle and pious man. As we have seen, he had a great interest in education and founded not only Eton (for seventy poor boys) but King's College, Cambridge. We are told that he dressed humbly in 'round-toed shoes and boots like a farmer's' and when he had to wear more regal attire, 'he would always have put on his bare body a rough hair shirt'. He prayed frequently and, when he dined at table, he had brought to him an image of the Five Wounds of Christ.

His violent death led him to be considered by many a martyr. In the words of the Carthusian, John Blacman, 'like a true follower of Christ, he patiently endured hunger, thirst, mockings, derisions, abuse, and many other hardships and finally suffered a violent death of the body'. Henry was buried in obscurity at Chertsey Abbey and the authorities hoped that he would be quickly forgotten. However, the tomb soon saw an outburst of miracles. His statue was placed on the choir screen of York Minster within two years of his death and many other churches followed suit. Even to this day his image can still be found in the Norfolk churches of Binham Priory, Barton Turf, Gately and Ludham. The dagger with which he was killed was kept in a little chapel on Caversham bridge.

In 1484 Richard III removed the remains to St George's Chapel, Windsor, hoping that honourable burial would cool down the cult. However, the translation of the relics had the opposite effect. At the turn of the sixteenth century his shrine seems to have been more popular than that of St Thomas at Canterbury. A contemporary print now kept at the Bodleian Library gives us some idea of the shrine. Around the figure of Henry a number of clients are kneeling, with evidence of the miracles he wrought—a woman with a knife in her throat and a gentleman pierced with an arrow. In the background, *ex voto* images hang from the wall—parts of the body, crutches, fetters, a ship—and there is a tablet, presumably with an account of his life and miracles. Moreover, one of the king's hats was placed on the heads of devotees who suffered from headaches and it was the custom for people who promised to make a pilgrimage to Windsor to bend a coin in the king's honour and then offer the coin at the shrine. Large candles were also presented, the measurements being based on the height plus the breadth of the pilgrim's body asking for Henry's intercession.

The canonisation of Henry VI was the personal dream of Henry VII, motivated by a combination of devotion and politics. The plan was to transfer the king's remains to Westminster Abbey, which was deemed the most fitting place for a royal saint. This led to a long dispute, showing just how emotive sanctity could be on the eve of the Reformation. The abbot of Chertsey asked for the return of the relics, since Richard III had removed them 'illegally' to Windsor. The dean and chapter of Windsor claimed that Chertsey had agreed to the translation of the body and that the abbot himself had participated in the exhumation ceremony. Meanwhile, the abbot of Westminster provided evidence that Henry VI had expressed a desire to be buried at Westminster. Despite the on-going dispute, plans were drawn up for a new shrine chapel at Westminster. In 1503 a chapel at the east end of the high altar and the adjoining 'White Rose' tavern were pulled down so that the foundations could be built. However Henry remained in his tomb at Windsor and the magnificent chapel built at Westminster is now known as the 'Henry VII Chapel'.

The twentieth century saw a revival in the cause: Cardinal Bourne showed an interest in reviving it and the memory of the king was promoted by the Henry VI Society. Perhaps one day this hapless king will be raised to the altars of the Church. In the meantime, we can be thankful for his legacy, especially in the field of education, and the example he set for all those in public life.

FARNBOROUGH, HAMPSHIRE

'Irreclaimedly French'

On arriving at Farnborough in Hampshire, nothing appears out of the ordinary beyond its proud claim to be the birthplace of British aviation. The town centre (as is so often the case) is a non-descript maze of shopping centres and car parks. It would be quite easy to miss the small sign pointing towards St Michael's Abbey and the *Chapelle Impériale*.

After a short walk through the gates and up the hill, the visitor sees an extraordinary collection of buildings that provide a neat synthesis of French architectural styles. The magnificent church is flamboyantly gothic and stands over a Romanesque crypt. The central section of the neighbouring monastery is quite different; it is almost as if a Renaissance Loire chateau has been dropped into the Hampshire countryside. Finally, an imposing extension is based on the great monastic buildings at Solesmes, designed by Benedict Williamson, the gifted architect who went on to become a priest and re-establish the male branch of the Bridgettines. Ronald Knox, who was received into the Catholic Church at Farnborough, thought that the abbey is 'a little corner of England which is forever France, irreclaimedly French'.

The abbey is 'irreclaimedly French' in more ways than one. Its origins lie with France's defeat in the Franco-Prussian War and the fall of the Second Empire (1870), when the imperial family were forced into exile in England. Napoleon III did not survive long and died at Camden Place, near Chislehurst (Kent), in 1873. He was buried in the local Catholic church of St Mary. Here he was joined six years later by his son and heir, the Prince Imperial, who had been killed in a Zulu ambush while serving with the British Army. The distraught Empress Eugénie decided to build a fitting monument that would not only keep their memory alive but (much more importantly) ensure prayers for their souls. There seemed little hope of making the church at Chislehurst into a suitably grand imperial mausoleum and, besides, the place had unhappy memories for the empress. And so, in 1880, she purchased Farnborough Hill, which had previously belonged to the Longman family (of publishing fame), and began building an imposing church on a neighbouring hill.

The architect was Hippolyte Alexandre Destailleur, also responsible for the Rothschild's manor at Waddesdon (Buckinghamshire). The church building, completed in 1888, was an appropriate tribute to the Bonapartes, not only echoing the dome of Les Invalides in Paris (where Napoleon I is entombed) but also evoking the French Middle Ages and Saint Denis (the historic burial place for French kings).

An imperial mausoleum needed a community of religious to offer prayers and Masses for the dynasty. At first, a group of French Norbertines from Storrington (West Sussex) fulfilled the role but left abruptly in 1895. It seems that they had fallen out with the empress, perhaps because she thought their pastoral labours in the area distracted them from praying for her dead loved ones. Thus, the Abbot of Solesmes sent a contingent of Benedictine monks to take over, under the direction of Dom Fernand Michel Cabrol.

By this time, Farnborough had attracted many distinguished visitors, including Queen Victoria, Empress Frederick (mother of the Kaiser) and the King of Sweden and Norway. The curious also flocked to the church to see the imperial tombs and perhaps catch a glimpse of the aged empress, a relic of a now bygone era. One of the abbey's most memorable moments came in 1920, following Eugénie's death at the grand old age of 94. Her Requiem Mass provided a unique spectacle in England, at least in the centuries following the Reformation, when the reigning sovereigns of Great Britain and Spain, as well as the former King of Portugal, attended Mass together.

The Benedictines also made the abbey (as the priory became in 1903) famous for its scholarship and publications, notably the multi-volume *Dictionnaire d'Archéologie Chrétienne et de Liturgie*, still considered a standard work in the field. Some of the monks became household names among educated Catholics—including not only Abbot Cabrol (who produced a popular *Missal* for the laity and many other works) but André Wilmart, Louis Gougaud and Henri Leclercq.

The last of these was something of a monastic rarity. Astonishingly prolific, Dom Leclercq got up early each morning, celebrated Mass, joined his brethren in choir and then caught the train to London, in time for the opening of the British Museum reading room at 9am. He could often be seen waiting at the entrance while looking at his watch and muttering in French, 'they must have found it by now'. He was normally the last to leave the British Library and sometimes arrived back at the abbey late—on one occasion he had to climb into the enclosure through a window, assuring a startled guest that everything was in order and that he really was one of the monks. His name became synonymous with Farnborough and yet he was unpopular with the other monks since he was hardly an active member of the community. After Abbot Cabrol stepped down, it was decided that this irregular situation could not carry on any longer and Leclercq was asked to leave Farnborough. He became a priest of the archdiocese of Westminster and also an Oblate of the Benedictine house of Sainte Marie in Paris, which allowed him to retain the monastic habit.

By the outbreak of the Second World War, the community at Farnborough was diminishing in size and increasing in age. Still predominantly French-speaking, it was proving difficult to attract vocations. In 1947 (the 1400th anniversary of St Benedict's death) the arrival of five monks from Prinknash Abbey (Gloucestershire) ensured continuity of monastic life. One superior from this period was Dom Bede Griffiths, who later became famous for his work in India. These Benedictines of the Subiaco Congregation remain to this day.

St Michael's Abbey continues the tradition of the Solesmes monks by publishing books and seeking liturgical excellence. Within easy reach of London and only a short walk from the main station, many come here for their retreats and days of recollection. 'Irreclaimedly French' it may be, but it serves an important role in the English Church.

FOLKESTONE, LYMINGE AND MINSTER, KENT

The Royal Saints of Kent

It is interesting how many of the early English saints were blue-blooded — convert kings, pious queens, regal martyrs, princely abbesses and so on. It was almost as if there was a connection between high birth and holiness, as if the government was 'hagiocratic' (rule by saints). And it is certainly true that members of the various royal families in Anglo-Saxon England played a key role in supporting the evangelisation of their kingdoms and founding churches and monasteries.

It is well-known that St Ethelbert of Kent was the first Saxon ruler to be baptised, thanks to the mission of St Augustine in 597 and the prayers and persuasion of his consort, the Christian Queen Bertha — who strangely has never been venerated widely as a saint. Various members of his family followed him not only to the font but in being raised to the altars of the Church.

This was driven home to me when I visited a friend in Kent and toured the beautiful countryside. On the exterior of the charming church at Lyminge, for example, after you walk through a lone flying buttress, a plaque announces that this was once 'the Burial Place of St Ethelburga the Queen, Foundress of this Church and First Abbess of Lyminge'. A small recess inside the church, on the south wall, is thought to have once been her shrine, until her relics were moved to Canterbury in 1085.

St Ethelburga (also called Tate or Æthelburh) was the daughter of St Ethelbert of Kent. She went north to Northumbria to become the wife of the powerful King Edwin, on condition that she would be free to practise her Faith without hindrance and that the king himself would consider being baptised. Edwin took his time in making a decision, seeking the counsel of his followers and interpreting the 'signs of the times', such as a child being born to him the same night he survived an assassination attempt. He was eventually baptised, thanks largely to St Ethelburga and her chaplain St Paulinus, originally one of St Augustine's monks who became first Bishop of York.

However, when St Edwin died in battle against the pagan Penda of Mercia, St Ethelburga fled to Kent and, in 633, founded a religious community at Lyminge, one of the first in England. The nunnery survived for several centuries, until being destroyed by the Danes in the ninth century. Although her community have long since disappeared, the site remains a remarkably peaceful spot and the saint is not only remembered in the dedication of the church (St Mary and St Ethelburga) but also in a nearby 'holy well'.

Another Kentish saint is commemorated down the road at Folkestone, in the church of St Mary and St Eanswythe. The day of my visit was idyllic—the sun was shining and hoards of schoolchildren were leaving the church after a special service anticipating Palm Sunday, for they were happily waving their palms about. The main focus of our attention, though, was the shrine of St Eanswythe, granddaughter of St Ethelbert, who, according to tradition, turned down an arranged marriage with a Northumbrian prince and was given leave to establish a monastery at Folkestone, possibly as early as 630 (which would make it the first nunnery in England). Little is known of her subsequent life though various legends have been passed down—such as the story of how she had to collect water from a spring some distance away and how one day she struck the ground with her crozier and commanded the water to follow her uphill to the monastery. She was venerated as a saint after her death although the original nunnery was either destroyed by the Danes (as at Lyminge) or swallowed by the sea. It seems that she died at a relatively young age.

What is unusual is that her relics survive in the present church, having been discovered by workmen in 1885. They were found in a lead casket, part of which may have re-used a Roman sarcophagus. In 2020 the 'Finding Eanswythe' project tested the bones and confirmed that they came from a young woman who lived in the mid-seventh century and had no evidence of malnutrition.

The Kentish royals produced many other saints, including St Domneva (or St Ermenburga) a great-granddaughter of St Ethelbert. Her youth had been traumatic for internal politics had resulted in the murder of her two brothers. As compensation, King Egbert agreed to give her as much territory as a hind could cover in a single run so that she could build a monastery. The resulting religious foundation was based at Minster and ruled over by St Domneva and two other royal saints, St Mildred (her daughter) and St Edburga; the hind became the symbol for Thanet.

Here there is another continuity. The community of nuns was re-founded in 1937 and the nuns live essentially the same life of prayer and work as their Saxon forebears. The abbey sundial has the inscription *The time glides on: they perish and are laid to our charge*—time does indeed glide on and circumstances change but the Gospel preached so vigorously by our distant Saxon ancestors and these royal Kentish saints are now laid to our charge.

FROYLE, HAMPSHIRE

Hampshire's Village of Saints

Apart from the presence of church buildings, there are few public signs that we live in a Christian country. Go overseas, though, and there are constant reminders: wayside crosses, street shrines, even private houses placed under the patronage of a favourite saint.

There are odd exceptions in these colder climes and one of them can be found in the little Hampshire village of Froyle. Situated between Farnham and Alton, near the Pilgrim's Way that leads from Winchester to Canterbury, a writer in 1941 stated that 'great events, like the main road, have by-passed Froyle, so that its history ... is that of the yeoman families whose names are still borne by many of their houses' and who grew rich thanks to the hops and the wheat. The place name is said to have originated with the Norse goddess, Freya, and the hill that was once dedicated to her (Froehyll) seems to have been Christianised as 'Saintbury'.

The village church has the relatively unusual dedication of the 'Assumption of the Blessed Virgin Mary' — shared with only nineteen other Anglican churches in England — and this is often explained with reference to the fact that before the Reformation the manor was in the hands of the nuns of St Mary's Abbey, Winchester. It is an interesting little church, with a fourteenth-century chancel and an 'Easter Sepulchre' — an arched recess representing Christ's tomb where the Blessed Sacrament was placed on Good Friday and hidden by a curtain until the Easter alleluias were sung. When a local man, John Mott, died in 1377 he left 'money for candles to burn at the Easter Sepulchre'.

Much of the charm of the church, though, is of a more recent origin. It is clearly 'High Church', influenced by the Oxford Movement which rediscovered the Catholic roots of the Church of England, and full of statues, lamps and banners. Many visitors must wonder whether this is indeed a Catholic church. There is even a statue of St Gregory the Great (complete with tiara) and a display case showing off a baroque 'fiddleback' vestment.

Much of the charm of Froyle can be attributed to its last 'lord of the manor', Sir Charles John Hubert Miller, 8th Baronet, who died in 1940. In his youth he had served as a captain with the Coldstream Guards, before taking up residence at Froyle in 1892. The Millers had been the premier family of the village for over a hundred years; his grandfather rebuilt the nave of the church and his father opened the local school. Sir Hubert, as he was called, was himself a devout Anglo-Catholic and a close friend of Lord Halifax, president of the English Church Union (a society dedicated to the promotion of Catholic principles and practices within the Church of England). Spending the winter each year in Venice, Sir Hubert was inspired by continental liturgy and devotion and tried to introduce 'Italianate' elements into his little patch of rural Hampshire.

From Catholic Europe he brought back pictures, sacred vessels and sets of vestments, some of which dated back to the sixteenth and seventeenth centuries. He opened a 'mission church', made of corrugated iron, for the villagers of Lower Froyle, thus saving them a two-mile walk to Sunday service. The inside of this unprepossessing 'tin tabernacle' contained a rood screen, a forest of sanctuary lamps, an altar with the 'big six' candlesticks, and Stations of the Cross around the walls. The building was sadly knocked down in the 1960s.

Most famously, Sir Hubert placed images of the saints on the houses and cottages that were part of his estate. These can be found scattered around the village, though most are in the vicinity of the church. Thus, St Paul stands with his sword and book on a plinth on what used to be the vicarage and is now 'St Paul's House'; St Michael slaying the dragon can be found on Sir Hubert's former home of 'Shrubbery House'; the Sacred Heart is on 'Misselbrook Farm'; St Anthony Abbot at 'The Chestnuts' and St Katherine (with her wheel) on the house Sir Hubert built for his erstwhile (and no doubt very busy) sacristan. One of the most attractive statues is that of St Hubert, the baronet's patron, shown with a stag on what used to be the post office. Overall, there are nineteen images. It is little wonder that Froyle is known as the 'Village of Saints'.

What the people of Froyle think of these saintly figures on their houses a hundred years on I do not know. It is, from the perspective of faith, a most attractive idea and it made me wonder what we can do in our parishes to help people know the saints better and seek their patronage. The visitor to Froyle should, I think, applaud the bold and in many ways unconventional vision of Sir Hubert.

HEVER CASTLE, KENT

Hever's Catholic Past

Hever Castle (Kent) is just the sort of home that Americans might imagine the English to typically inhabit. In its picture postcard perfection, it has everything you could wish for: a drawbridge and double moat, water lilies and swans, turrets and battlements, two mazes, stunning gardens, topiary and an idyllic looking 'Tudor village'. For aficionados of Anne Boleyn, this is one of the main pilgrimage sites for it was here that she spent much of her childhood and her beguiling face can be found throughout the castle shop, on thimbles, tea towels, cards and jewellery.

Look again and much of what you see is not quite as it seems. The castle is indeed historic and Hever was the seat of the Boleyn (or Bullen) family between 1462 and 1539. But what visitors see today is largely the creation of William Waldorf Astor, the wealthy American who purchased the property in 1903. He had a great love of England and ten years previously had bought the Buckinghamshire estate of Cliveden. He aimed to turn Hever into a comfortable modern home that also celebrated its colourful history.

Thus a 100-room extension was built in the form of a Tudor village on one side of the castle, still known as the 'Astor Wing' and used for luxury bed and breakfast. The interiors of the castle were 'Tudor-ified', with exquisite oak panelling, a minstrel's gallery in the 'Great Hall' and rooms boasting titles such as 'King Henry VIII's Bedchamber' and 'Anne Boleyn's Bedroom'. An impressive collection of Tudor portraits was amassed, second in importance to the National Portrait Gallery, and treasures obtained such as two Books of Hours that once belonged to the ill-fated queen. One, produced in Bruges around 1450, has the inscription *'Le temps viendra* [The time will come], *Je Anne Boleyn'*. The other, which was printed in Paris, is believed to have been taken by Anne to the scaffold. Perhaps shortly before her death she wrote on one page, 'Remember me when you pray that hope doth lead from day to day'. The manuscript contains evidence of the turbulent times in which she lived and for which she was a catalyst: the name of the pope has been crossed out, as well as references to St Thomas of Canterbury. In another room there is a collection of instruments of torture and five German beheading swords, appropriate enough given the fate of Anne.

Although the ghost of Anne, which is said to walk the castle grounds, may not recognise much of the interior, the modern visitor is grateful to the Astors for allowing them to so easily soak up the atmosphere of a Tudor household. The Astors only sold the property in 1983 and surely felt a great sympathy with their Tudor precursors. Like them, the fortunes of the Boleyns had dramatically gone from rags to riches within a few generations and Sir Thomas, Anne's father, made many additions to the castle, most notably by adding the Long Gallery above the Great Hall, which King Henry himself would have known.

It might be thought that, being the home of the woman over whom Henry broke with Rome, there would be few Catholic connections here. But, surprisingly, the family who lived at Hever for the longest length of time — the Waldegraves — were well known for their Catholic faith. In 1557, after the death of Anne of Cleves, who had been granted Hever as part of her divorce settlement, the property passed to Sir Edward Waldegrave, a Privy Councillor to Mary I. He had been imprisoned in the reign of Edward VI for tolerating the celebration of Mass in Mary's household and he would die a prisoner in the Tower under Elizabeth because of his Catholic Faith.

The family remained Catholic until the end of the seventeenth century. Next to the so-called 'Waldegrave Bedroom' there can be seen a small secret chapel. Here Mass would have been celebrated regularly, although its current arrangement is courtesy of the Astors, complete with a nineteenth-century painting of the 'Virgin in Ecstasy' and a baroque rock crystal crucifix.

There is further evidence of the house's recusant past downstairs in the Morning Room, where a priest hole lies hidden behind the china cupboard. 'One of the many ghostly tales surrounding Hever', explains the guidebook, 'suggests that one such priest perished here and that his unhappy spirit still lingers'. Talking of ghosts, it is interesting that another onetime Waldegrave property, Borley in Essex, was associated with a high profile haunting in the early twentieth century.

Under the Catholic James II, the owner of Hever became Baron Waldegrave — encouraged in part by the fact that he had married Henrietta FitzJames, the illegitimate daughter of the new king and his onetime mistress Arabella Churchill. Henry remained loyal to James after the 'Glorious Revolution' and died in exile at St Germain-en-Laye in 1689; his memory is celebrated at Hever by an interesting collection of Jacobite relics, including a rare 'Rhyming Blade Sword' with the words 'With this sword thy cause I will maintain; And for they sack [sake] O James breath [break] each vein'.

However, his son, James, decided to renounce the Catholic Faith and become part of the Anglican establishment—as ambassador to France, Privy Councillor and Earl Waldegrave. His growing status caused him to sell Hever, as it was considered rather small.

Despite the legacy of its most famous daughter, Hever Castle should not be forgotten as a secret Catholic stronghold and a monument to those who risked everything to follow their conscience. As I sat in the garden just before closing time and the shadows lengthened, I imagined generations of Boleyns and Waldegraves walking the paths and enjoying this wonderful spot and I prayed they were now at peace.

Remember me when you pray that hope doth lead from day to day.

HYDE ABBEY, HAMPSHIRE

The Head of St Valentine

Quite how St Valentine's Day originated as a feast for lovers is somewhat unclear. Was it a continuation of a pagan festival of fertility? Or a recognition of the saint's own defense of marriage? Or perhaps a link to Chaucer's observation that on 14 February 'every fowl cometh ... to choose his mate'? To add to all the confusion, the traditional *Roman Martryology* gives two different St Valentines for 14 February. One was a priest who 'after many wondrous works of healing and teaching, was scourged with rods and beheaded under Claudius Caesar' in Rome. The other was Bishop of Terni who, after a period of imprisonment and torture, 'was brought out of his prison in the silence of midnight and beheaded'. Some have thought that these Valentines are actually one and the same person.

There are many relics of St Valentine around the world. One was given to St John Henry Newman and lies under the altar of St Athanasius at the Birmingham Oratory; another was acquired by the Irish Carmelite, John Spratt, and housed at the church on Whitefriar Street in Dublin. In medieval England relics could be found at Reading, Salisbury, St Albans and Windsor. But the most famous of them all, the saint's head, was kept at Hyde Abbey, just outside the city walls of Winchester.

Little remains of Hyde Abbey today but it was once one of the greatest monasteries in England. Founded as the 'New Minster' by Edward the Elder in 901, it originally stood beside the old cathedral in the heart of Winchester and became the royal mausoleum for the House of Wessex. It was here that Alfred and his queen were buried, together with Edward the Elder and the teenage King Eadwig. The abbey, along with the royal tombs, was moved to a new location just outside the north walls in 1110 to allow for the rebuilding of the cathedral. The abbey became the first stop for those setting off from Winchester to Canterbury along the 'Pilgrim's Way'.

Hyde Abbey gained much wealth and power. It owned a large portfolio of land and property, including the famous Tabard Inn in Southwark, where Chaucer's pilgrims began their journey. The abbey also gained an extensive collection of relics. These included the bodies of the Breton St Judoc and St Grimbald, a French scholar at the court of King Alfred who was involved in the monastery's foundation. A relic of St Barnabas was the focus of miracles after the apostle appeared to a local sick woman in a vision; this was commemorated each year at the abbey with the unique feast of the 'revelation' (*revelatio*) of St Barnabas on 12 December.

The head of St Valentine was the gift of Emma of Normandy, the mother of St Edward the Confessor and wife of two English kings, Ethelred 'the Unready' and Cnut (Canute). Following the death of her son, King Harthacnut, in 1042 she 'gave to the New Minster for his soul the head of St Valentine the Martyr'. She was a great benefactress to the abbey and had previously given, along with her husband Cnut, a gold cross adorned with precious stones and holding the relics of St John the Baptist and St Peter and St Paul.

The head of St Valentine became one of Hyde's great treasures, represented on the abbey seal. As can be seen in the surviving Hyde Abbey Breviary, the saint's feast was celebrated solemnly each year with its own octave. In 1116, shortly after being moved (translated) to Hyde, the reliquary was opened and the head washed by the monks.

Four centuries later the abbey was dissolved. In April 1538 the last abbot, John Salcot, surrendered the monastery to Henry VIII and the house was emptied of its treasures. Thomas Wriothesley, the royal commissioner, wrote proudly that 'the silver thereof will amount to near two thousand marks' and added that he hoped 'to sweep away all the rotten bones that be called relics, which we may not omit, lest it should be thought that we came more for the treasure than for avoiding the abominations of idolatry'.

The site was subsequently used for a variety of secular purposes. Hyde House was built for Richard Bethell, a wealthy politician and mayor of Winchester, and at the end of the eighteenth century part of the abbey precincts was used as a prison. John Milner, the future Catholic bishop and antiquary of Winchester, wrote that 'miscreants couch amidst the ashes of our Alfreds and Edwards; and where once religious silence and contemplation were only interrupted by the bell of regular observance, and the chanting of devotion, now alone resound the clank of the captive's chains and the oaths of the profligate!'

The head of St Valentine is long gone but, if you look closely, there are various remnants of Hyde Abbey. Most obvious is the fifteenth-century gateway and the church of St Bartholomew, formerly the monastery's parish church. 'An ancient stoup' from the abbey was placed in the church porch in 1879 and inside there are capitals from the cloister. Bones found nearby were, at one point, proudly claimed to be those of Alfred but have been recently dated to several centuries after his lifetime. Nevertheless, they have been buried respectfully in the graveyard. Visitors can stroll along the 'Monk's Walk' following a stream that once stood within the abbey precinct; here you can find some of the peace that must have surrounded the medieval monks and their guests.

Most poignant of all is the Hyde Abbey garden, opposite a leisure centre and surrounded by rather nondescript housing. At first it is difficult to imagine that the chancel of the abbey church once stood here. However, in 2003 a specially designed garden was opened to reflect the lost sacred splendour. A glass panel depicts the gothic interior, three ledger stones represent the royal tombs, flint paving marks the design of the church and holly trees and hedges mark the site of the church's chapels and buttresses. You can just about imagine a lost world of monks and pilgrims, of magnificent buildings and glittering reliquaries, where one of our greatest kings awaited doomsday and prayers were muttered to the patron of lovers.

KEMSING AND OTFORD, KENT

Two Kentish Holy Wells

As pilgrims made their way to Canterbury there were many 'side attractions' that merited a pause or even an overnight stay. An example is provided by two Kentish 'holy wells' at Otford and Kemsing, not far from Sevenoaks, which are situated on the ancient path that led from Winchester and Canterbury.

Pilgrims would undoubtedly have stopped at Otford as they passed the manor house that had belonged for centuries to the archbishops of Canterbury. They would remember that this had been St Thomas's favourite residence. On one occasion, it was said, he was so distracted in his prayers by a singing nightingale that he forbade birds of that kind to sing again in Otford. Another charming legend asserts that the saint struck the ground with his staff, like a new Moses, and a spring issued forth, providing a much-needed supply of fresh water for his residence. St Thomas's Well can still be seen to this day.

Otford has an additional draw for modern visitors: one of the lost palaces of Tudor England. Little remains today beyond the remnants of a turret and the lower gallery, now converted into cottages. It is hard to believe that when the palace was rebuilt by Archbishop William Warham just before Henry VIII's break with Rome, it was one of the great houses of Europe, built in the latest style and boasting the largest inner courtyard in England. When Wolsey took over as Lord Chancellor in 1515, he began the construction of his own palace at Hampton Court, hoping to rival the splendours of Otford. The Kentish palace remained the larger one. It was spacious enough to host Henry VIII, who stopped here in 1520 on the way to the Field of the Cloth of Gold, with an entourage of nearly 3,500.

A short distance away is the village of Kemsing, home to another holy well, this time dedicated to St Edith. This saint, who was the illegitimate daughter of King Edgar and half-sister to Ethelred the Unready, was born at Kemsing in 961. She became a nun at the famous abbey at Wilton (Wiltshire) and, having lived a holy life and refused to become England's first queen regnant, died at the age of 23. The water of her well in Kemsing was known to be particularly efficacious for eye problems. There was also a folk tradition that if devotees threw water over the left shoulder, St Edith would grant their request providing they kept silent on leaving the well until someone spoke to them.

As well as cures at her well, St Edith's intercession was also sought for a good harvest, protecting it from 'blasting, mildew and other harm'. Locals brought grain to be blessed at the shrine and mixed it with other grain to produce a maximum return. There seems to have been a small chapel of St Edith in the churchyard of St Mary the Virgin, with a well-known statue and (it seems) a relic of her arm. The exact site of the shrine was recently suggested when a new gas pipe was installed on the east side of the church.

As pilgrims to Canterbury stopped at Kemsing, they may have been told that the knights who murdered St Thomas rode through the village after committing their sacrilegious crime. It is said that one of them haunts the churchyard to this day every 29 December, tethering his horse and slipping into the church to pray for forgiveness; one of several ghost stories linked to the martyr.

Chaucer's pilgrims may have told each other their tales but there were many others to discover along the route to Canterbury.

LANGLEY MARISH, BERKSHIRE

A Family Pew

> Come, friendly bombs, and fall on Slough.
> It isn't fit for humans now,
> There isn't grass to graze a cow.

John Betjemin's words are well-known. They still cause frustration to locals and, indeed, the poet later expressed regret for his sentiments, written a few years before the outbreak of war and the horrors of the Blitz. Surprising though it may seem, Slough has its treasures and Betjemin could not have wished any bomb to fall on the medieval church of St Mary the Virgin, located within the Slough conurbation but, as residents would proudly say, in the quite distinct area of Langley Marish.

This 'Jewel of Slough', as it has been called, can be found in a largely residential area, opposite a pub, like so many of our historic churches, and sandwiched on the other side by picturesque almshouses. The extensive and leafy graveyard includes the tomb of the war artist Paul Nash, whose atmospheric paintings of the desolate landscape around Ypres, full of trenches and blasted trees, have entered the popular imagination.

The key figure in the church's history was Sir John Kedermister, who had the prominent position of Keeper of Langley Park between 1607 and 1631. His fingerprint can be found throughout the church: the impressive family monument in the chancel, with numerous kneeling Jacobean children; the red-brick bell tower; the Tuscan pillars that separate the nave from the north aisle, which Sir John put in to replace the medieval arches and improve the congregation's visibility. He also founded a block of almshouses and presented the royal coat of arms that can still be seen within the church—given an added poignancy by the fact they predated the Civil Wars and Charles I's execution by two decades.

Most importantly, Sir John commissioned a magnificent family pew in the chapel south of the nave, raised by a flight of six steps and with an exterior painted ornately to resemble marble. The inside consists of a narrow gallery, with a long bench, Latin quotes from the psalms, and numerous heraldic shields of the Kedermisters and the associated families of Spencer, Harvey and Seymour. There is a clear view through the latticework of the church and pulpit, though no-one can easily see in. In case this was the cause of temptation, there are frequent depictions within the pew of the Eye of God, with the words *Deus Videt*—the minister may not see you, but God is most certainly watching! There was much indeed on which to meditate, for below lay the family vault, where their bones would one day rest.

The glory of the Kedermister Pew is in the adjoining and rightly famous library, probably built on the site of a pre-Reformation chapel. It is the sort of room one expects to find in the stateliest of homes, in a French chateau or an Italian palazzo, rather than a 'church' in Slough. The neatly bound volumes are kept on shelves behind elaborately decorated panelled doors. There are paintings of prophets and apostles, as well as scenes of various places, real and imagined, including nearby Windsor Castle and a mansion that may have been the Kedermisters home in Langley Park. The books—numbering 307 in a catalogue of 1638—largely consist of the Fathers and Doctors of the Church—Augustine, Gregory, Bede, Aquinas—as well as more contemporary authors—Luther, Calvin, Jewel, Andrewes. Of particular value is the eleventh-century Kedermister Gospels, now deposited in the British Library, a pre-Reformation Missal, and the family medical book or *Pharmacopolium*, full of (to our eyes) unusual prescriptions. The books were for the benefit of the parish clergy, 'as well of ministers of the said towne and such other in the County of Buck as resort thereunto'. It was a library endowed by the laity for the benefit of the clergy, though one wonders whether family members occasionally wandered through to browse the shelves during an especially onerous sermon.

Private pews were partly a result of the Reformation: the emphasis on the Word and the sermon meant that seats became a necessity and were gradually introduced into churches. Medieval churches were 'standing room only' and the faithful were, one could say, more physically involved in the Mass—standing, kneeling, straining to view the elevation, venerating images, reciting beads. There was less need for sitting.

Moreover, since much church land passed into the hands of the nobility and gentry, the lord of the manor was often patron of the church, with power to present the incumbent. A family pew was a way of expressing this local hierarchy, as well as providing privacy, warmth and distance from the less desirable elements of the congregation. As with the Kedermister Pew and Library, many had private entrances, and fireplaces or stoves.

Another expression of social status, elsewhere in the church, was the practice of collecting pew rents—paying for the use of a pew, the more expensive ones having a better position. For many an incumbent it was a substantial source of income, though by the mid-nineteenth century it became the subject of controversy and free, open seating was increasingly promoted. Some thought it smacked of popery, though the custom was not unknown 'across the Tiber'. An article in *The Rambler* of 1851 states: 'what a fearful sight it is to see a Catholic chapel at Mass with its largest portion, and all its best parts, half empty, sometimes not a third or a quarter full, while below the bar, where the box keeper sits, a multitude of poor persons sits crushed together'. Perhaps a residue of this still exists in the twenty-first century: welcome members of the faithful into a typical church and they will seldom sit at the front. Better be squeezed in discomfort at the back. The cheap seats. The escape route is clearer and there is no charge.

LOSELEY PARK, SURREY

On Mulberry Trees

Loseley Park, near Guildford, is the home of the More-Molyneux family. It is perhaps best known these days for its Dairy Ice Cream, which can still be purchased at many cinemas in its distinctive tubs. The present house dates largely from the second half of the sixteenth century, much of the stone having been recycled from the recently dissolved Cistercian abbey of Waverley, about eight miles away. This, says the guidebook, 'contributes greatly to the mellow appearance and atmosphere of the House', as if the stones brought with them the peace of the cloister.

The present house was built by Sir William More, a close advisor to Queen Elizabeth. She liked to visit her courtiers but thought that Loseley 'was not mete for her to tarry at'. The queen seems to have liked the new house, for she stayed there four times. Another Elizabethan guest was the Earl of Southampton, who was kept at Loseley under house arrest for three years because of his Catholicism, though he seems to have treated with kindness.

A further link to the turbulent times of the Reformation can be found near the car park, where a sign points to a small meeting space named after St Thomas More, next to a (non-Catholic) chapel. The saint almost certainly visited Loseley, for his stepmother, Alice, was the sister of Sir William's father, Sir Christopher More, who had bought the original manor in 1508. St Thomas's portrait also hangs in the Drawing Room. Curiously on the adjacent wall there is an oval portrait of Anne Boleyn, whose marriage to Henry VIII he so vehemently opposed.

The More family has a curious motto that shows its long association with mulberries. *Morus* is both the Latin form of the surname and the botanical name for this species of tree. It led to the pun that forms the motto: *Morus tarde moriens morum cito moriturum*, the Mulberry tree is slow to die but its fruit quickly decay. It was a rather stark warning that while the family lives on, generation by generation, its individual members pass through this world only briefly.

Mulberries can be found aplenty at Loseley: in the plasterwork frieze and the fireplace in the drawing room and in the garden. One venerable specimen is said to have been planted around 1570 by Elizabeth I herself. It fell down in the 1940s but, to the family's relief, still flourishes.

Mulberries were introduced to England by the Romans, who valued their fruit and medicinal properties. They were often grown in medieval monasteries and enjoyed a renaissance under James I, who encouraged the planting of 10,000 trees to bolster the English silk industry. Silkworms are particularly fond of mulberry leaves, although the king's efforts were marred by the fact that black rather than white mulberries were planted; the latter are better for silk.

England has many examples of mulberries associated with famous people: 'Milton's Mulberry' at Christ's College, Cambridge; Dr Johnson's mulberry in Streatham Park; a mulberry associated with Thomas Gainsborough at his family home at Sudbury (Suffolk), and the tree that Shakespeare planted at New Place, Stratford-upon-Avon. It no longer exists largely because the wood was used to make souvenirs.

Then there is St Thomas More's mulberry. The martyr planted several mulberry trees in his garden at Chelsea. It was an idyllic, peaceful place, where he loved to spend time with his family, his friends and his books. There was even a raised area from which he could admire the distant skyline of the City of London, dominated by old St Paul's. His great-nephew, the Jesuit Ellis Heywood, wrote that it was 'an enchanting spot, as well from the convenience of the situation—from one side almost all the noble city of London being visible, and from the other the lovely Thames, being crowned with lovely flowers, and the sprays of the fruit trees so admirably spaced and interwoven, that looking at them they appear like a veritable piece of living tapestry made by nature herself'.

Chelsea has many mulberries; there is even a road called 'Mulberry Walk'. In the eighteenth century there was an attempt at producing Chelsea Silk, led by an entrepreneur, John Appletree of Worcester, but he was eventually declared bankrupt. Many of Chelsea's mulberries are linked to this project but there is one, in the garden of Allen Hall seminary, which claims to be one of St Thomas's original trees.

It is attractive to think of the future martyr sitting underneath it on a summer's evening and enjoying witty discourses with his loved ones. *Morus tarde moriens*. This mulberry tree is indeed slow to die but the heroic witness of its famous Tudor owner continues to bear much fruit.

NORTH MARSTON, BUCKINGHAMSHIRE

The 'Jack-in-the-Box' Priest

One finds in most parishes those who follow devotions which are still awaiting formal approval by the Church, often centred around the latest visionary or mystic. Sometimes they are eventually recognised by the Church, other times they simply fade away. It is interesting to reflect that this is not a new phenomenon and that unofficial cults could be found, with surprising frequency, in England just before the Reformation. A case in point was the veneration of a country priest called Sir John Schorne (medieval priests were often called 'Sir' rather than 'Father'). Despite never being canonised, Schorne was actively regarded as a 'saint' for over two centuries.

Although he was the subject of much devotion, Schorne's life was never written, perhaps because he was a secular priest and thus did not interest monastic writers. Thus, little is known for sure about the details of his life. He may have studied at Oxford and served as rector first of Steppingley in Bedfordshire and then North Marston in Buckinghamshire, both livings under the control of the Augustinian priory at Dunstable.

Schorne was a pious man and we are told that 'his knees became horney by the frequency of his prayers'. The will of a John Schorne is kept at the British Library, in which he rendered to God what belonged to God (his soul), to the earth what belonged to the earth (his body), while his goods would provide for the welfare of the poor and prayers for his soul.

Schorne became particularly associated with two miracles during his lifetime. On one occasion during a drought he struck the dry ground with his staff and a spring of water burst forth. The parallels with Moses were unmistakable. The water, naturally rich in gypsum, Epsom salts and carbonic acid, was said to cure gout, ague, eye disorders and other afflictions. Perhaps on account of his powerful assistance for sufferers of gout, Schorne was also celebrated for trapping the devil in a boot. As a local rhyme put it, 'Sir John Schorne/ Gentleman borne/Conjured the devil into a horn' (or boot).

At his death around 1315, Schorne was buried near the high altar at North Marston and pilgrims began to visit his tomb, together with the nearby spring of water. Depictions of the Buckinghamshire priest appeared in churches as far afield as Hennock in Devon and Gateley in Norfolk. In Binham, also in Norfolk, Richard Easingwold left directions in his will for his body to be buried 'before the holy ymage of maister John Shorn' (1508). Archaeologists have discovered many pilgrim badges in the south-east depicting Schorne holding the devil in a jackboot or preaching in a pulpit wearing his master's hood and holding a staff. Up until the eighteenth century, an old road-way sign near North Marston could still be seen pointing in five directions, including that of the shrine.

The popularity of the pilgrimage meant that the church at North Marston could be extended. However on 7 April 1478 a licence was issued by Pope Sixtus IV to move Schorne's bones to St George's Chapel, Windsor. Although the cult was never formally approved by the Church this papal permission gave the devotion some respectability. It seems that the authorities in Windsor hoped that pilgrims would bring the revenue needed to complete the building of the chapel. The King, Edward IV, also hoped to divert attention from the tomb of his rival, Henry VI, in nearby Chertsey, the base of another unofficial cult. As it happened, the relics of 'Good King Henry' joined Master Schorne at St George's in 1484, making it a popular religious centre.

Pilgrimages continued to both Windsor and North Marston right up until the Reformation. As with the other English shrines, that of Sir John Schorne was dismantled in the 1530s. The image of the priest kept at North Marston was sent to London for destruction in September 1537 and the shrine chapel at Windsor was eventually re-used for the tomb of Edward Clinton, Earl of Lincoln. However, popular devotion took longer to extinguish. As late as 1552 Hugh Latimer complained of pilgrims 'running hither and thither to Mr John Shorn or to Our Lady of Walsingham'. More recently the holy well at North Marston has been renovated and both a local walk and a grouping of twelve local Anglican churches bear his name.

This obscure medieval cult has left its mark on our culture. Schorne's imprisonment of the devil in a boot is supposed to have led to the children's toy, the 'jack-in the box' (in French, *diable en boîte* or 'boxed devil'). Perhaps readers have such a reminder of Sir John Schorne sitting in their nursery or attic. Old devotions rarely die completely.

PENN, BUCKINGHAMSHIRE

A Buckinghamshire Doom

It was a perfect day off: a drive into the countryside, a visit to my favourite second-hand bookshop (now sadly no more) and a pub lunch. After a busy week there is nothing quite like sitting in an old-fashioned hostelry with a pint of real ale in one hand, a newly purchased book in the other, the pub cat 'Chablis' on my lap, high expectations of the ham, egg and chips that had just been ordered and the company of a good friend.

As if the day could not get any better, we found the local church open on the way back. Holy Trinity in the Buckinghamshire village of Penn does not look particularly extraordinary on the outside: an old flint church with a short tower and a rambling graveyard. But inside there are plenty of reminders of its medieval past, chief of which is its 'Doom', a fifteenth-century painting on wooden boards depicting the Last Judgement. Only a few such Dooms exist in the country.

A forage in the porch to find the light switch illuminated the interior and allowed the Doom to be clearly seen. With one flick it was as if the centuries suddenly disappeared and we were back in 1400, a time when the area enjoyed considerable prosperity. This was largely because of the production of 'Penn tiles' which were used in many prominent buildings, including Westminster Abbey, Windsor Castle and the Tower of London. Some existing examples of this local craft are displayed in the floor of the church's Lady Chapel.

The Doom would have been part of a whole scheme of wall-paintings, a small section of which can be seen by the pulpit in red and yellow ochre. It is always satisfying to look for pre-Reformation traces when visiting our old churches. At Penn the eagle-eyed can see the entrance to the Rood loft, now long blocked-up, and the beam over the chancel arch which still has the socket for the great cross and the hooks that would have supported statues of Our Lady and St John. One particularly poignant relic are the grooves on the arch near the west door, left by many years of the *sanctus* bell rope being pulled at the consecration.

The Doom was only uncovered in 1938 when extensive repairs were being carried out in the church. The workmen removed some decayed boards from the bay of the roof above the chancel arch. They had been whitewashed and covered with lath and plaster and the men thought nothing of them as they broke them up and left them in the churchyard so that they could be taken to the dump. One of them, Tom Randall, luckily removed part of the whitewash and plaster on one piece of boarding and, much to his amazement, saw that he had uncovered a painted face. He told the vicar and soon what had been discarded as rubbish had carefully been placed in the Old Schoolroom nearby. Clive Rouse, an expert on medieval wall-paintings, quickly arrived on the scene and found himself combing through the rubbish tip for the pieces that already been taken there. It raises the question of how many church treasures have been mistakenly thrown away and how many are still awaiting discovery.

The painting was reassembled and placed back in its original place. It shows Christ in majesty sitting on a rainbow with his feet resting on a sphere and His hands showing the Precious Wounds. On either side are Our Lady and St John, with the other apostles, and, in the sky, angels holding the instruments of the Passion and blowing trumpets. Immediately below Christ are the dead rising from their tomb, including a tonsured cleric. Scrolls read in Latin: 'Rise ye dead and come to judgement'; to the right of the Lord 'Come ye blessed of my Father, inherit your kingdom' and to the left 'Go ye evil-doers into eternal fire'. Unusually, there are no depictions of Heaven or Hell, and originally the Doom would have included the image of St Michael weighing souls in a set of scales. It seems that around 1480 the rood loft was rebuilt and the Doom repainted and cut down to fit into this new position. The original purpose remained the same: to remind the good people of Penn of the Last Things: that life is short, death is certain and judgement real.

The local family that took its name from the village and acted as patrons of the church is an interesting one. Sybil Penn had the distinction of being the future Edward VI's nurse and foster mother after the death of Jane Seymour. Her modern-day descendant, Earl Howe, treasures a pearl necklace presented to her by a grateful Henry VIII and a velvet cap that is said to have been given by Edward. She was also awarded a generous annuity and the advowson of the parish, meaning that the Penns could appoint each successive vicar.

It is intriguing that Sybil was so close to this most Protestant of princes since, until the early seventeenth century, the family seem to have been largely Catholic in sympathy. That is not to say that they did not benefit from the dissolution of the monasteries, which in fact trebled the family's property, but there is evidence of their opposition to the religious changes. This was probably shared by Penn's priest, William Egleston, who was heard by his own churchwardens to utter 'opprobrious words', possibly in criticism of the king. As a result he found himself behind bars in Aylesbury. Nevertheless he remained in office and died in 1553 just as England was returning to the Old Faith under Mary Tudor. An inventory dating from the previous year lists three chasubles, two silk copes and a pyx in his possession.

Sybil's son, John, and his wife Ursula were certainly recusants, listed as absentees from the Anglican services in 1584. The following year they paid a fixed annual fine in return for exemption from further penalties to which they were liable as Catholics. This did not prevent John from being appointed to a lucrative post in the county and it may be that his family connections with the royal family kept him in favour at court.

Catholicism was truly alive and active in this corner of Buckinghamshire. In 1587 John Gardiner of Seagraves Manor, the village's other great house, was imprisoned for sheltering Catholic priests. The Penns continued to be loyal to the Old Faith until the death of Martha Penn in 1635. Of course, the most famous 'Penn' was another sort of dissenter: the Quaker William Penn, founder of Pennsylvania. There is some uncertainty about whether he was related to the Penns of Penn but he clearly thought he was and in 1753 a vault was created under the nave of the church in which six of William's grandsons were buried.

When the last trumpet is sounded, as depicted on the Doom, quite an assembly of the dead will rise up in Penn churchyard; saints and sinners from every background. There will be the local worthies buried within the church, the Penns and Curzons and former vicars, and the hundreds of (to us) unknown men, women and children who lie beneath the ground without a monument. The more recent memorials that do exist in 'God's Acre' there contain some interesting names, representative perhaps of every spectrum of the human condition: Donald Maclean, the British diplomat who acted as a Soviet spy, and Louisa Garrett Anderson, the suffragette who ran the only military hospital during the Great War to be staffed entirely by women; David Blakeley, the racing car driver shot by his lover Ruth Ellis, and Alison Uttley, author of the *Little Grey Rabbit* stories.

Yes, the trumpet shall one day sound in this charming corner of Buckinghamshire and the dead shall be raised incorruptible.

RAMSGATE, KENT

St Augustine and the Conversion of Kent

'Noticing some fair-haired children in the slave market one morning, Pope Gregory, the memorable pope, said (in Latin), 'What are those?' and on being told that they were Angles, made the memorable joke— '*Non angli, sed angeli*' ('*not* Angles, but *Anglicans*') and commanded one of his saints called St Augustine to go and convert the rest.

That's how W. C. Sellar and R. J. Yeatman summed up the story of England's convrsion, tongue firmly in cheek, in *1066 and All That*. It went through my mind as I joined a procession starting from Pegwell Bay for St Augustine's feast. The small group of pilgrims met at a signpost that gave directions to Ramsgate, Sandwich and, rather unusually, Rome, many miles distant over the Channel.

There is something timeless about the British coastline. The fresh sea air makes our cheeks ruddy and enlivens our spirits today much as it has done over the centuries and millenia. Indeed the sea wind has been the agent of historical change. It has brought across the Channel new ideas, new cultures and new dynasties.

The area around Pegwell Bay is a good example. The Romans landed near Richborough in AD 43 and eventually made it the grand entrance to Britannia, complete with triumphal arch. Then, in the aftermath of the fall of Rome, these shores witnessed the arrival of Hengist and Horsa, brother chieftains from Jutland—the *Adventus Saxonum*, the coming of the Saxons. In later centuries, it was the turn of the Vikings and Normans.

The sea wind can bring power not only in the natural order but also in the supernatural—in 597 the strong Channel wind acted as the agent of the Holy Spirit, swelling the sails of a boat full of Roman monks and bringing to these shores grace, truth and salvation; the power of the Almighty.

Christianity first arrived on these shores in the first or second century, though 'whence it came' we have no certainty of knowing—a soldier, a merchant, perhaps even a disciple like St Joseph of Arimathea. But we can be more sure when it comes to a figure like St Augustine of Canterbury. He was the principal instrument through whom the English people were converted—initially starting in the kingdom of Kent. It was a long process and supplemented by the Celtic missionaries in the north and the presence of the surviving Romano-British

Church. But it was St Augustine who inaugurated a new chapter in our Christian history, who founded, directly or indirectly, the sees of Canterbury, Rochester and London, and who firmly bound these isles ever more closely to the See of Peter.

It was fitting, then, to mark his feast by processing from Pegwell Bay through the local roads to St Augustine's Cross, near the reputed site of his meeting with the powerful King of Kent, St Ethelbert. St Augustine himself, though a familiar name to us all, is a rather elusive figure. He remains the eternal monk since he always stands in the shadow of his former abbot and master, St Gregory the Great. In St Bede's *Ecclesiastical History*, it is the pope who remains the key figure in the account of the Roman mission and it is St Gregory rather than St Augustine who is known as 'Apostle of the English'.

Despite our lack of information about St Augustine, Bede thankfully does not present him as a plaster statue saint. Setting out for England in 596, Augustine and his monks got cold feet as soon as they reached the south of France. They had heard rumours that the English were barbarous unbelievers and, feeling nervous and unprepared for the task at hand (the monks had no knowledge of the Saxon or Frankish languages), Augustine was sent back to Rome to appeal to the pope. Perhaps their fear is not surprising for they were going into the unknown.

Mgr Ronald Knox, in the mid-twentieth century, said in a sermon:

> the Britons, in the classical authors, are always used as a synonym for the extreme limit, the outside edge of mankind—those Britons, tucked away right at the edge of the world, much as we should say 'Borneo' or 'Patagonia'. And I should think in St Gregory's time, owing to the invasion of the Angles and the Saxons, England was a still more inaccessible and unheard-of region. And that is where St Gregory sent St Augustine to convert you and me when we were little heathens.

St Augustine soon returned with a papal letter of exhortation, together with testimonials for the Frankish authorities they would meet as they travelled through France. This allowed them to pick up a number of Frankish clergy, who were able to act as interpreters and negotiators with the English. Moreover, St Augustine was almost certainly consecrated bishop before he boarded the boat for Kent.

And so this 'miniature church' landed on the Isle of Thanet. The monks sent word to King Ethelbert, 'saying that they had come from

Rome bearing very glad news, which infallibly assured all who would receive it of eternal joy in heaven and an everlasting kingdom with the living and true God'. The king met them in the open air, for fear of hostile magic, but greeted the missionaries with courtesy. They carried 'a silver cross as their standard and the likeness of our Lord and Saviour painted on a board'.

Fishermen say: 'Wind from the East, fish bite the least', but the wind that drew St Augustine westwards resulted in a very healthy catch. St Ethelbert was converted and baptised—probably something he had been considering for years, thanks to the ministrations of Queen Bertha (the unsung heroine of the whole episode), her chaplains and perhaps the indigenous clergy. Along with St Ethelbert, his kingdom was effectively 'baptised' and claimed for Christ.

The power of the Holy Spirit broke forth from Kent, like a strong wind, bringing the Faith to neighbouring territories and ensuring, within a few years, a whole network of dioceses, churches and monasteries. In Kent itself religious houses for women were quickly founded at Folkestone by St Eanswythe (granddaughter of St Ethelbert) and Minster by St Dumneva (possibly the king's great-granddaughter).

And all this was undoubtedly was a Very Good Thing.

ROCHESTER, KENT

Rochester and St William

Rochester is a quintessential English cathedral city. Charles Dickens, one of its most famous sons, summed up its historic associations in the *Pickwick Papers*, where Alfred Jingle vividly (though rather inaccurately) described the 'old cathedral': 'earthly smell—pilgrims' feet worn away the old steps—little Saxon doors—confessionals like money-takers' boxes at theatres—queer customers those monks—popes and lord treasurers, and all sorts of old fellows, with great red faces, and broken noses, turning up every day—buff jerkins, too—matchlocks—sarcophagus—fine place—old legends, too—strange stories: capital'.

Rochester is the second oldest diocese in England, set up in 604 by St Augustine of Canterbury, who consecrated one of his companions as bishop: St Justus. Indeed, the first few bishops of Rochester were members of the Augustinian mission. When St Justus was translated to Canterbury, he was replaced by Romanus—a name suggesting his origins. Little is known about him beyond the fact that he drowned in the Mediterranean in 627 while travelling to Rome on business. He was succeeded by another member of the mission, the great St Paulinus, who had been the first Bishop of York but had to flee to the south for safety.

The Saxon cathedral was dedicated to St Andrew and built on the site of the present cathedral. St Justus also founded what is now known as the King's School, which along with the similarly named school in Canterbury, claims to be one of the oldest continuously running school in the world.

The presence of the Norman castle opposite the cathedral reminds us that the place had a key defensive significance. The castle was built by one of the most remarkable bishops of Rochester, Gundulf, formerly a monk of Bec and a close associate both of William the Conqueror and Archbishop Lanfranc. He is chiefly remembered today, however, not so much as a shepherd of souls but as a gifted architect and the 'King's Engineer'. He also designed the White Tower in the Tower of London.

Under Gundulf, the relics of his predecessor, St Paulinus, were translated to a magnificent new shrine. However, by the thirteenth century a new saint had superseded him: St William of Perth. He was a Scottish baker, well known for his piety and his generosity to the poor, giving every tenth loaf to the poor. In around 1201 he started out on a pilgrimage to Canterbury and possibly eventually to Rome and the Holy Land.

Like many pilgrims, he stayed three nights at Rochester but was brutally murdered as he left the city, some say by his adopted son or his apprentice, who were accompanying him on the journey. His body was taken to the cathedral and, we read, 'he moulded miracles plentifully at his tomb'. It is little surprise that fellow pilgrims would have found him a particularly accessible saint. His cult was approved in 1256; some claim he was formally canonised but no papal bulls to this effect have been found. His shrine attracted many pilgrims and, with them, offerings. It is remarkable that, within a short space of time, the increased income allowed for the extension of the east end and the rebuilding of the choir, which was completed in 1227.

Despite such glories, Rochester was a poor diocese for much of its history and seen by many of its bishops as a stepping stone to greater things. It was indeed telling that its most famous bishop, St John Fisher, refused offers of promotion and stayed there for thirty-one years. He told a fellow bishop, 'though others may have greater revenues, yet I have the care of fewer souls, so that as I must before long give an account of both, I would not wish them one whit increased'. He compared his diocese to a wife and stated he had no desire to swap her for another. Unlike many of his colleagues, Fisher spent most of his episcopate (perhaps as much as 90 per cent) resident in his diocese, though its close proximity to London and the royal court must have been an advantage. He was also unusual in conducting parochial visitations himself, living simply and ensuring his clergy were learned and assiduous in their duties. Little wonder that the great Tridentine reformer, St Charles Borromeo, had such a deep devotion to Fisher and hung his portrait in his study at Milan.

ROMNEY MARSH, KENT

The Churches of Romney Marsh

According to the famous line in *The Ingoldsby Legends* (with apologies to Australian readers): 'The World, according to the best geographers, is divided into Europe, Asia, Africa, America, and Romney Marsh'. There is something eerily distinctive about the latter. Situated on the border between Kent and East Sussex, this area of a hundred square miles was originally under the sea but over the centuries drained and reclaimed. Yet it is still a land apart.

The landscape is flat, bleak and often covered by mist. One of the area's most distinctive features are its churches, many in an excellent state of restoration, even though some of them are no longer in use and in desolate locations. This is largely due to the work of the Romney Marsh Historic Churches Trust.

Given the relatively small population on the Marsh, some of the churches are surprisingly large—like those at Ivychurch and Lydd, both of which claim to be the 'Cathedral of Romney Marsh'. Churches, here as elsewhere, were built not only for the glory of God but as a statement by their patron, whether it be (in the case of the Marsh) the Archbishop of Canterbury or the local grandee. They also testified to the wealth brought to the region by the famous Romney Marsh sheep.

The churches are full of interesting details. A favourite for many is the attractively named St Mary in the Marsh—quintessentially English, in a deserted position but opposite a pub and a red telephone box. Beside the 'priest's door' in the chancel are the remains of a 'Mass dial'—a primitive sundial that indicated when the bell should be rung for Mass in the Middle Ages.

St Augustine's, Brookland is famous for its separate octagonal belfry, dating from the thirteenth century. It looks like a steeple that has blown down and settled next to the church. Many legends have arisen to explain its bizarre location, including the claim that it descended in amazement when a confirmed old bachelor married a venerable spinster. Inside, there is a medieval wall-painting of the martyrdom of St Thomas of Canterbury, reminding us that before the Reformation church interiors were a riot of images and colours, and a fascinating Norman lead font, showing the signs of the Zodiac and the occupations associated with each month. Thus, for April there is an image of Taurus and a female figure holding a spray of foliage in each hand. At the back of the church the visitor can see a collection of scales, weights and measures used to work out the tithes due to the church—so that the appropriate amount of, say, corn, cloth and wine could be measured. There is even a chest, once used to keep the parish archive, which is said to have come from a Spanish ship wrecked during the Armada of 1588.

Given its isolation, its proximity to France and its frequent mists, it is little wonder that Romney Marsh is so closely connected with smuggling. Indeed, there is a tradition that a tunnel connects St George's, Ivychurch to the Bell Inn, next door, and that the church vaults were used to hide contraband. The church authorities were involved and turned a blind eye—on one occasion the rector, arriving at the church to prepare for a service, was met by the sexton who declared: 'Bain't be no services s'morning, Parson, pulpit be full o'baccy and the vestry be full o'brandy'.

Many of the churches have box pews, dating from the eighteenth century. The ones at St Clement, Old Romney, are painted a light pink. This was not a Georgian colour scheme, however, but a decision made by the producers of the film *Dr Syn* (about a fictional smuggler), which used the church as a location in 1963. The colour has stuck ever since. Others have a handy little 'sentry box' called a 'hudd', which was carried to the graveside for a burial service and used by the parson to keep his powdered wig and book dry.

Romney Marsh is only an hour from central London and is well worth an excursion. There is a sense of entering a lost world and the churches are not only open museums of social history but testament to the Christian roots of our nation.

ST ALBANS, HERTFORDSHIRE

The Protomartyr and his Companions

St Albans Cathedral towers above the landscape as cars hurtle round the M25. It has only been a cathedral since 1877 and locals still refer to it as 'the Abbey'. It was, before the Dissolution, one of the country's wealthiest monasteries, reflected in the size of the church, with the longest of all cathedral naves. The city itself, despite its proximity to London, still has a proud identity: a place where two battles were fought in the Wars of the Roses, where travellers once crowded the coaching inns, and where there are memories of the only English pope (Adrian IV), who grew up nearby and who (it is said) was rejected as a youth by the monastic community. All around are reminders that this was once Roman Britannia's second-largest city—Verulamium—though such was the triumph of Christianity that its name now bears that of a Roman martyr.

The story of St Alban is well known. As a prominent pagan citizen of Verulamium, he hid a priest who was fleeing from persecution. So impressed was he by the priest's example that he took instruction and became a Christian. When the soldiers came to search for the priest, St Alban put on the fugitive's cloak and was himself arrested. After refusing to worship the pagan gods, he was taken to the hill where the abbey now stands and beheaded—the punishment reserved for Roman citizens. Such was the scandal of this execution that, according to tradition, the headsman's eyes fell out at the moment of martyrdom. The date for St Alban's martyrdom has been variously given as 209 (under Septimus Severus), 254 (under Decius) or 303 (under Diocletian). Whatever the true dating, St Alban testifies to the early existence of Christianity in Britain.

A cult quickly grew up around the martyr. St Germanus of Auxerre visited the shrine as early as 429 and in the eighth century St Bede referred to the 'beautiful Church worthy of Alban's martyrdom where miracles of healing took place'.

We often think of St Alban as a one off—this country's proto-martyr and, if he was indeed martyred in 209, one of the earliest known Christians from northern Europe. However, it is likely that he was not the only martyr to be produced by the Romano-British Church, even if the others have been largely forgotten in the mists of time. There is evidence, moreover, that when St Augustine made his mission to Kent he encouraged the veneration of Roman saints rather than British ones.

In the twelfth century, the priest hidden by St Alban was given the name St Amphibalus (possibly derived from the Greek name given to a cloak) and was himself venerated as a martyr. According to William the Monk's largely fanciful *Alia Acta SS Albani et Amphibali et Sociorum* ('Other Doings of SS Alban and Amphibalus and their Companions') St Amphibalus fled to Wales after St Alban's death together with a thousand converts he had made at Verulamium. Eventually they were discovered by the pagans and massacred.

Another tradition, preserved in the eleventh-century *Martyrologium Hieronymianum*, names two of these martyr converts as SS Socrates and Stephanus, who were honoured on 17 September. St Amphibalus himself was taken back to Verulamium in chains and disembowelled, scourged, stabbed and finally stoned to death.

In 1178, shortly after the *Alia Acta* was written, the body of St Amphibalus was discovered (or, to use the technical term, 'invented') in a small mound at Redbourne, three miles outside St Albans. According to the chronicler Matthew Paris, St Amphibalus was found with a large iron spear head and nine other bodies. The monks had almost certainly stumbled across an early Anglo-Saxon burial, and it remains questionable whether any of these bones were those of a Romano-British martyr. Nevertheless, the relics were placed in a shrine at first next to that of St Alban; then, around 1222, to the east end of the nave, before being finally translated to a worthier place in the retro-choir.

St Bede tells us that SS Aaron and Justus were martyred around the same time as St Alban, at the *Legionum urbs*—widely translated as the 'city of the legions'. We are told that 'they were racked by many kinds of torture and their limbs were indescribably mangled but, when their sufferings were over, their souls were carried to the joys of the heavenly city'. It seems that their cult was based around two chapels near Caerleon in Monmouthshire. St Aaron also gave his name to a holy well and the saints are still commemorated in the Welsh Calendar, together with St Alban, on 20 June.

The sixth-century writer, St Gildas, stated in his *De Excidio Britonum* that many others suffered for Christ and that their 'places of burial and of martyrdom, had they not for our manifold crimes been interfered with and destroyed by the barbarians [i.e. the Saxons], would have still kindled in the minds of the beholders no small fire of divine charity'. Moreover, those who survived 'hid themselves in woods and deserts, and secret caves, waiting until God, who is the righteous judge of all, should reward their persecutors with judgment, and themselves with protection of their lives'. Likewise, St Bede states that 'many others of both sexes' suffered throughout Britannia. The majority of these are long forgotten but in some places traces of their *cultus* remains.

The cult of St Alban is still very much alive in his city. There is an annual Alban Pilgrimage, featuring a medieval fair, and giant puppets retelling his story. The cathedral has resurrected the Alban Bun, a precursor to the Hot Cross Bun dating back to the fourteenth century. Most significantly, the pilgrim can still pray at the restored shrines of St Alban and St Amphibalus, which had originally been destroyed at the Reformation. The latter shrine was completed shortly after the Covid-19 lockdown and among the faces peering out of the stonework is one wearing a mask. A very twenty-first-century touch for England's oldest sanctuary.

SILCHESTER, HAMPSHIRE

Calleva Atrebatum

Driving along the country lanes between Reading and Basingstoke, a sign pointing to Silchester suggested a place of some importance, where perhaps we might find a hostelry for refreshment. We were surprised to discover that Silchester itself was a small village but just outside there were the remnants of an important Roman town: 'Calleva Atrebatum'.

The name 'Calleva' dates back to the Iron Age settlement which stood on the site, while 'Atrebatum' referred to the local British tribe, the Atrebates, whose territory stretched from Wiltshire to Surrey and from Oxfordshire to Hampshire. 'Silchester' itself is a Saxon name, meaning 'castle in the wood'.

Most Roman towns are still populated — think of London, York, and Colchester — but Silchester was deserted some time in the fourth century AD, for reasons that are not immediately clear. Roman Silchester now consists of about 100 acres of fields encircled by the Roman wall, built into an older earthen rampart, which emerges out of the trees and bushes to form a pathway popular with dog walkers. The bustling streets are now grazing ground; the citizens largely sheep, cows and even llamas.

The town was situated on the roads to London, Dorchester-on-Thames, Bath and Winchester, and so would have been an important administrative and trading centre. Walking across the fields, it is hard to believe that these once would have been full of shops, houses and workshops; there were baths, too, a market (or forum) and administrative centre (basilica). Near the south gate was an inn that supported the Empire's courier service. Nowadays in dry summers the grid of streets sometimes reappears on the parched grass, as if the past is trying to rise into the present.

Just beyond the walls there is an impressive amphitheatre, which would have seen gladiators, wild beasts and public executions, and could have accommodated up to 7,250. Outside there would have had stalls selling food and souvenirs. Walking into the arena today, with the high circular mounds surrounding on every side, is still a highly dramatic experience and it is easy to imagine the noisy spectacles once held there. 'What scenes have taken place in this now silent and deserted spot!', wrote one Victorian antiquary. 'The lion's roar, and the tiger's howl, have echoed through these woodlands. The shrieks of the torn victim have here rent the air, while the shouts of the multitude, as cruel as the beasts which afforded them such a sanguinary pleasure, were still more awful'. Perhaps among those victims were Christian martyrs, whose names are now known only unto God?

Unsurprisingly, all sorts of legends have grown up around Silchester. It was said that it was the abode of giants, one of whom was called 'Onion'. The Roman coins found here were at one time called by locals 'Onion's pennies'. King Arthur was also supposed to have been crowned here and such was its importance that he appointed one Maugannius as Bishop of Silchester. Excavations in 1866 resulted in the discovery of a wingless bronze eagle, which at the time was thought to have belonged to one of the Roman legions stationed there. It inspired Rosemary Sutcliff to write her popular novel *The Eagle of the Ninth* (1954) and more recently made into a Hollywood film. Subsequent excavations by the Society of Antiquaries of London and the University of Reading have unearthed many other items, including a stone head of Serapis, Egyptian god of fertility. Some of the mosaics found on the site were moved to the Duke of Wellington's house at Stratfield Saye, where they could be admired in the floor of the entrance hall.

The only buildings in view today within the walls at Silchester are a farmhouse and the medieval church of St Mary's. Like all our old churches, this is full of interest, with a fine fourteenth-century tomb of a local worthy and an early Tudor rood screen that was removed at the Reformation and then, having been discovered in a nearby barn, placed back in its rightful place in 1865. It features roses and pomegranates, the symbols of Henry VIII and Catherine of Aragon.

What is particularly fascinating, though, is that St Mary's is almost certainly not the first place of Christian worship at Silchester. A small building, to the west of the present church and now completely covered by grass, may well have been a church, built around 340 AD. Within the apse was found a geometric mosaic of black and white chequers, of which the central motif is a cross. A tiled area near the porch has been interpreted as the setting for a baptistry. Perhaps a member of the congregation dropped the fourth-century leaden *bulla* or seal, found in the Basilica, that bears the Christian monogram.

Silchester is indeed the 'Pompeii of Hampshire'.

STEYNING, WEST SUSSEX

The Boy with the Wooden Cart

It is hard to believe that Steyning was once a prosperous port with a market and a mint. This thriving centre for trade was known as the *Portus Cuthmanni* (Cuthman's Port), named after the local saint. Although the sea has long since receded, the memory of St Cuthman still lingers around the streets of his former home. A new statue of the saint has been placed near the ancient parish church and his picture appears on the town sign, which shows him pushing his mother around in a wooden wheelbarrow (his somewhat bizarre iconographical symbol). The village still celebrates his feast on 8 February.

St Cuthman was a shepherd, probably born in the late seventh century. Some say that he was baptised by St Wilfrid himself, the 'Apostle of Sussex', and he certainly showed signs of his closeness to God from an early age. One day, while tending his sheep, he drew a line around them with his staff so that he could get away to collect food. On his return, he found that the flock had not left the invisible boundary. This miracle may have taken place in a field near Chidham, which for centuries was known as 'St Cuthman's Field' or 'St Cuthman's Dell'. It was said that a large stone in the field, 'on which the holy shepherd was in the habit of sitting', held miraculous properties.

A turning point in Cuthman's life was the death of his father, which left both him and his mother destitute. They decided to leave their home and journey eastwards—in the direction of the rising sun. By this time, Cuthman's mother was an invalid and so he had to push her in a wheeled wooden cart. A rope that stretched from the handles to the saint's shoulders helped carry the burden. When the rope snapped, he made a new one out of withies but realised that this would be only a temporary solution. So, he decided that once this rope of withies broke, it would be a sign from God to settle at that place and build a church. This happened at Steyning and the saint soon began his work of erecting a sanctuary in honour of the One who had guided him safely along his journey. Many of the local inhabitants helped him in this great task and on one occasion, according to the legend, he even received divine assistance. The builders were having trouble with a roof-beam, when a stranger appeared and provided them with a solution. When asked his name, the newcomer replied: 'I am He in whose name you are building the church'.

Cuthman's time at Steyning continued to be accompanied with amazing portents, one of the most astonishing linking him to the formation of the 'Devil's Dyke', the world's deepest dry valley situated in the South Downs. St Cuthman lived at a time of intense evangelisation and church building in the area. The Devil became so angry at the propagation of the Faith, that he decided to dig a channel through the hills by night to let in the sea and drown the Christians of Sussex. Fortunately, St Cuthman found out the Devil's plan and tricked him by holding a candle behind a sieve and knocking the local cock off its perch. When the Devil saw the light and heard the cock crow, he fled the scene, leaving his great plan unfinished and giving us the 'Devil's Dyke'.

Such are the stories that grew up around St Cuthman, who came to Steyning from afar to preach the Gospel and shepherd the local flock. He built a wooden chapel, probably on the site of the present church of St Andrew's. This building was certainly well established by 857, when King Ethelwulf (father of Alfred the Great) was buried there. It seems, also, that pilgrims visited the tomb of St Cuthman and that his intercession led to many cures.

During the reign of St Edward the Confessor, the church at Steyning was given to the Abbey of the Holy Trinity at Fécamp, Normandy. This Benedictine house, founded in the seventh century, is famous for its 'Benedictine' liqueur, which today is commercially produced in the grounds of the old abbey. It was to this monastery that the Black Monks took the body of St Cuthman and his feast was celebrated at many of the religious houses of Normandy. Thus, St Cuthman became well known on the continent—as can be seen in a mid-fifteenth-century German engraving of the saint by Martin Schongauer and in the writings of the seventeenth-century Bollandists.

Meanwhile, the church at Steyning was rebuilt and dedicated to St Andrew. However, St Cuthman was not forgotten in his beloved land. A 'Guild of St Cuthman' was in existence at Chidham on the eve of the Reformation and a misericord in Ripon Cathedral supposedly depicts him pushing his mother in a three-wheeled barrow.

In more recent times, St Cuthman achieved fame by becoming the subject of a play by Christopher Fry, *The Boy with a Cart* (1939). This was performed at the Lyric Theatre, Hammersmith, in 1950, directed by John Gielguid and with Richard Burton playing the part of St Cuthman. The saint's story presents us with a charming example of filial piety, prayer, evangelisation and church building in Saxon England. In the words of Christopher Fry:

It is there in the story of Cuthman, the working together
Of man and God like root and sky; the son
Of a Cornish shepherd, Cuthman, the boy with a cart,
The boy we saw trudging the sheep-tracks with his mother
Mile upon mile over five counties; one
Fixed purpose biting his heels and lifting his heart.
We saw him; we saw him with a grass in his mouth, chewing
And travelling. We saw him building at last
A church among whortleberries ...

WAVERLEY, SURREY

The Abbey in the Water Meadow

Yorkshire has no monopoly of Cistercian ruins. There is even one in the Home Counties, just a few miles away from Farnham: Waverley Abbey. Indeed, it was the first English Cistercian house to be established, in 1128 by William Giffard, Bishop of Winchester. The Cistercian Order, let us not forget, was in part an English foundation: one of its founders, St Stephen Harding, was a Dorset man and former monk of Sherborne.

The Cistercians liked to build their abbeys in wild, remote spots, and despite its Surrey gentility this location was not without its challenges. The River Wey often flooded; in 1201, for example, the abbey was 'almost submerged and greatly imperilled'. The name 'Waverley' means, appropriately enough, 'water meadow'.

Initially 'colonised' by an abbot and twelve monks from France, sixty years after its foundation the abbey boasted 70 monks and 120 lay brothers. Eventually the church was rebuilt and at its dedication in 1278 over 7,000 guests gathered for a splendid banquet—a colourful company of abbots, knights and 'so great a multitude of both sexes' who, when the day was over, 'returned to their homes glorifying and praising God'.

Hear the name 'Waverley', however, and one thinks of Sir Walter Scott's popular *Waverley Novels* and the Edinburgh station that bears the name. Some have suggested that Scott was working in the Public Record Office one day when he stumbled across the *Annals of Waverley Abbey*, which gave him the inspiration for the name of his 1814 novel. It is possible that he read about or visited the abbey but the story itself does not involve monks and monasteries. Scott himself admitted to choosing 'Waverley' because it was a noble but 'uncontaminated name, bearing with its sound little of good or evil, excepting what the reader shall hereafter be pleased to affix to it'.

Nevertheless, a perusal of the monastic *Annals* brings these bare ruins to life. There are accounts of royal visits, criminals seeking sanctuary and 'miraculous' escapes from accidents. There is mention of Matilda (or Maud) of London, a benefactress who was known as 'Mother to the Convent'; 'almost all her goods, as well in life as in death, she gave to Waverley'. Indeed, the monks had good cause to thank her generosity twice a year: 'a portion of bread and fish was dealt to each monk on the 6th of the Ides of February annually, on which day the donor died, and another of fish on the feast of St Lucy, being the obit of her husband'.

In 1216 the spring that provided fresh water throughout the monastery dried up. Fortunately, we read, Brother Simon came to the rescue: he 'girded himself bravely to the task of searching and digging for new veins of living waters; and these after diligent search, he discovered, and with great labour and energy compelled them all to discharge their waters through underground pipes into one place; and there he made by art a living fountain which never ceases to flow, and which still supplies the Abbey most plentifully with water'. Some of these lead pipes were dug up in 1740, showing the ingenuity of medieval Cistercian engineering. Brother Simon's excavations may have helped form a local cave, which became associated with a local 'good' witch, Mother Ludlam.

Waverley was never a wealthy abbey and it seems to have escaped the major scandals that old-fashioned writers associate with medieval monasticism. It founded several daughter houses, including those at Garendon (Leicestershire), Forde (Dorset), Coombe (Warwickshire) and Thame (Oxfordshire). It was finally dissolved in 1536 and the last abbot, William Ayling, wrote to Thomas Cromwell 'beseeching your good mastership for the love of Christ's Passion to help the preservation of this poor monastery'. The abbey estate passed to Sir William Fitzherbert, treasurer of the royal household.

The abbey buildings were ravaged by time, weather and locals, who regarded it as a convenient quarry. 'The walls have been peeled like an orange', lamented the Victorian historian of Waverley, Rev. Charles Kerry, 'until nothing but the very rubble remains ... Much of the monastic pile has been altogether swept away; there is not the slightest trace of the Gateway, with its Chapel of St Mary, the Infirmary of the Seculars, nor of the Chapel attached to the Infirmary, all of which are mentioned in the *Annals*'. When the antiquarian John Aubrey visited in the seventeenth century, there were still roundels of stained glass to be seen, depicting such scenes as 'St Michael fighting the devil' and 'St Dunstan holding the devil by the nose with his pincers, and having retorts, crucibles, and chemical instruments about him'. These have long since disappeared.

When William Cobbett, a native of nearby Farnham, visited in October 1825, he was more interested in his childhood memories. He showed his youngest son, Richard, 'a tree, close by the ruins of the Abbey, from a limb of which I once fell into the river, in an attempt to take the nest of a crow' and a hollow elm, 'into which I, when a very little boy, once saw a cat go, that was as big as a middle-sized spaniel dog, for relating which I got a great scolding, for standing to which I, at last, got a beating; but stand to which I still did'.

My friend and I were the only visitors the day we went to Waverley. A venerable yew, with a thick trunk and intertwining roots, grew near the site of the high altar and made us think of those who lie buried beneath the grass, awaiting the day of resurrection. The soft breeze, the dappled light and the swans gliding gracefully on the river gave a glimpse of the peace that the monks sought here and now (we pray) enjoy eternally.

WEST GRINSTEAD, WEST SUSSEX

'The Little Cottage in the Forest'

Our Lady of Consolation at West Grinstead is the first Catholic Marian shrine to be erected in this country since the Reformation—in the 1870s. The founder, a Breton priest, Mgr Jean-Marie Denis, chose 'Our Lady of Consolation' as a title that would not only have been familiar to Englishmen before the Reformation but was still popular on the continent. Turin was the centre of devotion to the *Consolata* and this link not only allowed the shrine of West Grinstead to tap into the spiritual treasury of the Universal Church but opened the doors to international fund-raising.

Mgr Denis was certainly direct in his approach. In 1867 he wrote to an English Catholic newspaper:

> A small bank, which can afford to depositors the largest interest, has been established here on the best securities. Others give only three and five per cent, whilst this one will give ten times as much. Besides, it has over all other banks the great advantage that pennies, as well as pounds, can be invested in it, and that a large, though a proportional, interest will be returned for the smallest sum. This bank is the fund for building a church at West Grinstead, and the interest returned is the kingdom of Heaven. Who can refuse to invest at least a part of his savings in a bank which offers such an interest?

Such tactics seemed to work and in 1876 a splendid gothic church was opened. The title 'Our Lady of Consolation' also fitted in with the spirit of the times. After long centuries of persecution and enforced discretion, English Catholics were coming out of the catacombs and enjoying a 'Second Spring'. A shrine church such as the one at West Grinstead was a way of giving thanks for this revival. Indeed, it is perhaps appropriate that one of the most influential writers of this newly confident Catholic community, Hilaire Belloc, chose to be buried in the shadow of the shrine church (in his beloved Sussex soil).

Generations of Catholics at West Grinstead had suffered much for the Faith. The most important local family in the seventeenth and eighteenth centuries, the Carylls, was staunchly Catholic and sheltered a number of chaplains. By the 1670s they sponsored three priests — one to act as family chaplain and the other two as 'riding missionaries' in Sussex and Hampshire. The Carylls were related to Charles Carroll, the only Catholic to sign the Declaration of Independence, and John Carroll, first Bishop of Baltimore and founder of Georgetown University. The poet Alexander Pope was a friend of the family and wrote his famous *The Rape of the Lock* while sitting under a tree in the park.

The current presbytery of the shrine claims to be the oldest continuously occupied (Catholic) priest's house in England. It stood on the Caryll's estate and was in former times even more hidden than today, known locally as 'the little cottage in the forest'. Here generations of priests would stay, keeping a low profile among the local Downland shepherds. Visitors to the shrine can still see the hiding holes and the secret chapel in the loft, where the Sacred Mysteries were celebrated until the erection of Mgr Denis' church. In 1925 a slate altar stone and a small pewter chalice were found beneath the floor boards there, dating from the seventeenth century and providing a vivid link to recusant times.

'The little cottage in the forest' was positioned conveniently near the coast and the road to London. Tradition suggests that priests were brought up the River Adur and dropped off at a spot nearby, at the point where the reeds were marked with crosses. One of the priests who said Mass here was Blessed Francis Bell, a Franciscan who had worked at the English convents overseas before serving on the 'English Mission'. He had a great devotion to Our Lady and, it is said, was so proficient linguistically that he would recite her *Little Office* in Latin, Hebrew, Greek, Spanish, French, Flemish and English. Captured at Stevenage in 1643, he was condemned 'for being a popish priest' — evidence of this treasonable offence including 'having said Mass at West Grinstead at one time'.

It is pleasing to see how the connection between West Grinstead and the priesthood continued into modern times. One of Mgr Denis's curates was a certain Francis Bourne, who would later become Archbishop of Westminster and Cardinal. While at West Grinstead, he did much work in the orphanage near the shrine and started preparing some of the boys for Holy Orders (inspired perhaps by his hero, Don Bosco). They formed the nucleus of the new seminary set up by the diocese of Southwark in 1889, with Bourne as rector, which was initially located just down the road at Henfield (and later moved to Wonersh).

WEYBRIDGE, SURREY

The Chapel on the Heath

History is full of twists and turns. Who would have thought, for example, that a Korean Presbyterian church in Surrey once held the tomb of a King of France?

Go to Heath Road in Weybridge and you will see the striking church of St Charles Borromeo, attached to a later Victorian extension. The original chapel was built by James Taylor, a noted architect of the Catholic Revival at the turn of the nineteenth century. Taking advantage of the new-found freedoms provided by the Catholic Relief Acts of 1771, 1778 and 1791, Taylor designed the new church of St George, London Road, Southwark (later to be replaced by Pugin's gothic cathedral) and an impressive college building at St Edmund's, Old Hall Green (Hertfordshire). Here he came to know one of the masters, Fr John Potier, whose brother, a Dominican, was trying to set up a Catholic mission in Weybridge. This was especially necessary since the Catholic Southcote family had recently sold Woburn Park, which had acted as a Mass centre.

Taylor purchased a site of thirty acres in Weybridge and built a house for his family, which he initially called 'Waterloo Cottage', with a splendid neo-gothic chapel attached, consecrated by Bishop Bramston on 4 November 1835, the feast of St Charles Borromeo. It was small, in the shape of a Greek cross, with a dome and painted glass windows. Two medieval carved heads were incorporated into the design, expressing continuity with the abbeys of Chertsey and Waverley that once stood nearby.

Little did the Taylors know that their chapel would soon become a footnote to an internationally important event. After his abdication as King of France after the 1848 Revolution, Louis Philippe moved to England and lived at Claremont House, Esher (Surrey). This had originally been built for Clive of India and had been the home of Prince Leopold and Princess Charlotte, the only child of George IV. She had died there in 1817, mourned by all. Louis Philippe and his wife, Marie Amelie (niece of the ill-fated Marie Antoinette), enjoyed a quiet life in Surrey, occasionally travelling into London or to St Leonards on the Sussex coast. Known as the Count and Countess of Neuilly, they regularly attended Mass at St Charles Borromeo. The gallery, originally used by the Taylor family, became a royal tribune and between 1850 and 1869 no less than eleven members of the Orleans family were buried in the little church.

The 'Citizen King' himself died at Claremont on 26 August 1850, aged 76. The diarist, Charles Greville, writing in Brighton, noted that 'not long ago his life was the most important in the world, and his death would have produced a profound sensation and general consternation. Now hardly more importance attaches to the event than there would be to the death of one of the Old Bathing-women opposite my window'.

His obsequies were notably devoid of any pomp or ostentation and 'scarcely differed from those which would have been observed in the case of a wealthy country gentleman'. Indeed, many of the guests, including foreign nobles and diplomats, who arrived at Esher railway station, had to make the lengthy walk to Claremont, where the king's body lay in semi-state. It took ten 'stout' men to carry the coffin to the hearse, which was drawn by eight black horses to Weybridge, along narrow lanes and through the villages of Esher and Hersham, where many of the locals had gathered out of curiosity and sympathy. Some had closed their shutters and blinds. At St Charles's chapel, there was little room for the distinguished congregation. The Requiem Mass was celebrated by Dr Whitty, Vicar General of the London District, shortly to become the first Vicar General of the newly created archdiocese of Westminster. When the queen died sixteen years later, the Prince of Wales and Duke of Cambridge were present at the Requiem.

Louis Philippe had been replaced in 1848 by Louis Napoleon, who became the Emperor Napoleon III. He eventually lost his throne in 1870, as a result of the Franco-Prussian War, and, like Louis Philippe, became an exile in England. He was eventually buried at St Michael's Abbey, Farnborough—not a million miles from Weybridge. The transition from Second Empire to Third Republic in 1870 meant that it became possible for the bodies of Louis Philippe and family to return to his mausoleum in Dreux—all except that of the Duchesse de Nemours, at the explicit request of her husband. She was a favourite cousin of Queen Victoria, who sometimes visited her tomb by use of a discreet side entrance. The body of the duchess was finally taken to France in the 1980s.

The church, recently restored, is no longer in Catholic hands and is now in the care of the World Mission Korean Presbyterian Church. It remains a fascinating memorial to a French dynasty and a reminder of this little-known part of our history.

WINDSOR, BERKSHIRE

The Treasures of St George's Chapel and an Apostate Dean

Windsor Castle, a favourite residence of Elizabeth II, is one of the world's most famous buildings. However, it is not just a working palace and a tourist attraction. A quarter of its buildings are taken up by the College of St George, with the magnificent chapel at its centre—a burial place of monarchs and home of the Most Honourable and Noble Order of the Garter.

There is, of course, much to interest the pilgrim. The chapel was originally staffed by a dean and twelve secular priests or canons, who were assisted by the vicars choral. Many of the original buildings of this community still survive. Inside the chapel are splendid chantry chapels and reminders of the 'holy places' once visited by pilgrims: the shrines of Henry VI and John Shorne and the 'Cross Gneth', a relic of the True Cross which had been captured by Edward I from Prince Llewelyn of Wales.

Towards the back of the chapel is a more recent Catholic connection: a monument to the Prince Imperial, the only son of Napoleon III who was killed during the Zulu War in 1879. His effigy lies here among kings and princes but his actual remains are buried in the Imperial Crypt at St Michael's Abbey, Farnborough.

Look at a list of deans of Windsor and they contain, as one would expect, names of a distinctively English character: Christopher Wren (not the architect), Henry Beaumont, George Neville-Grenville. The eagle-eyed will spot Christopher Bainbridge, an early Tudor dean who went on to become Bishop of Durham, Archbishop of York and a prominent cardinal in the Rome of Julius II.

But one early seventeenth-century name does not seem to fit into this series of respectable English ecclesiastics: Marco Antonio de Dominis, who—uniquely—came from what is now Croatia and had previously been a Jesuit and Archbishop of Split. How did such a character, with an impressively Catholic pedigree, come to occupy one of the most privileged positions within the Church of England?

De Dominis was born in 1560 on the island of Rab, just off the Croatian coast. At the time of his birth, he was a Venetian subject for the Serene Republic held sway over the Adriatic and the fabled city was only 120 miles away. A member of a well-established noble family, he was educated in Italy at Loreto, joined the Society of Jesus and taught at the universities of Padua and Brescia.

If he is chiefly remembered today for his bewildering spiritual odyssey that took him from Rome to Windsor and then back to Rome again, it is easy to forget that he also made a name for himself in the world of science, writing on such subjects as the theory of tides and optics. Isaac Newton was familiar with his work and said that he was the first to develop the theory of the rainbow by focusing on the refractions of light in a raindrop.

In 1597 he resigned from the Society of Jesus and became Bishop of Senj (sometimes Italianised as 'Segna'), which was controlled by the Habsburgs. He succeeded an uncle who had been killed by Turkish raiders. In 1602 he was translated to Spalato or Split and back under Venetian rule, although parts of his large diocese came under the Ottomans. De Dominis found himself on the edge of Christendom and on multiple borders between Christians and Muslims, and Catholics and Orthodox. It is little wonder that he developed such firm ideas about the unity between Churches!

As archbishop, he fought many battles with the papacy over his jurisdictional rights. As a loyal subject of La Serenissima, he also sided with Venice in its long dispute with Rome. The Venetian authorities had forbidden the erecting of churches, monasteries, hospitals and the purchase of real estate by the Church without the permission of the State and, with the backing of the theologian Paolo Sarpi (a friend of De Dominis), had banned the publication of the subsequent papal censures. As a result, Venice was placed under Interdict and excommunicated in 1606 and a diplomatic crisis ensued, in which (it should be noted) England sided with the Venetians. The turn of events led De Dominis to develop his thinking on the relationship between Church and State and the authority of the pope, which would eventually find its mature expression in *De Republica Ecclesiastica*, published in England between 1618 and 1620. He favoured a reunion between Catholics and Protestants, the reform of the Church and the reduction of papal power over national churches.

The archbishop's views increasingly came under the suspicion of the Roman Inquisition. Having stepped down from the see of Split, and helped by his friendship with the English ambassador to Venice, Sir Henry Wootton, De Dominis decided to travel to London. Not only was it a safe haven, far away from the eyes of the Inquisitors, but the archbishop saw in King James a kindred spirit, who hoped to seek reconciliation in the aftermath of so much religious division, and reform the Church Universal.

De Dominis arrived in England on 6 December 1616, having departed on his long journey disguised as a Ragusian merchant. He was initially much-feted and wrote several works attacking the errors of Rome. He was granted precedence over all English bishops, except Canterbury and York. At the end of 1617 he was awarded doctor's degrees at both Oxford and Cambridge and took part, as assistant bishop, in the consecrations of the new bishops of Bristol and Lincoln. In 1618 he became dean of Windsor, master of the Savoy Hospital in London and prebendary of Canterbury — all prestigious appointments with a comfortable income.

England, however, was a far cry from Rome and his native Dalmatia. It is unclear whether he ever fully mastered English and he probably preached sermons in Latin and Italian. His hopes of pushing forward his vision for the Church were dashed when he realised that not all Anglicans were like the king. Moreover, negotiations concerning a marriage between Prince of Wales and the Infanta of Spain made De Dominis increasingly afraid of his position. He remained widely unpopular, not only because of the favour shown him but also because of his difficult personality — he is described by several commentators as bad-tempered, vain, pretentious and avaricious.

Such feelings were only confirmed when he decided to return to Rome in 1622, seeing the newly elected Gregory XV as a potential ally. The pope welcomed him back with open arms and formally absolved him of the sin of apostasy. De Dominis published several works attacking the errors he had found in England and the future seemed rosy and bright. But everything in seventeenth-century Rome depended on papal patronage and the situation was reversed when Gregory died in July 1623. The former dean of Windsor came once again under the scrutiny of the Inquisition and was imprisoned in Rome's Castel Sant'Angelo while his writings were once again examined. There he died of fever on 9 September 1624. His body remained unburied while the Inquisition completed its investigations. A few weeks later it came to the conclusion that he had died a relapsed heretic and his remains, along with some of his books, were burned on the Campo de'Fiori on 21 December 1624. No doubt students from the nearby Venerable English College were among those in the crowd.

What can one make of this unusual figure? A brilliant mind born before his time who showed that there was no contradiction between faith and science or an unscrupulous turncoat? A pioneer ecumenist or a greedy ecclesiastic? Sadly, the jury will probably always remain out for Marco Antonio de Dominis.

LONDON & MIDDLESEX

Entrée: The Catholic Underground

Londoners take the Underground for granted. They spend so much time squashed in those tubular carriages, avoiding eye contact with fellow passengers—on average, according to one source, spending eleven and a half days a year on the network (most of which, of course, is actually above ground). They also like to moan about the inevitable delays, travelling conditions and weekend engineering work. But they forget that without the Underground, London simply would not work and be a very different place.

The process of urbanisation and the growth of the suburbs over the last 150 years went hand in hand with the building of the railways. The opening of an Underground station normally meant the erection of lots of Edwardian villas or 1930s semi-detached houses. Another consequence, which perhaps is often forgotten, was the opening of new parishes as London got bigger and bigger. The Underground thus contributed to the expansion of pastoral provision in the metropolis.

When I sit on the tube, studying the map on the wall above, I try to spot as many station names with Christian associations as possible. You could almost draw up a Catholic guide to the Underground. Here are just some examples:

Barking: once celebrated for its abbey, one of the oldest in England. Founded by St Erkenwald (later Bishop of London) in 666, his sister, St Ethelburga, was appointed its first abbess—the first of seven saints who belonged to the community. The Saxon abbey was destroyed by the Danes in 870 but later re-founded. Abbesses included four members of the royal family, all of whom were called Maud—the queens of Henry I and Stephen and the daughters of Henry II and John.

Blackfriars: the mainline station takes its name from the Dominican priory founded here in the late thirteenth century. Blackfriars was not just a religious house—it was used as a state archive and a meeting place for Parliament, the Privy Council and the Court of Chancery. It was here, for example, that Wycliffe's teaching was condemned in 1382, and that the Legatine Court met to discuss Henry VIII's marriage to Catherine of Aragon in 1529. The monastery attracted wealthy patronage—including the parents of Catherine Parr, who were buried in the church. After its dissolution in 1538, the property was used for various purposes—including as the residence of the French ambassador, which was a meeting place for Catholics. On 26 October 1623 a large congregation met here to hear the Jesuit preacher, Fr Drury. Half an hour into the sermon the floor collapsed, and many were killed. The event was long known as the 'Fatal Vespers'.

Covent Garden: now celebrated for its restaurants, street-life and theatres, Covent Garden was originally the 'Convent Garden' of Westminster Abbey. At the Reformation, the land reverted to the Crown and was eventually given to the earls of Bedford.

Hornchurch: the name may be an Anglicisation of the Latin *Monasterium Cornutum*, the name of the priory of St Bernard in Savoy which owned land here and built a church. Or perhaps the name is explained by the church's horn-shaped gables?

Kensal Green: in 1858 St Mary's Catholic Cemetery was opened here, alongside the larger Anglican cemetery. The chapel and some of the tombs are clearly visible from the Bakerloo Line. It was the original resting place of Cardinals Wiseman and Manning, although their bodies were later moved to Westminster Cathedral.

King's Cross St Pancras: St Pancras station is named after one of London's oldest churches—reputedly founded in 314. The graveyard was popular with Catholics in penal times.

Marble Arch: it is said that the modern Marble Arch (originally designed as a ceremonial entrance to Buckingham Palace) was erected with the help of money confiscated from English Catholics, originally paid to them as compensation for the loss of properties during the French Revolution. It stands near the famous execution site of Tyburn, where 119 of our martyrs suffered. These are commemorated at nearby Tyburn Convent.

Monument: in 1671 Sir Christopher Wren erected a monument to commemorate the Great Fire of London. Ten years later, during the frenzy of the fictitious 'Popish Plot', anti-Catholic sentiments were added to its inscription: 'this pillar was set up in perpetual remembrance of the most dreadful burning of this Protestant city, begun and carried on by the treachery and malice of the Popish faction ... in order to the effecting their horrid plot for the extirpating the Protestant religion and English liberties, and to introduce Popery and slavery'. These were removed shortly afterwards by the Catholic James II, restored by order of William III and finally erased in 1831.

Parsons Green takes its name from the property used by the vicar of Fulham and first mentioned in 1391.

Preston Road lies near the site of Uxendon Manor, owned by the Bellamys and used as a Catholic base in the reign of Elizabeth. St Edmund Campion stayed here shortly before his martyrdom in 1581, and St Robert Southwell was arrested here in 1592. Many of the Bellamy family suffered for the Faith—Catherine, Robert and Bartholomew all died in prison and Jerome was hanged for supporting the Babington conspirators in 1586.

St John's Wood: in the Middle Ages, this was the part of the Great Middlesex Forest owned by the Knights of St John of Jerusalem.

St Paul's: Wren's cathedral stands in a long line of cathedral churches on the site. The first cathedral church was built in the seventh century by St Mellitus, first Bishop of London and enlarged by St Erkenwald and again in the ninth century. Fires necessitated rebuilding in 962, 1087, 1136 and (most famously) 1666.

Temple: this celebrated church was built by the Knights Templar, based on the design of the Holy Sepulchre and consecrated by Heraclius, the Patriarch of Jerusalem, in 1185.

Tower Hill: five of the English Martyrs won their palms of martyrdom on Tower Hill—St John Fisher and St Thomas More (1535), Blessed Adrian Fortescue and Venerable Thomas Dingley (1539—both Knights of St John), and Blessed William Howard, Viscount Stafford (1680).

As modern Londoners hurtle through the tunnels in their crowded carriages, they can think of the layers of history, both sacred and profane, that lie above and around.

CENTRAL LONDON

CHARTERHOUSE

A Silent Corner of the City

I remember watching at London's Barbican cinema that wonderful film, *Into Great Silence* (2005), documenting the monks at the Grand Chartreuse. Afterwards, before catching the bus home, I wandered down 'Carthusian Street' and gazed at the gatehouse of the London Charterhouse, where for 150 years up until the Reformation, monks had lived the same life I had just observed on the silver screen. Much had changed in the world around but in the silent life of the cloister, with its daily routine of prayer, penance and work, little separated the monks of the sixteenth and twenty-first centuries. As the Carthusian motto puts it: *Stat crux dum volvitur orbis*, 'the Cross stands still as the world goes round'.

The Charterhouse was one of the spiritual hearts of pre-Reformation London, famed for its monks' piety and learning. It was also one of the city's newest monasteries—founded in 1371 on the site of a cemetery for victims of the Black Death and established as 'the House of the Salutation of the Mother of God'. By the early sixteenth century it boasted a prior, thirty monks and eighteen lay brothers, and attracted patrons and friends from the highest echelons of society. These included St Thomas More, who was closely linked to the monastery as a young lawyer studying at Lincoln's Inn. He took part in the Carthusian way of life and is said to have even considered joining the community. It is interesting to speculate that, had things been different, we might well have been celebrating the memory of 'St Thomas More, Carthusian and martyr'.

By 1533 a number of portents began to disturb the peace of the Charterhouse and these are documented by Maurice Chauncy, the chronicler of the Carthusian martyrs. A bright comet was seen over London, and a member of the community, returning from Night Office, saw the beams glance off a tree onto the monastery bell-tower. Later that year, a large red globe was seen floating in the air over the monastery. Then there was a plague of flies, 'of divers colours and oblong', which 'appeared in great quantities; now approaching, now retreating, now returning they seemed to cover the whole surface of the convent. More often and for longer periods they would settle on the church and cells'. Finally Prior Houghton, who was also Visitor of the other English Carthusian houses, had to travel to the Yorkshire monastery of Mount Grace and, after the long journey from London, had his clothes washed. When they were hung up to dry in the monastery garden 'a quantity of crows' appeared and 'with grasping claws they violently dragged our father's garments from the poles on which they hung, plucked them with curved beaks and mangled them bit by bit', while the other clothes hanging there were left untouched. Chauncy concludes rather dramatically that 'beyond all doubt this portended nothing other than the rending and mangling of our father's limbs by the black satellites of Satan'.

The community cannot have been surprised, then, when the Royal Commissioners arrived in the spring of 1534, to ask the monks to subscribe to the Act of Succession, which made it treason to reject the validity of the king's marriage to Anne Boleyn. The prior replied that it was not their business to interfere in royal affairs but eventually advised his community to take the oath. Chauncy noted that they added the words, 'so far as it is lawful', a qualification which apparently satisfied their consciences.

The Act of Supremacy followed shortly afterwards—the monks once again were asked to take an oath, this time recognising King Henry as 'Supreme Head of the Church and Clergy of England' and renouncing the authority of the pope. This sat less well with their consciences. To prepare themselves for the trials that inevitably lay ahead, the prior ordered a Solemn Triduum, which was closed by a Votive Mass of the Holy Spirit, during which the monks had a mystical experience. According to Chauncy, Houghton 'was overpowered with so great a fullness of divine illumination ... that for a long time he could not proceed with the office of the Mass. The convent also stood astounded, hearing indeed a voice and feeling a marvellous sweet operation in their hearts, but knowing not whence it came or whither it went'.

In April 1535 St John Houghton was arrested, together with two other Carthusian priors from other houses (SS Robert Lawrence and Augustine Webster). Here their story becomes joined with several other opponents to the royal supremacy—St Richard Reynolds the Bridgettine and two secular priests, Blessed John Hale and Richard Feron (who was later pardoned). They were taken to Westminster Hall and sentenced to death. They perhaps little thought that less than 500 years later the pope himself would stand in Westminster Hall addressing the country's politicians.

They were hanged, drawn and quartered at Tyburn on 4 May 1535. St Thomas More had looked out of his cell window that morning and saw the men on their way to execution. He turned to his daughter, who was visiting him, and said 'Lo, dost thou not see, Meg, that these blessed Fathers be now as cheerfully going to their deaths, as bridegrooms to their marriage'. Houghton's mangled arm was nailed to the gatehouse of his monastery as a warning to all. Other members of the community followed—many of them left to starve in prison.

The Charterhouse itself was suppressed in November 1538, although a group of exiled English Carthusians gathered overseas and eventually settled at Sheen Anglorum at Nieuwpoort in Flanders. Meanwhile the site of the London Charterhouse went on to have a distinguished history; today it is an almshouse, with its male pensioners known as 'brothers'. Many of the monastic buildings survive, including the atmospheric Brick Cloister and chapter house (now the chapel), and there are regular ecumenical events commemorating the martyrs.

MITHRAEUM

Secrets of Bucklersbury

Very few people have heard of Bucklersbury, a small area in the City of London around Bank station. In ages past it straddled the River Walbrook and in Shakespeare's time it was renowned for its herbalists and druggists. Falstaff spoke of 'these lisping hawthorn buds, that come like women in men's apparel, and smell like Bucklersbury in simple time'.

It was here that St Thomas More had his first marital home, at a property known as the 'Old Barge'—so-called, no doubt, because the Walbrook was navigable at that spot. It was here that his children were born and his friend Erasmus wrote the original version of his famous *In Praise of Folly*.

The 'Old Barge' is long gone, taking with it many of its memories, and the Walbrook now continues its course underground. Bucklersbury, as far as it still exists, consists of towering office blocks, which would have amazed More and his contemporaries. Yet the past is never far away. In the basement of one of these futuristic-looking buildings is a vivid link to London's distant history, taking us back to the origins of the city. For beneath Bloomberg's European headquarters is a Roman Temple of Mithras, now open as a free museum.

Descending two levels beneath the modern world of corporate London, there is a clear sense of travelling back in time. The temple itself, which can be seen on the lowest level of the museum with appropriate sound and lighting effects, was probably built in the third century but the whole area has produced numerous finds, dating back to the first century, many of which are on display. The waterlogged earth around the Walbrook helped the preservation of fragile organic materials such as wood and leather—hence we can see part of a wooden door and shoes dating from just a few decades after the life of Christ. There are tablets, also, bearing the first written texts from London—such as one that was sent to a man called Mogontius during the first century.

What was this temple of Mithras? The cult is highly enigmatic to historians, largely because no original texts or eyewitness accounts have survived. It was based around the god Mithras, whose cult may have originated in Persia or the Danube provinces. He is often shown killing a bull, a heroic deed or act of sacrifice that was part of the creation story, as it was supposedly believed that all living creatures, including the first human couple, came from the bull's blood.

The Mithraic cult was centred around small temples, often arranged rather like churches with a rounded apse, central nave and two side aisles, and dimly lit with few or no windows, perhaps alluding to the god's cave that formed a central part of the myth. The communities were exclusively (or at least predominantly) male and open only to those who had been initiated; many followers seem to have been low-ranking soldiers or military veterans, which accounts for the Mithraeum on Hadrian's Wall at Carrawburgh (near Hexham). There were seven hierarchies within the cult, each under the protection of a planet. Indeed, astrology played an important part and images of the zodiacal signs have often been found in Mithraeums. Though little is known of the rituals celebrated in the temple, they involved a hearty banquet on reclining couches, a reflection perhaps of the banquet that lay ahead in the next world.

Mithraeums can be found across the Empire. Many subsequently had churches built over them, such as the Roman basilicas of San Clemente and Santa Prisca. The Norman builders of the church tower at St Peter-at-Gowts (Lincolnshire) reused an ancient relief that was thought to show St Peter but may have been an image from a nearby Mithraeum.

The London temple was excavated between 1952 and 1954, the work of archaeologists being helped by German bombs that had fallen a decade earlier. It was huge news at the time and thousands of people queued to peer at the ruins. Since it was located on prime real estate, it was decided to move the venerable stones a hundred metres away and erect them as a memorial to the lost world of Roman Londinium. However, many criticised the inaccuracies resulting from this reconstruction and, after Bloomberg acquired the temple site in 2010, it was decided that the ruins should be returned. Most of the stone and bricks that can be seen today are original, though there are some modern replacements to fill in gaps and the whole structure has been moved slightly to the west since some of the original temple still survives underground. It was thought best to leave this undisturbed.

The Mithras cult has sometimes been described as an early rival to Christianity. In 1882 the controversial French scholar Ernest Renan claimed that 'if the growth of Christianity had been arrested by some mortal malady, the world would have been Mithraic' — unlikely given the closed nature of cult. There are also suggestions that many Christian beliefs, rituals and images were based on Mithraism. Christmas is meant to have been 'borrowed' from the birthday of the Persian god, though scholars are more certain that 25 December was the celebration of the triumphant sun (Sol Invictus). Even today websites still argue that Mithras was born of a virgin, had twelve disciples and held a last supper before his crucifixion. Mithraic initiation rites are supposedly linked to Christian baptism, the ritual banquets to the Eucharist. There is little evidence for these claims and some scholars have argued that Christianity actually pre-dated Mithraism, so that it may be more accurate to speak of the mystery cult borrowing from the Church. The cult declined with the conversion of the Empire in the fourth century and some suggest that Christians destroyed some of the temples with their pagan imagery.

Nevertheless, a trip to the London Mithraeum brings us into contact with our Roman ancestors and the milieu into which the Good News first reached this land.

ST GILES-IN-THE-FIELDS

London's Most Hallowed Space?

I write this having attended a memorial service at the London church of St Giles-in-the-Fields, just off Charing Cross Road and Shaftesbury Avenue. It was, I thought, an appropriate location for such an event, for the deceased gentleman had had a great love for English literature and at this church the children of Milton, Shelley and Byron were baptised and the poet Andrew Marvell interred. The church building itself is typical of Georgian respectability and was designed by Henry Flitcroft, the son of William III's gardener. Unusually for central London churches, it is surrounded by a green space, once used as its churchyard and full of surprising secrets.

The church originated as a leper hospital founded in 1101 by Matilda of Scotland, wife of Henry I. St Giles was a popular patron for lepers, cripples and beggars and his churches can often be found on the outskirts of towns. The medieval hospital located at this isolated spot was run by the one of the lesser-known military orders founded at the time of the crusades: the Order of St Lazarus. During the fourteenth century, there were criticisms that the Lazars (as they were called) were putting the affairs of the Order ahead of caring for the lepers. On several occasions the king, who continued to see St Giles as a royal foundation, intervened by making appointments to the hospital management and briefly transferred the institution to the care of the Cistercians.

At the Reformation the institution was dissolved, as was the leper hospital at nearby St James's, which was transformed into a royal palace. In 1542 the old hospital chapel of St Giles became the parish church for the little village that had grown up around it. The area was at first sparsely populated, with a population of around 350 in the 1550s, but it soon grew into a crowded suburb, where rich and poor lived alongside each other. The poor—many of them, by the eighteenth century, Irish Catholic immigrants—lived in slums known as the 'Rookeries' and gave William Hogarth the inspiration for his famous 'Gin Lane' cartoon. As a reflection of the growing suburb, the church of St Giles was rebuilt in the contemporary style twice in the 1620s and 1730s.

According to Peter Ackroyd, 'the invocation and loneliness first embodied in the twelfth-century foundation has never entirely left this area; throughout its history it has been the haunt of the poor and the outcast'. 'It was in every sense a crossroads', continued Ackroyd, an 'entrance and exit' and a 'crossroads between time and eternity'. The graveyard at St Giles was the final resting place for the rich and the poor, the good and the bad, and many of the victims of the plagues that regularly hit London, including the Great Plague of 1665.

For many years, a gallows stood near the churchyard, where Flitcroft Street now meets St Giles High Street, and on their way from Newgate to Tyburn condemned criminals would stop at the churchyard gate to drink a strengthening ale from the 'St Giles Bowl'. The condemned often reached the 'Triple Tree' inebriated, which was perhaps a small mercy.

I wondered whether any of the Catholic martyrs were fortified here in such a way. Some of them certainly returned to the churchyard for burial—a favourable option given the alternative of the remains being flung into a mass grave or displayed across London as a deterrent to others. These include eleven of those martyred in 1679 as a result of the fictitious Popish Plot to assassinate Charles II. The first to be buried here, in January 1679, were Blesseds William Ireland, a Jesuit priest, and John Grove, described by Challoner as 'a Catholic layman, employed as a servant by the English Jesuits in their affairs about town'. Ireland's kinsman, Richard Pendrell, had been buried at St Giles eight years previously and is described on his memorial as 'Preserver and Conductor to His Majesty Charles the Second of Great Britain after his Escape from Worcester Fight in the year 1651'. Blessed William himself protested a similar loyalty on reaching Tyburn, which he called 'the last theatre of the world', where he prayed that God 'shower down a thousand and a thousand blessings upon his Majesty'.

The following month it was the turn of Blessed Robert Greene, 'an ancient feeble man, cushion-keeper of the Queen's chapel', and his servant Blessed Lawrence Hill, both accused of murdering Sir Edmund Berry Godfrey, the magistrate involved in investigating the alleged plot, whose sudden death increased the anti-Catholic frenzy. The two men strenuously denied the allegations made against them. The executions and burials continued: the Benedictine Blessed Thomas Pickering, the five Jesuits Blesseds Thomas Whitebread, William Barrow (alias Harcourt), John Fenwick, John Gavan and Anthony Turner, and the barrister Blessed Richard Langhorne.

The most high profile martyr to be buried at St Giles, however, is no longer there: St Oliver Plunkett, Archbishop of Armagh and Primate of All Ireland. After being hanged, drawn and quartered on 1

July 1681, his body was buried in two tin boxes beside the five Jesuits on the north side of St Giles. In 1683 the remains were successfully exhumed, even though a woman had been buried above him, and smuggled to the English Benedictine monastery at Lamspringe, near Hildesheim in Germany. A member of the community, Dom Maurus Corker, had befriended Plunkett while imprisoned at Newgate and had assisted him in his last days. He was at the time President of the English Benedictine Congregation and may have admitted the archbishop as a 'confrater' of his abbey shortly before his execution. It was fitting, then, that the martyr's body was enshrined in the abbey church, alongside other relics, such as the head of St Thomas of Hereford; Corker's desire, writes one modern historian, was to create 'a pantheon of English saints and martyrs which proclaimed the holiness and continuity of the English Catholic community'. The body was later translated to Downside Abbey. Plunkett's head, meanwhile, was brought to Rome and then transferred to Armagh and Drogheda, where it can be venerated at the church of St Peter to this day.

The churchyard of St Giles may appear to the casual passer-by as a convenient green space to sit down, enjoy a sandwich and catch up with the social media. In actual fact it is one of London's most hallowed spots, with the remains of eleven beatified martyrs hidden beneath the ground, silently witnessing to the Faith and awaiting the day of resurrection.

ST JAMES'S PALACE

An Apostle of the Sacred Heart

St James's Palace is the senior palace of the sovereign; indeed, the Royal Court is still officially designated as the 'Court of St James'. Today it is the home of several members of the royal family, containing some important offices and fulfilling a number of ceremonial functions. Yet, it remains one of the least known of London's royal residences.

St James's is full of interest for the Catholic. Built by Henry VIII on the site of the medieval Hospital of St James the Less, which had cared for 'maidens that were leprous', the turreted gatehouse, built in Tudor red brick, faces St James' Street to this day. The Queen's Chapel, where the bodies of Princess Margaret and the Queen Mother rested before their funerals, was commissioned in 1623 as a Catholic chapel for the Infanta of Spain, during negotiations for her marriage to the future Charles I. Designed by Inigo Jones, it was subsequently used by the three Catholic consorts of the Stuarts: Henrietta Maria, Catherine of Braganza and Mary of Modena. Of course, such a chapel required a team of Catholic chaplains, often brought over from the continent. Indeed, nearby 'Friary Court', where the accession of a new monarch is proclaimed by Garter King of Arms, commemorates the Capuchin convent set up under Charles II.

One of these royal chaplains, who worked in the household of Mary of Modena, second wife of James II, while she was Duchess of York, was later canonised: St Claude de la Colombière. He also provides a surprising link between London and the private revelations of St Margaret Mary.

Born at Saint-Symphorien d'Ozon on Candlemas Day 1641, St Claude was educated at nearby Lyons and, in 1658, joined the Society of Jesus at Avignon. Clever, hardworking and a gifted preacher, the future seemed bright, especially when he began work as tutor to the sons of Jean Baptiste Colbert, Louis XIV's financial minister. It came as a surprise when, shortly after taking his solemn vows in 1675, he was appointed Jesuit superior at Paray-le-Monial in the Charollais. The town was a provincial backwater, only recently freed from Huguenot control; today, of course, it is well known as the home of St Margaret Mary Alacoque and, in words of Pope Leo XIII, 'a town very dear to heaven'. Devotion to the Sacred Heart had existed in the Church during the patristic and medieval eras, but took its modern form thanks to the private revelations given to this Visitation nun. She started receiving visions at the end of 1673, but had found it difficult to find a sympathetic spiritual director.

The coming of Fr Colombière had been promised to her by Our Lord Himself: 'I will send you My faithful servant and perfect friend who will teach you to know Me and abandon yourself to Me'. When the priest paid his first visit to the convent, on 15 February 1675, there was an instant chemistry between them. He could not help but notice her behind the grille, and, upon further enquiry, was told that she was 'a chosen soul of grace'. Meanwhile, as Margaret Mary listened to the priest's conference, she heard a voice in her soul—'This is he whom I am sending you'.

Over the next few months, St Claude listened to her testimony and set his seal of approval on the revelations, providing encouragement and joining her in a consecration to the Sacred Heart. However, after only eighteen months at Paray, the Jesuit was told to pack his bags and begin a very different ministry—as chaplain to the Catholic Duchess of York. Amazingly, Protestant London became the first place, after Paray, where devotion to the Sacred Heart was preached.

St Claude arrived in October 1676 and moved into a room at the front of St James's Palace. Despite the brilliance of the Restoration Court, Claude tried to live a life of great regularity and simplicity. He slept on the floor, making do without the coal fire, fitted up a small oratory in his room and gave much of his money to the poor. Forced to wear lay dress, due to the persecution of Catholics, Fr Colombière soon gained a reputation as a preacher and confessor. Moreover, he continued to keep in touch with the nuns of Paray and wrote letters of guidance to St Margaret Mary.

St Claude found the Duchess of York 'a princess of great piety'— 'she makes her communion nearly every week and sometimes oftener', he wrote, '[and] every day she devotes an hour to mental prayer'. The duchess and her confessor would have met frequently, though it is recorded that such was the priest's modesty that he never looked her in the face. In these meetings at St James's Palace, the future queen became one of the first devotees of the Sacred Heart, as revealed to St Margaret Mary. Indeed, she was fertile soil for St Claude's direction. Before her marriage, she had herself hoped to join the Visitation Order, and it was long her desire to found an English house of the Order in France. Years later, when she and her husband were exiles at Saint-Germain, she would often visit the convent at Chaillot (itself founded by Henrietta Maria) and in 1696, with the encouragement of the nuns, she sent a petition to Rome begging authorisation for the cult of the Sacred Heart and a proper feast.

St Claude wrote in 1677: 'I realised that God wished me to serve Him in procuring the accomplishment of His designs of devotion to the Sacred Heart. These were revealed by Him to a person with whom He communicates intimately and through whom He has pleased to use of my weakness [St Margaret Mary]... I have already inspired this [devotion] to many people in England'. These included not only the duchess but at least one of the martyrs, St John Wall, who spent the Vigil of All Saints 1678 'in sweet converse on the love of Jesus' in St Claude's room. He even said 'Mass at the little Altar of the Sacred Heart, which Fr de la Colombière had erected in his oratory'.

Storm clouds loomed in the ridiculous allegations made by Titus Oates in 1678, which sparked off a period of anti-Catholic frenzy. Fr Colombière was soon implicated in this 'Popish Plot' and was arrested at 2am on 24 November 1678 and sent to the King's Bench Prison in Southwark, where his health, which was already weak, quickly deteriorated. However, he was saved from execution (unlike his friend, Fr Wall) by the intervention of the French ambassador and, after three weeks in prison, banished from England.

St Claude returned to France, his health badly broken by his sufferings for the faith. He never fully recovered and died peacefully on 15 February 1682, 'absorbed in the love of the dear Saviour Who had committed to his charge the abundant treasures of the Sacred Heart'. The following day, St Margaret Mary wrote: 'Weep for him no longer; rather pray to him and fear nothing, for truly he is more powerful to assist us than ever'.

St Claude's holiness and wisdom were well known at the time of his death, and in 1684 several volumes of his sermons and retreat notes were published, many of which dated from his ministry in London. With their teaching on the Sacred Heart and the references to a chosen soul, known to him personally, his writings spread the new devotion and directed increased attention on Paray-le-Monial. As an enclosed nun, there was little that St Margaret Mary could do to actively spread the message. It was St Claude who first promoted it—in Paray, at the English Court, to the hearts of young Jesuit scholastics and, through his published works, to the whole world.

St Claude was canonised by St John Paul II on 31 May 1992. On this occasion the pope stressed the great legacy of the new saint: 'The past three centuries allow us to evaluate the importance of the message which was entrusted to Claude de la Colombière. In a period of contrasts between the fervour of some and the indifference or impiety of many, here is a devotion centered on the humanity of Christ, on His presence, on His love of mercy, and on forgiveness'. True devotion to the Sacred Heart is the 'spiritual answer to the difficulties which the faith and the Church are facing' both in the seventeenth century and in the world of today.

ST PANCRAS

A Catholic Burial Ground

Despite having been drastically reduced in size by the various railway lines cutting across it, St Pancras burial ground is still one of those hidden corners of London where you can breathe the past. The presence of busy roads and the international terminus have not destroyed its rustic charm; indeed, up until the eighteenth century this was open country, with the metropolis clearly looming in the background and the River Fleet gently flowing by. Times change and the Fleet is now consigned to an underground pipe.

The church of Old St Pancras was drastically rebuilt in the nineteenth century. However, the sign boldly claims that the church has been 'a site of prayer and meditation since 314 AD'. According to tradition, it is one of the oldest surviving churches in the south-east, if not the whole country; the cartographer John Norden wrote in 1593 that, in terms of antiquity, the church 'is thought not to yield to Paules in London'.

There is no hard evidence for the claim and the earliest direct mention of the church is in two deeds from the second half of the twelfth century. However, the dedication to St Pancras, the Roman child martyr, is certainly a very ancient one and may have originated with St Augustine of Canterbury, who promoted the cults of Roman saints as part of his evangelisation of the English. In the nineteenth century what was thought to be a sixth or seventh-century altar stone was found and immediately dubbed 'St Augustine's Altar'.

Others argue that the church was on the site a pagan temple that was converted to Christian use in Roman times, long before St Augustine. The year 314, just after the conversion of Constantine, seemed a convenient date and Roman bricks and tiles were certainly used in the construction of the old tower. Perhaps the nearby 'Pancras Wells' were also part of this sacred site.

Whatever its origins, the most interesting dimension of Old St Pancras is its graveyard, which was particularly popular in the eighteenth and nineteenth centuries and saw the burials of the likes of J. C. Bach, Sir John Soane and Mary Wollstonecraft. Alongside the rich and the famous, however, were the graves of those on the margins of London society, including many foreign exiles, Jacobite sympathisers and Catholics.

Various theories are advanced to explain why these burial grounds were so favoured by London Catholics. Perhaps it was because of the cemetery's discreet location, away from the hustle and bustle of the city, and its venerable origins in the distant past. One tradition stated that the church was one of the last where Mass was said publicly after the Reformation. The Elizabethan incumbent, William Collier, a Marian priest, seems to have celebrated Mass in Latin well into the second half of the sixteenth century and was tolerated by the authorities. This sympathy towards adherents of the 'old Faith' seems to have continued at St Pancras after his death.

Others have suggested that the churchyard was further hallowed by soil from the Holy Land, brought back by a pious crusader, and by a connection with a church dedicated to St Pancras either in Rome or southern France where Masses were regularly offered for those buried there. Dr Johnson even erroneously believed that several Catholic martyrs had suffered on the site during the reign of Elizabeth I.

Whatever the motivation, many distinguished Catholics found their final resting place here. These included several of the Vicars Apostolic of the London District, who led the Catholic community before the restoration of the Hierarchy, and French émigrés, refugees from the Revolution, including many aristocrats and clergy. Indeed, their presence did much to break down old anti-Catholic prejudices; they were welcomed to England as victims of political radicalism rather than dangerous 'papists'.

One of the exiles buried at St Pancras is particularly interesting both in his life and death: Arthur Richard Dillon (1721–1806), last Archbishop of Narbonne. Born into a family of Irish Jacobites living in France, he was related to some of the leading British Catholic families. Despite this background, Dillon was destined for a very French ecclesiastical career: he studied at St Sulpice in Paris and went on to become Bishop of Evreux, Archbishop of Toulouse and finally Archbishop of Narbonne. This was a very rich diocese and with the office came the title 'Primate of the Gauls' and the presidency of the estates of Languedoc (the regional assembly). He was a power to be reckoned with in the area and undertook many building projects—not so much churches but roads, canals, harbours, silk factories and the like. He was criticised, however, for neglecting his parochial clergy.

Given his wealth and power, it is no surprise that Archbishop Dillon spent much of his time living as a *grand seigneur* in Paris (near the royal court) or on his estate at Hautefontaine, near Soissons (the other end of the country to Languedoc). Having said that, his niece, Madame de la Tour du Pin, recalled that he often had financial worries and in Paris 'kept noble state, but of a simple kind. Food was plentiful, but not extravagant'. When Louis XVI once questioned him on his fondness for hunting and suggested it gave a bad example to his clergy, he responded: 'Well, Sire, for them it would undoubtedly be a grave fault but for me it is only a taste I have inherited from my ancestors'. But the king, himself a keen huntsman, was jealous of the archbishop and 'nothing annoyed him more to hear about the exploits of the Hautefontaine pack'.

All this changed in 1790, when the archbishop refused to take the oath to the Civil Constitution of the Clergy, effectively setting up a State Church, and was soon forced into exile. He once said, 'My God, if I had only been a bishop I might have given way like the others, but I am a gentleman'. In 1793 he arrived in London and became a key figure among the other exiles. When his niece visited him one day at his 'modest five-windowed house' on Thayer Street, she found herself at dinner 'with the six aged bishops of Languedoc whom he boarded at his table'. He finally died in July 1806, of gout of the stomach, and was buried at St Pancras.

But that is not the end of the story. In January 2003, while Gifford were conducting excavations in the burial ground in preparation for a rail extension, Dillon's coffin was unearthed. His remains were temporarily placed in St Pancras Cemetery in East Finchley before being moved amid great splendour to his old cathedral at Narbonne in March 2007. The Narbonnaise provided him a warm welcome; he may not have been a very attentive spiritual leader but he had become a symbol of regional pride and of heroism during the storms of revolution.

ST THOMAS À WATERINGS
On the Road to Canterbury

The 'Thomas à Becket' pub on the Old Kent Road stands near the site of 'St Thomas à Waterings', a spring near the second milestone from the city. It was the boundary of the City liberties and a local landmark; indeed, in times past, those crossing it towards London said they were 'going over the water'.

The Old Kent Road, of course, is the Roman Watling Street, that great artery which linked London to Canterbury and Dover—and ultimately Europe. The pilgrims travelling to St Thomas's shrine at Canterbury would stop at the stream and water their horses. It was at this first stop that Chaucer's merry band discussed who would narrate the first tale:

> And forth we rode, a little faster than pace
> Until we reached Saint Thomas' watering-place.
> Our host then pulled his horse, began to ease
> And said: "Now, gentleman, listen if you please."

The pilgrims would have then continued, hoping to reach Dartford for their first night's sleep.

St Thomas à Waterings was also one of the main execution sites for Surrey. Amongst those who suffered there were some of the English Martyrs, including several lesser-known victims of Henry VIII. Four were put to death here on 8 July 1539 for supporting Cardinal Pole, although their exact identities are unclear. One was certainly the vicar of Wandsworth, John Griffith (sometimes referred to as Griffith Clarke) and another may have been 'Friar Waire' (though curiously he is not mentioned by Franciscan historians). The other two were possibly Griffith's curate and servant. Another early victim was Blessed David Gunston, a member of the Order of Malta who was hanged, drawn and quartered on 12 July 1541, without trial, for denying the king's supremacy.

Catholics continued to suffer at St Thomas à Waterings under Elizabeth, including two of the 'Forty Martyrs'. On 12 July 1598 St John Jones was hanged, drawn and quartered there. A Welsh Franciscan, he had (according to one tradition) briefly joined the friary at Greenwich when it was restored under Mary I. Subsequently he spent much of his religious life in France and Rome, before returning to England in 1592. He acted as Franciscan Provincial and travelled around the country, using the name 'Buckley', until he was arrested while visiting a recusant lady, Jane Wiseman, in prison. He was tortured by Richard Topcliffe, the famous priest-hunter, and after two years was brought to trial for treason. To be convicted, it was enough to be a priest on English soil: 'if this be a crime', he said, 'I must own myself guilty; for I am a priest and came over into England to gain as many souls as I could to Christ'. His execution was a drawn-out affair for it was discovered that the hangman had forgotten his rope. He had to wait one long hour, during which time he prayed and spoke to the crowd, stressing that his only crime was his Catholic Faith and priesthood.

The other canonised martyr of St Thomas à Waterings was St John Rigby, a Lancashire layman. He had been reconciled to the Church by the Jesuit, Fr John Gerard, though during his questioning Rigby said that it was St John Jones who had done this—presumably protecting Fr Gerard's name by naming a priest who had already been martyred. Rigby ended up in the service of a Catholic family and in February 1600 was sent to the Old Bailey to plead poor health as the reason one of the daughters of the house was unable to answer charges of non-attendance at church. Rigby himself was questioned about his religious position and admitted to having been reconciled to the Church. He was immediately taken to prison, tried and condemned to death. On hearing the verdict, he exclaimed: 'Praise be to thee, O Lord, King of Eternal Glory' and, in considering his death, thought it but 'a fleabite in comparison of what it pleased my sweet Saviour Jesus to suffer for my salvation'. It was perhaps more than a fleabite, for accounts of his execution on 21 June 1600 reveal the cruelty of his treatment—on being cut down, he was able to at first stand and was therefore fully conscious of his disembowelment, during which he muttered: 'May God forgive you. Lord Jesus, receive my soul'.

Today, St Thomas à Waterings bears little trace of Chaucer's pilgrims or the courage of the martyrs. Nearby, there is a large stretch of open land, Burgess Park, with an impressive lake, which presumably uses some of the water that had once drawn those *en route* to Canterbury. Beneath the modern streets of our cities lies a rich Catholic history, which needs to constantly be rediscovered.

ST PAUL'S
Before Wren

On 2 September 1666 a fire started in a baker's house on Pudding Lane and quickly spread to destroy much of medieval London. One of the world's greatest cities was changed for ever. Many historic buildings were lost but perhaps the most iconic casualty was St Paul's Cathedral.

Its origins were ancient. A cathedral had stood on the site since the time of St Mellitus, first Bishop of London and companion of St Augustine of Canterbury. It was once thought that it was built on the site of a Roman temple to Diana but no strong archaeological evidence for this has been found. Sadly, fires were a common feature in Saxon and medieval cities and at least two previous St Paul's were burnt down; the building destroyed in 1666 replaced the cathedral damaged in the fire of 1087.

This Norman cathedral became the largest building in medieval England, larger even than the present-day St Paul's, with a tall steeple (which collapsed in 1561), magnificent stained glass and thirteenth-century extensions which enclosed the nearby parish church of St Faith. The dispossessed parishioners were granted part of the cathedral crypt for their use as well as a separate bell-tower.

The cathedral was a centre for pilgrimage, especially to the shrine of St Erconwald, fourth Bishop of London, who was called by one medieval hymn the *Lux Lundoniae*, 'light of London'. Originally buried in the crypt, his remains were translated to a splendid new shrine during the reign of King Stephen. It was adorned with gold, silver and precious stones and seems to have had a pyramidal structure, though the cult disappeared at the Reformation, over a century before the fire.

A twenty-first-century visitor to 'Old St Paul's' would be surprised not only by its splendour and size but by its hustle and bustle. The long nave was known as 'Paul's Walk' and it was the custom for 'the principal gentry, lords, courtiers, and men of all professions not merely mechanic, to meet in Paul's Church by eleven and walk in the middle aisle till twelve, and after dinner from three to six, during which times some discoursed on business, others of news'. Unfortunately, thieves and prostitutes could also be found there and successive bishops tried to preserve the sanctity of the cathedral's space. The churchyard was a centre of the book trade and 'Paul's Cross' an important place for civic ceremonies and open-air sermons, especially during the Reformation, when it became the centre for debate and controversy. It has been called 'the public barometer of the nation's views'. St Paul's was much more than just a cathedral; it was the very heart of London.

A true 'son' of St Paul's was the martyr, St Edmund Campion, the son of a 'stationer' or bookseller in Paternoster Row. He was born in the north-east end of the Churchyard in 1540 and attended St Paul's School. The cathedral precinct formed the backdrop of his formative years and perhaps inspired his later ministry, very much based around the spoken and written word and the power of the printing press. Another famous English Jesuit, Henry Garnet, also had a connection to the cathedral for he was executed in St Paul's churchyard in 1606, in the aftermath of the Gunpowder Plot.

We normally think of St Paul's in terms of the architect, Sir Christopher Wren. It is often forgotten that before the Great Fire he was engaged in an attempt at restoring the deteriorating medieval building and envisaged a new design: 'the Gothic rectified to a better manner of architecture'. Inigo Jones had also recently added a neo-classical portico to the medieval church, creating a curious mixture of styles; even at the time it was judged by some as 'altogether incongruous with the old building'. The fire obviously made their vision a necessity.

It may seem strange that such a large stone building should burn down in the Great Fire. Indeed, many Londoners saw it as a safe place and placed their stocks and valuables there for safety, confident that the flames should never reach them. Ironically it was these that, along with the wooden scaffolding encasing some of the building, actually accelerated the destructive effects of the fire. It must have been a pitiful sight.

Returning to London shortly after the fire, John Evelyn wrote in his *Diary* that he was

> infinitely concern'd to find that goodly Church St. Paules now a sad ruine ... It was astonishing to see what immense stones the heate had in a manner calcin'd ... the ruines of the vaulted roofe falling broke into St. Faith's, which being fill'd with the magazines of bookes belonging to the Stationers, and carried thither for safety, they were all consum'd, burning for a weeke following ... Thus lay in ashes that most venerable Church, one of the most antient pieces of early piety in the Christian world.

The body of an old woman was found in the ruins, her identity and final moments known only to God.

Along with the structure, many treasures and monuments were destroyed, though according to one nineteenth-century dean, Henry Hart Milman, it was 'surprising how few famous men, before the Reformation, reposed under its pavement, or were honoured with stately monuments'. There were two Saxon kings (Sebba of the East Angles and Ethelred the Unready) and the powerful John of Gaunt (father of Henry IV); most royalty opted instead for Westminster or Windsor. More recent worthies were entombed there, including the poets Sir Philip Sidney and John Donne, the physician Thomas Linacre and the scholar John Colet. In the confusion of the fire, the tomb of the latter was broken open and his coffin found to be full of liquid, which was tasted and considered 'ironish, insipid'. Another burial to receive undignified treatment was that of a fifteenth-century bishop, Robert Braybrooke, whose mummified remains were found in the ruins. Londoners flocked to gawp at his body and Pepys famously described his skin as being like 'spongy dry leather'.

St Paul's was built again—probably the fifth to stand on Ludgate Hill—and Wren finally had his way in 'rectifying' the tired Gothic style. It became a national project and the cost partly defrayed by special subscriptions and taxes. Wren's cathedral is, of course, one of the landmarks of London, though its 'modern' style was criticised at the time and also thought to be 'popish' and alarmingly similar to St Peter's, Rome. The dome, second in size only to St Peter's, was supposed to be 'an Ornament to His Majestie's most excellent Reign, to the Church of England, and to the great Citie'.

Dean Milman thought that 'of England's more glorious cathedrals, it seems to me, I confess, none could be so well spared. Excepting its vast size, it had nothing to distinguish it ... a gloomy ponderous pile'. Yet on this anniversary of its destruction, I feel some regret that I never got to stroll down 'Paul's Walk', marvel at the famous rose window, pray at the site of St Erconwald's shrine and visit the bookstalls in the Churchyard. For Londoners Old St Paul's left a yawning gap that even Christopher Wren could not entirely fill.

TOWER OF LONDON

Locked in the Tower!

I was once locked in the Tower of London. I should add that I had gone to the Tower voluntarily, tickets having long been booked to witness the Ceremony of the Keys. This is a short but impressive ritual that has taken place every night for at least six centuries; it even went ahead one evening in 1941, despite the participants being blown off their feet by a bomb. As such, it is the oldest military ceremony in the world still in continuous use.

Having presented ourselves at the entrance, our small group was given an introductory talk by a Yeoman Warder (or 'Beefeater'), with the characteristic mix of crowd-pleasing banter and historical fact. We excitedly awaited the start of the ceremony in front of the gatehouse known as the Bloody Tower, which leads into the inner ward where the crown jewels are kept and the White Tower stands majestically. At 9.53pm precisely the Chief Warder appeared with a lantern and the keys to the Tower. At the Bloody Tower he met a detachment of four guardsmen, in their winter greatcoats and famous busbys, who then escorted him to the Byward Tower, the principle outer entrance. We could not see the Warder locking the heavy doors and the soldiers turning inwards and presenting arms, for the keys are the king's keys. However, my eyes wandered to the windows of the Byward Tower, behind which there is a fine medieval wall-painting showing Our Lady, St John the Baptist and St Michael, with pink wings and holding a pair of scales. A Tudor chimney piece sadly obscures the original centrepiece of the painting: the Crucifixion. It is a reminder that the Tower was not only a prison but a palace and at the centre of the royal administration. Indeed, it is thought that the painting once presided over the workings of the Royal Mint, formerly based at the Tower, and its subject matter would have inspired those who worked there to be honest and just in their dealings.

The warder and guardsmen then marched back to the Bloody Tower and, as they approached, the lone sentry levelled his rifle and issued a challenge. 'Halt! Who comes there?' The Chief Warder replied, 'The keys!' The dialogue continued: 'Whose keys?', 'King Charles's keys!', 'Pass, King Charles's keys, and all is well!' According to the late Geoffrey Abbott, a retired beefeater and author of a series of books on the Tower, the area around this gatehouse could claim to be 'the most historic airspace in the country... traversed by the kings and their families who lived in the Tower, the captive queens awaiting execution, royal captives such as Sir Thomas More, Sir Walter Raleigh and Guy Fawkes—a veritable host of those who had fashioned our past'. Observing the brief Ceremony of the Keys, he continued, 'it requires little imagination to envisage the same ceremony being enacted repeatedly over the past centuries, the Chief Warder or Porter, as he was once known, standing in exactly the same spot, shouting in the same stentorian voice "King George's keys!", "King William's keys!", "King Henry's keys!"' 'You may have read history', he concluded, 'there you can feel it!'

The keys party then marched through the arch of the Bloody Tower to the steps leading up to the Broadwalk, where a further detachment of Guards awaited. The keys were saluted and the Chief Warder doffed his iconic bonnet, shouting 'God preserve King Charles!', to which all present responded 'Amen'. As the clock chimed ten o'clock, the Last Post was sounded by a bugler and the ceremony concluded.

As we watched the soldiers march away into the darkness, the realisation dawned that we were now officially locked into the Tower. And we were not to escape for a little while, for there was a sudden commotion. It transpired that some drunkards had foolishly trespassed into the moat and that the Tower was in lockdown while this was investigated. It may have been a stupid prank but this is His Majesty's royal palace and fortress and any threat to its security is taken very seriously. It was, though, a happy fault because the incident allowed us to soak up the atmosphere of the Tower by night. It is a time when the Tower becomes itself again, after its loud, glitzy, tourist-centred day—in the silence of night it was once again an official royal residence and the working home to the Constable, the warders and many support staff.

As we waited for the crisis in the moat to pass, I looked around me. The Tower has worn many hats over the years, including those of fortress, palace, records office, mint, zoo, museum and prison. Its first prisoner was a Norman Bishop of Durham, Ranulf Flambard, accused of extortion in 1100. Not only was he the first known state prisoner at the Tower but the first also to escape, thanks to a rope smuggled to him in a gallon of wine. The number of prisoners increased dramatically during the sixteenth century, largely due to the religious turmoil of the times and well-known paranoia of Henry VIII.

Although the Tower's role as state prison was only incidental, it has given the place its sinister reputation, much promoted by artists, novelists and tour guides over the years. William Harrison Ainsworth's novel *The Tower of London* (1840) was one particularly influential trend-setter, describing the torture chamber as 'lighted by a dull lamp from the roof, and furnished as before with numberless hideous implements — each seemingly to have been recently employed'. Little surprise, then, that the queue for the present-day torture exhibition is normally second only in length to that of the Crown Jewels.

Everywhere I looked, there were memories of unfortunate prisoners and heroic martyrs. If I looked to my left down Water Lane, I could clearly see the Bell Tower, so-called because of the bell on its turret. It was here that both St Thomas More and St John Fisher were confined before their execution. They never met there but seem to have sent messages to each other and perhaps heard each other moving about. The knowledge of the other's presence must have given them much comfort during the months of imprisonment and soul-searching.

One of the most moving memorials of the martyrs can be found in the Beauchamp Tower, just off Tower Green, where many prisoners inscribed their names on the walls. In part, this must have alleviated the boredom of imprisonment, but it also made a strong statement and, in some cases, was done out of devotion. Some carved simple crosses or religious emblems such as the Sacred Heart, giving them comfort amid the anguish of confinement. Other prisoners were more ambitious: the Jesuit St Henry Walpole carved his name and those of St Peter and St Paul and the four great Doctors of the Latin Church, SS Jerome, Ambrose, Augustine and Gregory. Blessed Thomas Abel left behind him a large letter 'A' with a bell.

As I looked to my right, I could just make out the Salt and Cradle Towers. The first of these, reputed to be heavily haunted, still bears the marks of many prisoners in the form of inscriptions on the walls, including a 'signature' left by St Henry Walpole. Another Jesuit confine here, John Gerard, was able to communicate with a fellow Catholic, Francis Arden, imprisoned in the Cradle Tower, exchanging notes written in that most cunning of invisible inks: orange juice. Fr Gerard obtained permission to celebrate Mass at Mr Arden's cell and then brought back with him to the Salt Tower twenty-two consecrated hosts, which he hid in the chimney. The priest was eventually moved to the Cradle Tower and from there made his daring escape with Mr Arden one night in 1597.

Our understanding of the past is so often exaggerated. We seem to think that 'in olden times' all gaolers were sadistic torturers, looking for any excuse to use their ingenious devices. In actual fact, torture was used rarely and (at least on paper) had to be sanctioned by the Privy Council. Between 1540 and 1640 this permission was only given forty-eight times. Nevertheless, this statistic would have been of little comfort to those who were tortured, many of whom were Catholic priests in the reigns of Elizabeth and James I—and it must be admitted that hagiographers played a key part in constructing the blood-soaked myth of the Tower which so enthrals today's tourists.

Let us not forget that one martyr, the Jesuit lay brother St Nicholas Owen, was tortured to death at the Tower in 1606. 'They tortured him with such inhuman ferocity', we read, 'that his stomach burst open and his intestines burst out'. The authorities tried to cover their tracks by claiming that Owen had committed suicide by stabbing himself in the stomach, though it was pointed out that his hands were so crippled that he could not feed himself, let alone hold a knife. John Gerard, an Elizabethan Jesuit who managed to escape from the Tower in 1597, wrote in his autobiography: 'we went to the torture room in a kind of solemn procession. The chamber was underground and dark. It was a vast place and every device and instrument of human torture was there. They pointed some of them to me and said that I would try them all'. He was suspended by the manacles: 'The pain was so intense', he wrote, 'that I thought I could not possibly endure it, and added to it, I had an interior temptation. Yet I did not feel any inclination or wish to give them the information they wanted. The Lord saw my weakness with the eyes of His mercy, and did not permit me to be tempted beyond my strength'. After being racked a third time, St Edmund Campion was asked how he felt: 'not ill', he replied, 'because not at all'.

Eventually we too were able to escape the Tower, though perhaps more reluctantly than Fr Gerard and his friend. We left the royal fortress with its many memories and shades behind us but took into the bustling streets of contemporary London the inspiration of its many saints and martyrs, who pondered eternity behind these strong walls. One of them, St Philip Howard, Earl of Arundel, wrote above the chimney breast in the Beauchamp Tower a sentiment that sums up their attitude: 'The more affliction we endure for Christ in this world, the more glory we shall get with Christ in the world to come'.

TYBURN

To Tyburn

The notable priest historian Canon Edwin Burton called the route to Tyburn London's *Via Sacra*. 'Every inch', he wrote, 'of that journey through Holborn, High Holborn, Bloomsbury High Street, and Oxford Street is holy in our eyes.' Newgate prison, where many of the martyrs were placed before execution, was connected to the gallows of Tyburn by means of what was then a country road, 'passing down Snow Hill to cross the Fleet River, and then ascending Holborn Hill, which in after days was to be called "the heavy hill to Tyburn."' Much of this route went through open country, though there were groups of houses along the way and places of more intense development like the village of Bloomsbury. On an execution day, though, the crowds would have been similar to the ones that we will no doubt experience; the atmosphere would have been that of a fair.

Many are the stories told of the martyr's last journey. Blessed Richard Leigh was a secular priest who suffered in the year of the Armada, along with four companions (including Blessed Edward Shelley, a Sussex gentleman, and Blessed John Roche, an Irish waterman). As they were dragged to Tyburn on their hurdles, a high born lady forced her way through the crowds and knelt down before the martyrs, asking for their blessing. She was soon taken away to prison. The martyrs continued along the *Via Sacra*, according to St Henry Walpole, singing 'their service by the way' (perhaps the Office of the Dead?). At the gallows, Leigh was given time to pray and, we are told, 'his colour changed and his legs began to bend, insomuch that it was thought that his soul had been already in Heaven'. However, 'the hangman pulling him by the sleeve, he came to himself, and looking about demanded what the matter was'.

The temptation is only to think of our martyrs' last heroic moments, thanks to God's grace, so that we forget the witness of the rest of their lives. For the martyr's crown was only the climax to a life spent in the pursuit of holiness; the final sacrifice made possible by many daily ones. Their life should be seen as a whole, not simply defined by the final chapter, no matter how glorious.

A good example of this is provided by the Irish bishop, St Oliver Plunkett. The Reformation in Ireland, of course, was very different from England. There was a majority Catholic population in a nominally Protestant kingdom. The Irish experienced much persecution but their one advantage was having a hierarchy, no matter how limited. In 1669 Plunkett, after many years studying and working in Rome, was appointed Archbishop of Armagh and Primate of All Ireland. Back in his homeland, he had at times to wear disguises, such as that of 'Captain Brown', with a costume including a wig, a pair of pistols and a sword. Near his home of Ardpatrick, you can still 'St Oliver's Oak' where he sometimes had to hide. But, especially in more tolerant periods, he was able to do much—visit the faithful, comfort the poor and sick, preach the Gospel (often in Gaelic), hold diocesan synods, ordain and confirm. One of the churches he used for such ceremonies measured only 18 feet by 28 feet, which must have put his master of ceremonies to the test!

Finally he was falsely charged during the Popish Plot with 'endeavouring ... the king's death, and to levy war in Ireland' with 20,000 French troops. The alleged crimes were ridiculous, the evidence lacking, the legal process corrupt—but St Oliver was brought over to London to be hanged, drawn and quartered on 1 July 1681, the last of the Tyburn martyrs. By remembering him we recall not only a heroic martyr but a saintly and zealous pastor.

Nor should we regard the martyrs as super-heroes, possessing a sanctity that we ourselves can never aspire to. The martyrs were human beings just like ourselves. We can see this humanity in their humourous and adventurous spirit but also in their weaknesses. The story of the English Catholic community at this time was one of division, as seen in the tensions between the secular and regular clergy or the lengthy debates about the nature of ecclesiastical government in this country after the Reformation. The martyrs themselves were quite prepared to side with a church party and enter into the polemic.

Likewise, the temptation to run away, to escape the terrible death of hanging, drawing and quartering would have been a natural human reaction for all the martyrs. So too would be the temptation to reach a compromise or accept the offers that were normally made promising clemency and even preferment in return for conformity in matters of faith. The martyrs probably lay awake in their prisons at night struggling with these thoughts, searching their consciences, thinking of their imminent death. But they realised that truth was more important than their personal well-being and safety.

Our martyrs have become a vital part of the identity of our 'native brand' of Catholicism. In his famous sermons of eighty years ago, Mgr Ronald Knox summed up our attitude towards these brave men and women: 'these are no distant figures from stained-glass windows; they are men of our blood, sharing our common speech and our national ways of thought'. He thought that the English Martyrs were typically English: 'How we love them for being so specifically English! English in their bluff directness, English in their obstinancy; English above all in their determination to face death, though the death were martyrdom with a jest. From St Thomas More refusing to have his beard cut by the axe, to [St] John Kemble having his last pipe and his last drink with the sheriff, they are of our blood. Different, somehow, from the other saints...'

WESTMINSTER ABBEY

Mass at the Confessor's Shrine

It was a privilege to celebrate Mass at the shrine of St Edward the Confessor in Westminster Abbey, an event organised each year by the Guild of Our Lady of Ransom. The shrine is not only at the spiritual heart of the abbey but one of the spiritual hearts of England. This is the place of coronations and royal weddings, the burial place of the great and the good, the setting for grand state occasions. All the abbey's magnificence is based around this eleventh-century king, who built a large Romanesque church on the site and a century later was canonised. He subsequently became not only the saint of Westminster but a patron of the monarchy and of England.

As I stood at the altar, I reflected on the congregation around me. There was, of course, our group of pilgrims, including friends and family, crammed into every nook and cranny in the small space around the shrine. But also present, very visibly, were at least five medieval kings and four queens, who asked to be buried on that spot, hoping for St Edward's intercession and for some of his sanctity to 'rub off'. So, joining us in our congregation, their splendid monuments forming the boundary of the chapel, we had Henry III, who rebuilt the abbey; Edward I, the famous 'Hammer of the Scots'; Edward III, whose reign saw the victories of Crecy and Poitiers; the unlucky Richard II, usurped and then murdered at Pontefract; and Henry V, victor of Agincourt, buried in an elaborately carved chantry chapel. Let us not forget St Edward's wife, Edith, the sister of King Harold and (according to one theory) one of the creators of the Bayeux Tapestry, who lies near her husband in an unmarked grave.

What is interesting is why so many monarchs looked to St Edward as a patron and model. The hagiographic tradition remembers him as a king of justice and peace but also portrays him as a reluctant ruler who was more concerned with the things of Heaven and whose most obvious legacy, beyond this abbey, was a contested succession and a brutal Norman Conquest. The saintly Confessor was remembered more for his piety, purity and miracles than his policies and triumphs.

In reality, this is not the full picture: a study of contemporary sources shows St Edward taking tough decisions, sending political enemies into exile and commanding his fleet against pirates. An early chronicler wrote that 'he was of passionate temper and a man of prompt and vigorous action'. Like most kings of the period, he enjoyed hunting, hawking and the telling of sagas.

Of course, there were always political motives behind the cult of the Confessor. St Edward's canonisation took place in 1161 and proved useful to the reigning monarch, Henry II, who was asserting the power of the Crown in matters ecclesiastical, a campaign which would put him in dispute with the Archbishop of Canterbury, St Thomas Becket, and create one of our great martyr saints. The Church's response is often seen in the canonisation of an Archbishop of Canterbury, St Anselm, in 1163, two years after St Edward. Like Becket, he had been a champion of the Church's liberty and endured many years of exile.

Moreover, St Edward was not only the last English king of the line of Alfred the Great but also half-Norman. He was thus a figure of continuity, able to heal the divisions of the past and give legitimacy to the current royal dynasty.

But such factors were not the only reasons for St Edward's popularity. One of his most fervent devotees was Henry III. By the 1230s he had chosen St Edward as his special patron: he rebuilt Westminster Abbey in the latest gothic style, erected a new shrine for his patron and named his son and heir after him: Edward I, the first in a long line of King Edwards. What attraction did Henry see in his saintly predecessor?

Firstly, St Edward was the sort of king that Henry wanted to be — a ruler who based his leadership on justice and peace, who enacted laws and lived in harmony with his people. This was what England needed in the aftermath of the Magna Carta and decades of division and violence. In the words of a recent historian, Henry's reign saw England 'transformed from being the private plaything of a French-speaking dynasty into a medieval state in which the king answered for his actions to an English parliament'.

On a personal level, Henry saw in St Edward a man who had been through many similar life experiences. Henry had become king at the age of nine, succeeding his unpopular father, John. With much of England occupied by rebels and most of his continental possessions still in French hands, Henry inherited a challenging situation and would have empathised with St Edward, who himself spent much of his youth in exile and succeeded to the throne in the aftermath of war and oppression. Henry, like the Confessor, had also been deserted by his mother and, as king, had to deal with treacherous advisers. Indeed, the abbey's late-twelfth-century wax seal shows St Edward trampling on one of them, Earl Godwine (with St Peter trampling on Nero on the other side). As one historian writes, 'Henry turned to an eternal mentor, who would never deceive or desert him, and would never let him down... [he] found a powerful spiritual protector at a time when he most needed protection'.

St Edward, in other words, was no cardboard cut-out saint but a man—a king—of his times, flesh and blood like us, with his own strengths and weaknesses. As I offered Mass in the abbey, I looked up to see a magnificent vista of the Confessor's shrine and then, high above me, the gothic vaulting. We were there because we trusted in his heavenly intercession. Although we are not Plantagenet kings and live nearly a millennium later, we can still imitate him in his ability to combine a busy life of worldly concerns with prayer and living faith, in his love of justice, and in his constancy in the face of adversity. As St Aelred of Rievaulx advised in the Prologue to his *Life* of St Edward: 'Entrust yourself to his careful protection, be sure to imitate his holiness as well, and so you will achieve happiness for ever with him. Amen!'

WESTMINSTER CATHEDRAL

'Cardinal Vaughan's Railway Station'

Westminster Cathedral is such an established part of the London skyline that it is hard to believe the foundation stone was only laid in 1895 and that the great building was opened in 1903.

From the moment the archdiocese of Westminster was established in 1850, speculation began about the location and design of a fitting cathedral. While funds were raised, pro-cathedrals were set up first at St Mary Moorfields, the parish church of the City, and then Our Lady of Victories in Kensington. Both were ultimately unsuitable: the former, too small; the latter, in the words of one Victorian journalist, 'all hidden behind shops, and has to be reached by a narrow courtway, which, when crinolines again come into fashion, will be too narrow for the ladies to pass'.

After the death of Cardinal Wiseman, his successor, Henry Edward Manning, expressed his desire to build a monument in his honour. However, there was no rush. The priority was opening schools rather than a grand cathedral. Money was gradually collected together—the Marquis of Bute, the richest man in England, contributed £5,000—and a plot of land eventually purchased near Vauxhall Bridge Road, not far from Westminster Abbey. As early as 1877, Manning was using the site for a temperance rally, organised by the League of the Cross. He explained how he was like an admiral without a ship and that any cathedral would have to be erected little by little—indeed, he would be content if it were finished in a hundred years; all were bound to do what they could in their own time.

The site had been that of a prison, variously known as the Tothill Fields Bridewell or the Westminster House of Correction. Erected in 1834, replacing an earlier prison nearby, it was circular in design so that wardens could maximise the number of prisoners observable from a central point; for most of its brief history, the inmates were women and juveniles (only the former from 1861). The entrance in Francis Street—where Clergy House and the diocesan offices now are—consisted of 'massive granite blocks and immense iron gates, ornamented above with portcullis work'.

It is curious to think of the cathedral being built directly on prison foundations and inmates picking oakum where the sacred liturgy is now celebrated. Yet how appropriate, given the Catholic community's long history of persecution and its preferential option for the poor, which is still visible in those who linger around the piazza outside the cathedral and seek refuge in the nearby homeless shelters.

Of course, Westminster Cathedral would become the great project of Cardinal Herbert Vaughan, the third archbishop—though neither he nor the architect, John Francis Bentley, lived to see the structure ready for worship. Vaughan favoured a cathedral in the Byzantine style since then it would not need to compete with the glories of Westminster Abbey a short walk away. This style was also relatively cheap and easy to build, allowing future generations to add the interior decoration. A wide nave also allowed the sanctuary to be as visible as possible, thus facilitating the participation of the congregation in the Sacred Liturgy. However, as the structure was erected critics dubbed it 'Cardinal Vaughan's Railway Station' and the 'Roman Candle'. Anti-Catholic rumours even spread that the foundations would serve as dungeons for a new Inquisition!

By the time of the consecration in 1910, the cathedral had already hosted a number of high-profile events. On 6 June 1903 Sir Edward Elgar conducted the London premiere of Newman's *Dream of Gerontius* with some well-known soloists, the North Staffordshire District Choral Society and the Symphonic Orchestra of Amsterdam. It proved a useful test of the building's deep acoustic. Then a fortnight later the cathedral received the body of Cardinal Vaughan and a solemn Requiem was offered on a temporary altar erected at the sanctuary steps. Later in the year the new archbishop, Francis Bourne, was enthroned. Under his stewardship the cathedral marked the thirteenth centenary of St Gregory the Great's death (1904), the translation of the bodies of Cardinals Wiseman and Manning from St Mary's Cemetery, Kensal Green to the crypt (1907) and the International Eucharistic Congress (1908), when seven cardinals were present in Westminster including, for the first time since the reign of Mary Tudor, a papal legate.

The ceremony of consecration was long, elaborate and highly symbolic. On the afternoon of 27 June 1910, the relics that would be placed in each of the thirteen altars were brought to the cathedral hall in procession and Matins and Lauds was sung. The following morning proceedings began at 7am and, fortunately, a dispensation had been gained from the normal fast in preparation for the feast of St Peter and St Paul—fortunate because the liturgy would take over seven hours. The cathedral choir sang Lassus's *Missa Quinti Toni* 'in spite of intense fatigue'. To mark the link with the pre-Reformation past, a special edition of plain-chant was prepared from the medieval Sarum *Pontificale* and *Antiphonale*. The day ended with Vespers and

Benediction and all concerned no doubt had an early night for there was yet another full day ahead of them on 29 June, designated as a 'National Celebration' for the sixtieth anniversary of the restoration of the hierarchy.

Thus, Westminster Cathedral was established as the mother church of England and Wales (at the time there was still only one archbishop in the country) and the spiritual heart of the Empire. It has heard the whispered prayers of millions and witnessed many grand ceremonies: two papal visits, the translation of the relics of St John Southworth (the martyr who once laboured among the Catholics of Westminster), national and diocesan celebrations, relic tours, priestly ordinations, and episcopal consecrations and funerals. Its award-winning choir is famous the world over; few churches can compete with the musical quality of its daily sung Mass. And the decoration has been added to generation by generation, most notably in the magnificent Blessed Sacrament and Lady chapels. As Manning said all those years ago, all are bound to do what they can in their own time. It is the work of generations.

MIDDLESEX

HAMPTON

Hampton Court

Hampton Court has always been my favourite of the royal palaces. As a child I was fascinated by stories of Catherine Howard's shrieking ghost running along the Haunted Gallery and the prospect of getting lost in the maze. For many years it was a popular family trip in the half-term holidays. Thus, it was a delight to return in February 2016 for the first Catholic Vespers (Evening Prayer) to be held there since the Reformation. It was celebrated by Cardinal Vincent Nichols, in the presence of the Papal Nuncio and with a sermon by the Bishop of London, in his capacity as Dean of the Chapel Royal.

Hampton Court is not perhaps particularly remembered for its Catholic past, being so often associated with Henry VIII and his break with Rome. Yet, the palace stands on the site of a manor and grange used by the Knights Hospitallers of St John of Jerusalem from the thirteenth century. Excavations reveal a large barn, where agricultural produce would have been stored. The location became an increasingly useful one, situated near the royal palaces of Sheen, Byfleet and (later) Richmond, and it was in demand by visitors to the royal court. The Knights rented out their property to high-profile tenants, such as Giles Daubeney, Lord Chamberlain to Henry VII, and then Thomas Wolsey, who leased the property in 1515.

It was Wolsey who transformed Hampton Court into a magnificent palace, with grand apartments and a processional route that led to an impressive chapel. The guest lodgings all had *en suite* lavatories — something of a luxury in the sixteenth century! It was a palace fit for a cardinal, inspired by ideas current in Renaissance Italy, and it would not have been out of place in Rome itself, complete with eight reliefs of ancient Roman emperors on the gatehouse. There was, however, a distinctively English blending of styles — perpendicular gothic meeting Renaissance classicism.

It was also a palace fit for a king. According to tradition, the opulence of Wolsey's court caused the jealousy of Henry, who soon got his greedy hands on it. Wags, like the poet John Skelton, wrote 'The king's court/ Should have the excellence/ But Hampton Court/ Hath the pre-eminence'. The cardinal's official line was that the magnificence of his court was not only supposed to be a reflection of Henry's glory but intended for his use, with state apartments reserved for the royal family. Nevertheless, once Wolsey fell from grace, having failed to obtain an annulment for the royal marriage, Henry was quick to acquire his palaces. York Place near Westminster would become the great Whitehall and Hampton Court became Henry's favourite country retreat, conveniently situated on the river and surrounded by over a thousand acres of parkland. He extended the buildings, making sure there were tennis courts, bowling alleys and tiltyards.

As I sat at the back of the chapel, praying the psalms, listening to the glorious music and occasionally smelling a waft of incense, I felt as if the drama of our nation's religious history was being replayed. After all, Hampton Court has become a symbol of the turbulence of Henry's reign and in this very chapel so many key events had happened: here he attended services with Catherine of Aragon and Anne Boleyn, here Edward was baptised and, shortly afterwards, the viscera of Jane Seymour buried under the altar; here Catherine Howard met her downfall, when a letter outlining her scandalous conduct was placed on his seat; here Henry married his sixth and final wife.

The Chapel Royal itself also had a sense of witnessing to this drama. The plain wooden altarpiece, devoid of images, is a stark contrast to the elaborate Tudor ceiling. It was, in fact, not until the mid-seventeenth century that the Chapel lost many of its Catholic elements, the ceiling being preserved because it was too high for the Roundheads to reach. Even the Protestant boy-king, Edward VI, decided to keep his father's chapel more-or-less intact. He would have probably seen the now demolished stained glass window that not only featured Henry and Wolsey but 'popish' saints such as St Anne, St Catherine and St Thomas Becket. It is uncertain when the last Catholic service was held at Hampton Court. It seems that Mary I heard Masses here and that the Catholic chaplains of the Stuart queens, Henrietta Maria and Catherine of Braganza, probably used the Queen's Holy Day Closet, overlooking the Chapel Royal.

At the centre of the Vespers was the Blessed Virgin Mary. 'May your Church be united heart and soul, held fast by love', we prayed. 'May the Virgin Mary intercede for us'. Here, as at her shrine of Walsingham, she was a source of unity, continuing to lead all to Christ and to soothe the hurt of the past. As St John Paul II wrote, 'why should we not all together look to her as our common Mother, who prays for the unity of God's family and who "precedes" us all at the head of the long line of witnesses of faith in the one Lord, the Son of God?'

As I left the reception that followed the Vespers, I walked through several empty state rooms, carefully watched not only by the palace staff but by the portraits of various kings and queens. In the Throne Room I passed the nuncio, who had had to take a phone call. This is not a sight that the palace has been accustomed to witness in recent centuries; a sign of the growing understanding between the Churches. Henry VIII would have been very surprised.

HAREFIELD

A Martyr's Secret Garden

Despite the ravages of HS2, Harefield remains a rare glimpse of what Middlesex once looked like: rolling fields, country lanes and quaint villages. Sit in the beer garden of The Old Orchard and you can admire a fine panorama of woods and lakes, all astonishingly within the M25. Visit St Mary's church, located down a tree-lined lane some way from the village centre, with its fine collection of monuments and ANZAC cemetery, and the bustling metropolis seems far away.

The church was for many years a 'private peculiar', meaning that the church lay outside the jurisdiction of the local bishop. This originated in the late twelfth century when the Knights Hospitaller were given the privilege of not only appointing priests to St Mary's but exercising other powers normally reserved to the bishop. At the Reformation this passed to the local Newdigate family. Indeed, in 1691 a jury declared that no bishop's writ had run in the parish for over 500 years and that Newdigates were 'the undoubted ordinary'. Peculiar jurisdictions such as Harefield were transferred to the bishop in 1847, though a number of 'Royal Peculiars' remain, directly under the monarch, including Westminster Abbey.

The north chapel is known as the 'Breakspear Chapel', named after the family which produced the only English pope—Nicholas Breakspear (Adrian IV). Born near Abbots Langley, he spent most of his life in France, Scandinavia and Rome. Some have suggested that the future pontiff was born in Harefield but there is no evidence for this, beyond the fact that his family owned land in the area during the fourteenth and fifteenth centuries. This is reflected in the house known as 'Breakspears' on 'Breakspear Road' as well as the names of a local pub and crematorium. The chapel at St Mary's, however, contains tombs not of the pope's kinsmen but of the Ashby family, who lived for many years at the house.

We are on more certain ground with Harefield's connection with the Newdigate family. From the fifteenth century they lived at the manor which once stood near St Mary's, accounting for the church's remote location. Of particular interest are John and Amphyllis Newdigate, whose memorial can still be seen at the church. That they were devoutly Catholic is shown in the lives of some of their seventeen children. Maria was a Bridgettine nun at Syon, and Sybil became the last prioress of Holywell (or Haliwell), a religious house following the Augustinian rule in Shoreditch. Jane married into the Dormer family and famously opposed the idea of her son marrying Jane Seymour, thinking the match beneath him. Her granddaughter, also called Jane, married the Spanish ambassador to England, the Duke of Feria. The two Janes, grandmother and granddaughter, went into exile in Flanders and Spain during the reign of Elizabeth and were prominent members of the English Catholic community there. Henry Clifford later wrote a biography of the Duchess of Feria (1643) which contains valuable information about the Newdigate family. Two brothers, Dunstan and Sylvester, were Knights Hospitaller, inspired no doubt by the local links with the order in Harefield. However, all families were affected by the religious divisions of the times and another brother, John, sat on the jury that condemned St John Fisher.

The glory of the family was Blessed Sebastian Newdigate, born at Harefield on 7 September 1500 and educated at Cambridge. He grew to become 'a gentleman of good parts' and a favourite of Henry VIII. He married Catherine Hampden and had two daughters, Amphyllis and Elizabeth, although little is known about them.

Sebastian was eventually widowed, and this proved a turning point in his life. His grief coincided with the growing crisis over the king's marriage. Jane Dormer became concerned lest the 'lustful' atmosphere at Court corrupt her brother. She invited him to her house in Buckinghamshire and 'advised him to take heed of the deceits of the world and the snares of the devil; to look to the duty of a Christian; and not to stain his soul and honour with so dangerous and pestilent contagions, as the bad example of so potent a master did lead him to'. Sebastian listened to her words and replied, somewhat cryptically: 'Sister, what will you say, if the next news you hear of me shall be that I am entered to be a monk in the Charterhouse?' Jane did not take him seriously and when Sebastian entered the Charterhouse shortly afterwards, she imagined his sudden conversion to be 'a delusion, and temptation of the devil; first carrying him to so high a pitch, and after to throw him down'. She voiced her worries to the prior, St John Houghton, but when she was allowed to see Brother Sebastian, her opinion quickly changed. 'It was not so much the alteration of his person and habit which did move her', Clifford writes, 'as his gesture, his retired speech, his grave humility and modesty astonished her; he so demeaning himself, as if he had been all his life in a monastery'.

Sebastian progressed in his vocation and was ordained subdeacon on 3 June 1531 (Ember Saturday) by St John Fisher, Bishop of Rochester, and deacon and priest shortly afterwards. However, he was not able to enjoy the peace of the cloister for very long. In 1534 the community reluctantly assented to the Act of Succession but refused to acknowledge Henry as Head of the Church in England. Houghton was arrested, together with two other Carthusian priors, and martyred at Tyburn on 4 May 1535.

Sebastian himself was soon arrested, together with Blessed Humphrey Middlemore (convent vicar) and William Exmew (procurator). The prisoners were taken to the Marshalsea prison, where they were chained to upright pillars for fourteen days 'with iron rings about their necks, hands and feet'. Even the king paid them a visit but when he saw his former courtier refusing to yield, he departed 'in a great rage threatening and cursing'. They were removed to the Tower, where the king interviewed Sebastian again. The monk told his former master: 'in matters that belong to the Faith and the glory of our Lord Jesus Christ to the doctrine of the Catholic Church and the salvation of my poor soul, your Majesty must be pleased to excuse me'.

On 18 June 1535 the three Fathers were tried at Westminster Hall and condemned to death. Before passing sentence, the Judge addressed himself to Sebastian, 'repeating to him the nobility of his blood, the honourable allies he had in that kingdom, the duty he owed to his Majesty having been his servant; the many favours he had received from him'. But he was resolved to make the ultimate sacrifice, and on hearing the sentence the Fathers cried out, *Deo Gratias*! The following day the monks were dragged on wooden hurdles to Tyburn. Sebastian was the first to suffer. Standing on the cart, with the noose around his neck, he 'intimated his own innocence both to the king and all the world, and that his death was only for the testimony and defence of the Catholic Faith'.

Henry Clifford ends his account of our martyr's life by saying,

> this was the violent death but most happy end of Father Sebastian, an approved valorous gentleman, a perfect Religious, and a glorious Martyr of Christ Jesus. He was a singular honour of his house and an immortal renown of his family ... who in the first risings and oppositions against the Catholic Faith in our country so valiantly stood for it, and for the defence thereof sealed it with his blood and life.

In 1586 the Newdigates exchanged Harefield Place for Arbury in Warwickshire. Their former manor rose to prominence at the turn of the seventeenth century, when it was the home of the Countess of

Derby, a notable patron of the arts, and visited by Elizabeth I shortly before her death. By 1675, though, the property was back in the possession of the Newdigates; after several further changes in ownership, it was demolished around 1813 and a new mansion built at a different location.

There is little evidence of the old manor today. The Newdigates would have been amazed to find, on part of the site, 120 First World War graves, mostly of Australians who died in the hospital at Harefield Park (now a famous hospital specialising in heart transplants), and the obelisk erected by their descendant, Sir Francis Newdigate, sometime Governor of Tasmania and Western Australia. Walk a little further down the lane, though, and there is another hidden Middlesex gem: Church Gardens. In 1995 Kay and Patrick McHugh purchased this derelict property and heroically restored the walled garden dating back to the Elizabethan period—among the oldest in the country and once forming part of Harefield Place. In the orchard is an unusual arcaded wall, which may been designed to protect fruit or house statues or even form the backdrop to a masque, entitled *Arcades*, written for Lady Derby by John Milton (who lived nearby) and with music by Henry Lawes. This was several generations after the Carthusian martyr but wandering around the grounds of his former home, and admiring the beauty of the gardens, one catches a glimpse of his spirit and the peace that he found at the Charterhouse.

ISLEWORTH

Parish Priest and Martyr

Blessed John Hale (or Haile), it could be said, was the only parish priest among the English Martyrs. Although many secular priests suffered under Elizabeth and the Stuarts, they were missionaries who moved from safe house to safe house and never formally enjoyed the tenure of a parish. Hale, therefore, is of special interest and a link to the generations of English secular priests who had the cure of souls up until the Reformation.

It seems that Hale studied at King's Hall, Cambridge and before gaining the benefice of Isleworth (Middlesex) in 1521 has been connected with the parishes of Chelmsford and Cranford. By the time Henry VIII's 'great matter' erupted upon the scene, he was already an elderly man and a seasoned pastor. Like many, no doubt, he had strong opinions on the matter and confided in his friends. This would prove to be his downfall. A brother priest in nearby Teddington, named 'Feron' or 'Fern', was later examined by the authorities and gave a full account of their conversations. According to this evidence, Hale asserted that the king was a heretic who was cruelly oppressing the Church and one of the worst princes to have ruled the kingdom. He referred to Anne Boleyn as 'a wife of fornication'.

Here, an unusual element enters the annals of the martyrs, one which gives an interesting insight into the Tudor mind. In his conversations about Henry, Hale referred to the 'Prophecies of Merlin. Attributed to the magician of Arthurian legend, though dating from a much later period, these had been passed down both in oral tradition and in numerous written sources, including Geoffrey of Monmouth's *History of the Kings of Britain* (c. 1136) and the rhyming *Prophecy of the Six Kings to Follow John* (c. 1312). Political prophecies such as these were highly influential and flexible enough to be used by all sides. Characters from Britain's legendary past could indeed be manipulated to suit a particular agenda.

These prophecies often involved animal symbolism. Merlin is said to have spoken of six kings identified by a particular beast. There would be a lamb, a dragon, a goat, a boar, an ass and finally a mole or 'moldwarp'. The evil mole would be 'accursed by God for his misdeeds' and finally defeated by a dragon from the north, a wolf from the west and a lion from Ireland. It had been applied to Henry

IV and there is a reference to this in Shakespeare's *Henry IV Part 1* (Act 3 Scene 1).

The crisis of the 1530s led to a great interest in political prophecy, which obviously reached the parish of Isleworth. Hale was heard identifying Henry VIII as the mole king and hinting that he would one day be defeated. Indeed, an expression he used that 'he himself would stand in the stead of a man' suggested that he thought it was justifiable to take arms against the king.

Hale was not the only one to speak of these prophecies; both Richard Bishop and John Bonnefant were executed for doing so in 1537 and 1539 respectively. The 'moldwarp' prophecy was on the lips of those involved in the Pilgrimage of Grace, that uprising against Henry in 1536, while the vicar of Muston (Leicestershire), John Dobson, was convicted for preaching the prophecies of Merlin and others the same year as Hale.

In being brought to trial, Hale was honest about the strength of evidence against him and acknowledged 'that he had maliciously slandered the king, queen, and the Council, for which he asked the forgiveness of God, the king and Queen Anne, and will continue sorrowful during his life, which stands only in the king's will'. He, together with Feron of Teddington, was found guilty of treason, although the latter was pardoned, presumably because of the evidence he had provided.

Already old and sick, Hale was dragged on a hurdle to the gallows at Tyburn on 4 May 1535, where a large crowd had gathered, including many of the leading men of the kingdom. He was the fourth to suffer that morning, after the three Carthusian priors. St Thomas More, on seeing the group leave the Tower, said to his daughter: 'Lo, dost thou not see, Meg, that these blessed Fathers be now as cheerfully going to their deaths, as bridegrooms to their marriage'. Few details have been recorded of Hale's last moments. He suffered bravely and, amidst the noise of the crowd and the screams of agony, would have heard the voice of his fellow victim, St Richard Reynolds, who was waiting his turn. We are told that, 'seeing them cruelly quartered, and their bowels taken out, [he] preached unto them and comforted them, promising them a heavenly banquet and supper for their sharp breakfast taken patiently for their Master's sake'. And so the old priest took his leave of this world and went joyfully to the eternal wedding feast.

SYON PARK

Syon Abbey

Henry V is celebrated as the victor of Agincourt but it is often forgotten that he founded several religious houses. The most famous of these was Syon Abbey, situated on the banks of the Thames, which was the wealthiest religious house at the Dissolution. The house built on the site is now the London home of the Duke of Northumberland.

Syon Abbey was the only English house of the Bridgettine Order. English interest in this new order is normally dated back to the wedding of Henry V's sister, Philippa, to Eric XIII, King of Denmark, Sweden and Norway, in 1406. One of her entourage, Sir Henry FitzHugh, visited the Bridgettine mother house of Vadstena and resolved to establish the order in England. Henry IV himself became enthusiastic about the plan. However, it was left to Henry V to make the dream into reality, laying the foundation stone on 22 February 1415.

Syon was intended to be one of a 'trinity' of new religious houses, the 'King's Great Work', opened in the vicinity of his residence at Sheen (Richmond). This was intended partly as reparation for the sins of his father, Henry IV, who had usurped the throne, been involved in the murder of Richard II and executed the Archbishop of York, Richard le Scrope, after an uprising.

There would be 'The House of Jesus of Bethlehem of Sheen', a Carthusian monastery opened in 1414; a community of Celestines (reformed Benedictines) at Isleworth, and finally 'The Monastery of St Saviour and St Bridget of Syon', located originally in Twickenham. The Celestine house was never opened, hardly surprising given that the monks were largely French and less than eager to comply with the king's wishes in the aftermath of Agincourt. The Bridgettines made the most of this by moving to their site in Isleworth in 1431, Twickenham being deemed too marshy.

Syon Abbey was a double house, made up of men and women, under the leadership of an abbess. By the time of the Dissolution there were seventy-three religious: twelve monks, five lay-brothers, fifty-two choir sisters and four lay-sisters. Their original aim was 'to celebrate Divine Service for ever for our healthful estate while we live and for our souls when we shall have departed this life, and for the souls of our most dear lord and father (Henry IV) late king of England, and Mary his late wife, etc'.

Over its short century or so of existence, it received many endowments and gifts of land. A large church was built, 323 feet long, making it larger than its rough contemporary, the chapel of King's College, Cambridge. The community became known for its learning and the brothers' library was one of the best of its kind in late medieval England, including many printed books and humanist works. Some of the brothers were authors in their own rights, such as Richard Whitford, who produced a dozen works, including the popular *Work for Householders*, directed at families, and *The Pipe*, a bold defence of the religious life at a time it was being criticised.

The abbey was also a place of pilgrimage. Although it had no major relics, it could offer an Indulgence, the 'Syon Pardon', on the feast and octave of St Peter in Chains (1 August). This proved to be popular and Margery Kempe was there in 1434 'to obtain her pardon through the mercy of our Lord'. By the time of the Reformation, Syon enjoyed the fourth highest pilgrim revenue in the country and pewter badges depicting St Bridget were taken away as souvenirs.

Syon was not to survive much past its centenary. Storm clouds were looming as Henry VIII tried to resolve his marriage difficulties. The abbey became a centre for the opponents of the royal divorce. St Thomas More and St John Fisher were frequent visitors, as was the 'Holy Maid of Kent', Elizabeth Barton. Indeed, while staying at Syon in 1533 she met with More in one of the side chapels. This had been arranged by a member of the community, St Richard Reynolds, a noted scholar, and his support for the Holy Maid and criticism of the king led to his execution on 4 May 1535.

The royal officials addressed the nuns at the end of 1535. Those who accepted the king's new title as Head of the Church were asked to remain seated, whilst those opposed were asked to leave the chapter house where they had gathered. All remained seated and later sent a request to Thomas Cromwell that he 'be a good master unto them and to their house'. They chose to play the long game and survive for as long as possible, though one nun, Agnes Smythe, who was described as 'a sturdy dame', tried to persuade the sisters not to hand over the abbey seal.

The community was pensioned off—a very generous £200 was given to the abbess, Agnes Jordan—but that was not the end of the story. Many remained committed to their way of life and so formed little groups, each with a senior sister and (where possible) at least one brother to celebrate Mass. The abbess herself moved to 'Southlands', a property near Denham (Buckinghamshire), and judging from her will was able to rescue from the abbey many of its images and hangings. On her death in January 1545, she was buried in the local church, where her brass can be seen to this day—dressed as a widow rather than a nun, but proudly identified as 'sometime abbess of the Monastery of Syon'.

The nuns began a long odyssey of wanderings: briefly restored at Syon under Mary I and spending many years of exile in the Low Countries, France and Portugal. In 1861 they returned to England and found a home in the West Country; with increasing numbers, they acquired an eighteenth-century manor house outside Totnes, Marley House, in 1925. However, they downsized in 1990 and finally closed in 2011, the surviving sisters moving to Nazareth House in Plymouth.

There is little trace now of the once magnificent abbey of Syon on its medieval site in Isleworth. However, it is remarkable to think that its religious traditions, stretching back to the year of Agincourt, continued into our own times.

UXBRIDGE

Conversation with a Gravedigger

November is a month when we visit cemeteries to pray for the dead and remember our loved ones. It is a praiseworthy practice and a work of mercy. This is why I always go to my local cemetery to bless the graves. It is a closed cemetery now, with no space for new burials apart from those who are interred in existing graves, and so only a handful of parishioners join me for the brief service; sometimes it's just me and the pastoral assistant. Yet it is important to commemorate locally the faithful departed — for is a parish made up only of the living?

The cemetery gets a steady stream of visitors every day, normally in ones and twos. One family of travellers comes daily and their family graves are magnificently covered in fresh flowers and always spotlessly clean. Other sections are neglected, consumed by an urban wilderness, with the Victorian tombstones heavily covered in ivy and almost impossible to read. There is something strangely reassuring about this. Just as the bodies below have returned to the dust, so their monuments also slowly return to nature. The cycle of life and death continues.

This particular cemetery (Uxbridge and Hillingdon Cemetery) was opened in 1856, one of the first of a new series of municipal cemeteries opened across the country. Up until the nineteenth century most burials were in graveyards beside the local church. The great and the good would be placed inside the church, with their own ostentatious monuments, and everyone else would be buried outside, their bodies often placed not in coffins but linen or wool shrouds. The numbers of burials can easily be seen by the fact that the ground is often significantly higher than the surrounding land. There were typically fewer burials on the 'un-consecrated' north side, which was reserved for suicides, criminals and other outcasts, and often this became considered a place for community recreations, such as football, cockfighting, wrestling or ninepins.

By the late 1600s it became the practice for tombstones to be erected, especially for the more prosperous members of the community, though few survive from this early period. However, churchyards were becoming crowded, especially in the cities, and health concerns began to be aired, especially in the light of the cholera epidemics. By the nineteenth centuries new cemeteries began to be opened, often on the outskirts of town and operated on a commercial basis. The first 'modern' inter-denominational cemetery was established in 1819: Norwich's Rosary Cemetery, which was located on Rosary Road (hence its Catholic-sounding name) and established by nonconformists. In the 1850s a series of Burial Acts allowed the creation of a system of public cemeteries, funded in part by the borough rate. A new era began for large cemeteries, with neat rows of gravestones and layouts that resembled a park.

I got speaking to my local gravediggers, who were unusually friendly. In my experience, they normally stay out of people's way, waiting for the crowds at a funeral to disappear before they resume their sombre job. Not surprising, perhaps, because in some cultures they are seen as 'untouchable' and, as one of them told me, people sometimes vent the anger caused by grief at them, blaming them for 'the slings and arrows of outrageous fortune'.

I ended up chatting to these gravediggers for well over an hour and their enthusiasm for the cemetery was catching. Having worked there for over fifty years between them, they knew every nook and cranny of the twenty acre site. They told me about the regular visitors they have got to know, so that when their time came to be buried there the gravediggers admitted to shedding a tear. They spoke of the den of foxes in the undergrowth and introduced me to 'Brian', a particularly bold fox who came sniffing the graves just a few feet away. They referred to their 'friendly' rivalry with the team that comes to look after the tombs of the Commonwealth War Graves Commission and stories of a ghostly figure seen walking across one part of the cemetery. They showed me the two gothic chapels designed by A. W. N. Pugin's friend Benjamin Ferrey, one of which has been adapted into their 'staff room'.

It was the stories behind the tombs that fascinated me the most. Here, waiting for the day of resurrection, were a Chartist poet, a Czech flying ace, two of my predecessors as parish priest, a winner of the Victoria Cross, the founder of the Church Lads' Brigade, a politician who lost three sons in military service, and a remarkable woman who set up a Catholic charity (St Francis Leprosy Guild).

This cemetery is not unique in all this. Each one is a largely untapped source of local history. It is there that previous generations lie at rest and a careful survey of the gravestones reveals many interesting names and connections. If you have a cemetery nearby, why not visit it and not only pray for those interred there but learn something about our fellow pilgrims who once trod the same streets and lived in our houses. For, in the words of the poet Thomas Gray:

Uxbridge • Conversation with a Gravedigger

Beneath those rugged elms, that yew-tree's shade,
   Where heaves the turf in many a mould'ring heap,
Each in his narrow cell for ever laid,
   The rude forefathers of the hamlet sleep.

WEST DRAYTON

A Suburban Tudor Mansion

West Drayton is not the sort of place you expect to find a Tudor mansion. There is a perpetual traffic jam on the High Street, numerous fast-food stalls, and a bustling railway station on the Elizabeth Line. But walk down Church Road and you will suddenly stumble across a Tudor Gatehouse, with faint echoes of Hampton Court. This, along with long sections of red brick wall, is all that remains of a substantial house—with a large hall, courtyard, gallery and some fifty chambers—built in the mid-sixteenth century by one of Henry VIII's most-trusted courtiers, Sir William Paget.

Nearby is the medieval church of St Martin, much of which dates from the fifteenth century. One author wrote, rather romantically, in 1908: 'visions of the varying customs and manners of the ages that have passed whilst these well-worn stones have remained in position, of the scenes gay and sad that have been witnessed within the old church walls, or the stirring incidents connected with the grand baronial hall—these are the thoughts that pass quickly through the mind as one contemplates the ancient tower or frowning gate-house, with their evidences of long-continued buffetings on the rugged shores of time' Many members of the Paget family are buried, without much fanfare, under the chancel, their coffins having been placed on end in arcaded niches in the continental manner. Like so many of our medieval churches, numerous interesting features disappeared during over-zealous restorations in the nineteenth century and then the 1970s; an old sexton remembered in 1936 seeing body armour that had once been worn by the Pagets and a fine collection of old flags.

Sir William Paget was one of the 'new men' who managed to make fame and fortune at the court of Henry VIII thanks not to their pedigree but their ability. The family seem to have originated in Staffordshire and were of modest means. Nevertheless, the young William had the good fortune to be educated as a scholar at St Paul's School, before proceeding to Trinity Hall, Cambridge, and the University of Paris. He became a skilful lawyer and enjoyed the support of the master of his old Cambridge college, Stephen Gardiner, who had become Bishop of Winchester. Patronage was everything for those of humbler birth; Gardiner gave him a step upwards, allowing him to participate in diplomatic missions. By 1534 Paget had transferred his allegiance to Thomas Cromwell, who with the gathering clouds of the king's divorce was becoming the man of the moment. Several important posts at court followed, including secretary to the king's third and fourth wives. Crucially, in 1543 Paget became a Privy Councillor and was knighted the following year; by 1547, the year Henry died, he was Chancellor of the Duchy of Lancaster and Knight of the Garter.

Paget was well thought of by the Emperor Charles V: once, on seeing him at court, the great man remarked, 'yonder is the man I can deny nothing to' and, in comparing the various English diplomats that had been sent, he remarked if Cardinal Wolsey's 'great train promised much, as his great designs did nothing', so Paget 'promised nothing and did all'. He continued to be prominent under Edward VI as a member of his Council. If he began the 1540s as an up-and-coming court official, he ended the decade as a political heavyweight, constantly in the monarch's presence, and bearing the title of Baron Paget of Beaudesert.

Navigating the twists and turns of Tudor politics was no easy task. Paget supposedly left behind him some maxims that give an insight into his methodology: 'Fly the court, Speak little, Care less, Desire nothing, Never earnest, In answer cold, Learn to spare, Spend in measure, Care for home, Pray often, Live better and Die well'. Despite such sage advice, his career was not a straightforward progress. Between October 1551 and June 1552 he was a prisoner of the Tower of London and degraded from the Order of the Garter due to charges of corruption; in 1553 he supported Lady Jane Grey, the 'Nine Days' Queen', but then managed to find favour under Mary I, who restored him to the Privy Council and the Garter. For reasons that remain unclear, his star waned under Elizabeth and he retired from public life. Perhaps he felt he had done his 'bit' or his increasingly pro-Catholic sympathies were out of step with the new regime (his support for Mary Tudor's marriage to Philip II had earned him a lucrative Spanish pension). He died on 9 June 1563 and was buried at St Martin's.

This Catholicism was most vividly seen in his son, Thomas, who eventually became 3rd Baron Paget. When not in London on parliamentary business, he spent most of his time in Staffordshire, leaving his widowed mother, Lady Anne, to use West Drayton as her main residence. Here where she maintained a priest in her household, ostensibly working as steward. Thomas was a man of culture: a great lover of books (by 1617 the inventory of the library at West Drayton ran to some fifty-one pages) and a patron of William Byrd, the great composer who lived for a time at Harlington and was also known for his secret Catholicism. He is known to have visited West Drayton and a room at Burton is described as 'Mr Byrde's Chamber'.

An impressive monument to Sir William was made in Italy at the cost of £700 and placed in Lichfield Cathedral in 1577, over the former location of the shrine of St Chad (a veiled reference to the family's Catholicism). Including four kneeling figures—Sir William, Lady Anne, and their eldest son and wife—all facing the altar, there is a suggestion that it was intended for St Martin's church but perhaps found to be too large or heavy. It was destroyed in 1643 during the English Civil War.

As a Catholic, Thomas sailed close to the wind. It is likely that he was aware of the secret conference of Jesuits held near Uxbridge in October 1580 and perhaps St Edmund Campion, one of England's most wanted men, visited West Drayton at this time. In 1583 Thomas became involved in a conspiracy to put Mary, Queen of Scots, on the throne—the Throckmorton Plot—along with his younger brother (Charles). They both fled to Paris, where they became embroiled in the Babington Plot, which had a similar aim. The brothers were attainted of treason and the Paget properties confiscated. Thomas died in Brussels in 1590.

The family's fortunes were eventually restored and its most famous member, Henry Paget, Earl of Uxbridge, was Wellington's second-in-command at Waterloo, even though relations between them were restrained following the former's elopement with the latter's sister-in-law some years previously. This adds an extra dimension to the (probably apocryphal) exchange they had on the battlefield when grapeshot hit Paget's leg: By God, sir, I've lost my leg', 'By God, sir, so you have!' If he lost a limb, he quickly gained the title of Marquess of Anglesey. Twice serving as Lord Lieutenant of Ireland, he was a supporter of Catholic Emancipation. On one occasion he stated 'I would gladly relieve [the Catholics] from all their disabilities. I would willingly place them upon a footing of perfect equality, in respect to political power, with the Protestants', though he thought it should never be at the expense of the establishment. Nevertheless, it was a hot issue with ever-changing administrations and briefly led to his dismissal. He sympathised with many of the demands of Daniel O'Connell, the 'Liberator', and can especially be praised for introducing state-aided education that affected 400,000 children.

The old Tudor house at West Drayton was largely demolished by 1750 and the manor was eventually sold to the De Burgh family, who lived at Drayton Hall. The last squire was Hubert de Burgh, who died in 1872 and was proud of once entertaining the exiled Napoleon

III — he delighted in pointing out to visitors 'Napoleon's Room' and the bed he used. His brother, Robert Lil, was the vicar at St Martin's between 1844 and 1879. He built a new vault for his family under the chancel window, since he disliked that of the Pagets and expressed a desire to have more air. In his old age he lived in the Gatehouse, from whence he could often be seen being wheeled out in a bath chair; by this time he had converted to Catholicism and there is a window in his memory at the beautiful Catholic church of St Catherine the Martyr, nearby.

WILLESDEN

London's Black Madonna

Willesden is a shrine with difference. It is located in a tired-looking suburb, just up the road from a major railway junction. It seems a far cry from the peace and beauty of Aylesford or Walsingham, and yet it speaks very powerfully of Our Lady's maternal presence even in the midst of a busy metropolis.

Things were not always so. It is amazing to think that the bustling roads were once quiet country lanes; that the rows of suburban houses stand on green fields. The annual May procession passes near Fortune Gate Road; the field that lies beneath the modern tarmac had the same name. Willesden has changed beyond recognition, but the remarkable thing is that the procession made on a May afternoon today would not have looked out of place on a similar May afternoon in the reign of Henry VII.

We do not know when people started making pilgrimages to Willesden and (unusually for a Marian shrine) no firm tradition has been handed down about an original vision or miracle. Stories, made faint by the passage of the centuries, speak of a holy well, an apparition by an oak tree and miracles involving the cure of blindness. All we know for sure is that by the end of the fifteenth century pilgrims were making their way there because 'Our Lady of Willesden' had shown herself to be a true Mother, interceding for her children and granting many favours.

People came to Willesden on pilgrimage for all sorts of reasons. For some, it was a day-out—and complaints were sometimes made about their rowdy behaviour. Others visited at some turning point in their life, asking for help. Devotees included the high and the lowly. Henry VII's queen, Elizabeth of York, paid 3s 4d to a man who went on pilgrimage to Willesden on her behalf in 1503, as she lay on her deathbed at the age of 37. Then in April 1534 St Thomas More prayed before the statue, as he had done many times before. He was arrested the following week and his pilgrimage was his last trip out of London. No doubt he suspected what lay ahead and prayed for strength.

When the medieval pilgrims went to Willesden, they had to walk not only through open countryside but the Middlesex forest, which could be dangerous. They may have gathered together for safety at certain well-known points, like 'The Red Lion' in Kilburn or Willesden Green. Indeed, when Cardinal Vaughan visited the parish in 1893 he said: 'in those days Willesden was a kind of wild forest to which people came from London in parties to seek sport and entrap game. Often times robbers infested the woods, and it was scarcely safe to traverse the paths which led to the forest unless there was a large company. And so at a certain point outside Willesden people from London and the neighbourhood used to meet, and in parties proceed to the church to pray and hear Mass, returning under similar protection to their homes'.

The shrine at Willesden enjoyed only a brief period of glory. At the Reformation the shrine was dismantled, pilgrimages suspended and the precious offerings of pilgrims (as far as they existed) transferred to the royal coffers. The well-known statue, which was dark in colour (possibly due to the burning of pilgrim candles), was unceremoniously thrown upon a bonfire in 1538, along with Our Lady of Walsingham and other images.

It was not until 1885 that the Catholic Church managed to establish a mission in Harlesden, dedicated to 'Our Lady of Willesden'. The first priest was Fr Bernard Ward, who would later become President of St Edmund's, Ware and first Bishop of Brentwood. Like so many suburban parishes, Mass was first offered in a private house until a temporary chapel was opened. In 1892 a new statue of Our Lady of Willesden was commissioned, carved from a piece of wood from an old oak overlooking the original shrine, and blessed by Cardinal Vaughan.

In 1903 annual pilgrimages to Willesden were formally started with the help of the Guild of Our Lady of Ransom. As one newspaper reported in 1908, 'the League of the Cross kept guard as usual, acolytes, cross-bearers, Ransomers, men and women, parishioners, school children, the girls in white, all with their distinctive banners, the excellent band of St Joseph's Orphanage, North Hyde, preceded the statue of Our Lady of Willesden, escorted by Children of Mary in their picturesque blue cloaks and white veils, and these were followed by the Confraternity of the Blessed Sacrament, St Stephen's Guild, and the clergy'. Such a strong display of local Catholic strength was likely to cause a reaction and, we are told, 'the Protestant Alliance emissaries showed their customary execrable taste and native intolerance by planting their rostrum at the end of the street and trying to lash themselves into an artificial fury'.

A beautiful Romanesque church was finally opened in 1931 as both parish church and a National Shrine. Our Lady of Willesden's greatest hour came during the Marian Year of 1954, when some 60,000 pilgrims visited the shrine. On 3 October 1954 a Marian pageant was held at Wembley Stadium in front of a crowd of 94,000. The climax of the celebrations came when Cardinal Bernard Griffin crowned the statue of Our Lady and she was carried back in procession to Willesden.

The founder of Opus Dei, St Josemaria Escriva, sometimes visited Willesden during his trips to London. On 15 August 1958 he made a private pilgrimage to the shrine, where he re-consecrated Opus Dei to the name of Mary (as he did every year). He returned on 17 August 1962, this time with his future successor, the Servant of God Alvaro del Portillo. They recited the Holy Rosary and bought some images of the statue to distribute to members of Opus Dei in Hampstead. Willesden can thus claim two saints among its pilgrims—a rare feat for a British shrine.

As already mentioned, Willesden has a new prominence today—not only because of its links with our Catholic past but also because of its location in the midst of one of the world's largest and most ethnically diverse cities. As Pope Francis put it, 'the Lord entrusts us to the Mother's hands, full of love and tenderness, so that we feel her support in dealing with and overcoming the problems along our human and Christian journey'. In the midst of all the joys and sorrows of urban life, Mary is there protecting and interceding for her children and leading them to her Son.

THE EAST OF ENGLAND

ANMER, NORFOLK

The Jesuits of Anmer Hall

Anmer Hall occasionally appears in the press because it is (at the time of writing) the private country home of the Prince and Princess of Wales, formerly the Duke and Duchess of Cambridge. If few have been there, many flock each year to Sandringham House, two miles away, which was purchased by the future Edward VII in 1862 and has been a favourite of many recent royals. Many princes and princesses have been baptised in the ornately decorated church in its grounds, and it is there that both George V and George VI died.

At first glance, Anmer Hall could easily be dismissed as a comfortable ten bedroomed country retreat with limited historical interest, beyond the fact that it was built in 1802 and passed into royal hands in 1898. It has had many different residents over the years but our interest is with the family who lived in an older house on the site during the reign of Elizabeth I. Several future Jesuit priests grew up there, including St Henry Walpole, one of the Forty Martyrs of England and Wales.

The Walpole family owned around fifty square miles in this part of Norfolk. There were Walpoles at Houghton, Herpley and Docking; a large house at the first of these was later built by Robert Walpole, our first prime minister. In 1575 Christopher Walpole of Docking purchased Anmer Hall and moved in with his large family. That they were of Catholic tendencies is revealed by the fact that four sons—Henry, Richard, Michael and Christopher—and a cousin, Edward, became Jesuits.

The most famous of their number, St Henry Walpole, was educated at the grammar school in Norwich and then at Peterhouse, Cambridge. He entered Gray's Inn and seemed intent on a comfortable legal career. However, at the end of 1581 he attended the public disputation between the recently arrested Jesuit, St Edmund Campion, and various distinguished Protestant divines, and on 1 December witnessed the priest's execution at Tyburn. Henry was splashed by the Jesuit's blood, which proved to be a moment of conversion. He felt called to continue Campion's mission.

Henry published a poem *An Epitaph of the Life and Death of ... Edmund Campion*:

> His quartered limbs shall join with joy again,
> And rise a body brighter than the sun,
> Your bloody malice tormented him in vain,
> For every wrench some glory hath him won.
> And every drop of blood, which he did spend,
> Hath reaped a joy, which never shall have end.

It was published anonymously and unsurprisingly attracted the attention of the authorities. The printer was fined and had his ears cut off; Walpole, meanwhile, went into hiding at Anmer Hall. Shortly afterwards he walked from Anmer to Newcastle, boarded a ship and escaped overseas, entering the English College, then at Rheims, in July 1582. The following year he moved to the Venerable English College, Rome, whose protomartyr, St Ralph Sherwin, had suffered with Campion. Henry was eventually ordained a priest in Paris on 17 December 1588.

He did not return home immediately but served the English and Irish Catholics who were fighting for the Spanish flag under Colonel William Stanley. Bearing arms for a Catholic power was an obvious career choice for those whose adhesion to the old Faith closed professional doors. However, when the Dutch town of Flushing (Vlissingen) was captured by the English at the end of 1589, Henry was captured. It was only because his family at Anmer were able to pay a ransom that he was freed in January 1590.

After spending time at Tournai (Belgium) and Valladolid (Spain), Henry was finally sent on the English Mission in December 1593, together with two companions. They intended to land on the Norfolk coast, not far from the Walpole estates, but bad weather drove the ship northwards, and so they landed at Flamborough Head—the north of England's only chalk cliffs—near Bridlington (East Riding of Yorkshire). Resting at an inn in Kilham, ten miles inland, Henry was betrayed by a fellow passenger and arrested. Taken to York Castle and then the Tower of London, he was interrogated and tortured fourteen times over a long period but refused to endanger the lives of his supporters and co-workers. The Jesuit inscribed his name into the stone walls of the Salt Tower, along with those of St Peter, St Paul and the Latin Doctors of the Church—they can still be seen today.

At the beginning of 1595 he was brought back to York for his trial. The result was a foregone conclusion, though Henry put his legal training into practice: he argued that the law only applied to priests who had not given themselves up within three days of arrival. Yet he had only been arrested less than a day after landing on English soil.

Nevertheless, on refusing to take the Act of Supremacy, he was condemned to death solely for being a priest and a Jesuit, he was hanged, drawn and quartered at Knavesmire—the York Tyburn—on 17 April, along with Blessed Alexander Rawlins. The executioner pushed him off the gallows ladder before he could finish the *Ave Maria*.

What of the other Jesuit members of the Walpole family? Michael wrote several treatises, corresponded with St Robert Bellarmine and ended his days at Seville. Christopher, who had been converted by the ministry of Fr John Gerard in Norfolk and Suffolk, became spiritual director at the English College, Valladolid.

Richard studied at the Venerable English College, Rome, then helped set up the English College in Seville, and joined the Society of Jesus in 1596. He was accused of a ridiculous conspiracy in 1598 by an English seafarer, Edward Squire (or Squier), who had been captured by the Spanish and brought to Seville. While imprisoned by the Inquisition, he toyed with becoming a Catholic and met with Richard, though the Jesuit doubted his sincerity. On returning to England, Squire alleged that 'he had received from Father Walpole a poisonous powder in a bladder, by sprinkling which upon the pommel of the queen's saddle (which might be easily effected by perforating the bladder), she might get it upon her hands, and thence by chance her nose and mouth, and thus cause death'. Similarly, he was told to poison the Earl of Essex's chair. On hearing of the allegations in the comparative safety of Seville, Richard dismissed them as 'the idle dreams of a silly fool'; they were, however, taken seriously, and Squire was executed for his part in the plot, though he recanted his confession on the scaffold.

A cousin, Edward Walpole, also joined the Society. He had long been attracted to the Catholic Faith and the decisive moment came around 1585 when he received a letter from Henry, which he felt was 'dictated by the Spirit of Truth': 'this letter was handed to Edward while sitting at table, who opened and read it there, and was so overcome by his feelings that, unable to repress or conceal them, he instantly rose from table and retired to a room alone, where falling upon his knees, with a loud voice and floods of tears, he acknowledged himself vanquished, begged mercy of God for so long resisting His grace, and yielded himself a conquest to the truth of the Catholic Church'. He was disowned by his family, even though he was the son and heir of his father, John Walpole of Houghton, and he went to Rome for the priesthood. He was ordained in 1592 and joined the Jesuits. Despite being outlawed under Elizabeth, between 1598 and his death in 1637 ministered quietly in England, using the name 'Rich'. Interestingly, he was pardoned in 1605, which meant he would have inherited his family estates on his mother's death seven years later. Nevertheless, he surrendered these to his brother, through whom they descended to Sir Robert the prime minister, and the earls of Orford.

Such are the twists and turns of English history that future monarchs now use the house where these future Jesuits—and alleged conspirators—once resided. Apparently, the saintly Jesuit still watches over its modern inhabitants. It is said his ghost wanders the gardens and that he can be heard calling when the strong Norfolk winds blow. When the royals moved to Anmer in 2014, it was suggested that Prince George would have a phantom friend (or, should we say, heavenly intercessor?), and the *Daily Express* revealed that the attitude of the royals was that 'no old home would be complete without its ghost'.

BUCKDEN, CAMBRIDGESHIRE

Buckden Towers

The Great North Road, now largely covered by the A1, is one of our principal thoroughfares. Traditionally running between London's Smithfield Market and Edinburgh, it is full of history and legend. It has seen magnificent processions, acted as the sinews of trade and commerce, connected towns and villages and borne the tread of thousands of men and women, most now long forgotten by posterity. Dick Turpin is even supposed to have galloped along it from London to York in just fifteen hours on his trusty 'Brown Bess', although historians now think this feat was performed instead by an earlier highwayman who gloried in the name of 'Swift Nick'.

The author found himself one lazy summer day following in the hoof-steps of 'Swift Nick', driving up the Great North Road to attend a Deanery Day of Recollection. As we reached the Cambridgeshire village of Buckden, we drove past several exclusive boutiques and up-market pubs, and then saw our destination: a red-brick Tudor palace, next to the medieval parish church, complete with a magnificent knot garden. It seemed as if we were doing a recollection at Hampton Court.

Buckden Towers is now a retreat centre run by the Claretian Missionaries. It was left by its last owner to the Bishop of Northampton to use for charitable purposes and transferred to the Claretians in 1956. The property was by then partly ruined and much had to be done to make it inhabitable and fit for purpose. For many years it served as a junior seminary and the chapel dedicated to St Hugh of Lincoln serves as the parish church.

A board in the gatehouse reveals its distinguished heritage. Between 1186 and 1838 Buckden Towers was as an important residence of the bishops of Lincoln, conveniently situated on the Great North Road between London and Lincoln. In the Middle Ages the diocese was particularly large and cumbersome, stretching from the Humber to the Thames; after the Reformation some of its territory was sensibly taken away to form the new sees of Oxford and Peterborough. Buckden's visitors include saints, monarchs and writers: Henry III in 1248, Edward I in 1291, Henry VIII and his doomed fifth wife in 1541 and Samuel Pepys in 1667.

Two visitors stand out. The first was St Hugh, the saintly Carthusian who became Bishop of Lincoln in 1186 and who was celebrating

Mass at Buckden one day when something strange and miraculous occurred. According to Adam of Eynsham, at the elevation 'God in His mercy deigned to open the eyes of a certain monk and showed him Christ in the likeness of a small child in the chaste hands of the venerable and holy bishop. Although very tiny, the child was very lovely and of a supernatural brilliance and whiteness beyond man's imagination'. On another visit an exasperated rural dean brought him a lady who claimed prophetic powers but whenever challenged entered into a 'flood of abuse'. The saint dealt with her gently but firmly and, we read, 'the familiar spirit which had before possessed her for evil purposes deserted her'. After St Hugh's death in London in 1200 his body rested overnight at Buckden as it made its slow journey along the Great North Road to Lincoln.

Another sorrowful procession reached the Towers in July 1533 when Catherine of Aragon was brought here with the remnants of her household. Since leaving Court in October 1531, she had lived variously at Rickmansworth, Hatfield, Hertford, Enfield and Ampthill. Despite having had her marriage to Henry 'annulled' by the Archbishop of Canterbury and been replaced by Anne Boleyn, Catherine was still appealing to Rome when she arrived at Buckden. She refused to consider extreme measures involving force or armed rebellion but she must have been buoyed up by public opinion, which was largely on her side. There were even reports that the crowds had refused to cheer or take off their hats during Anne's coronation procession in May 1533.

Perhaps nervous of this support on the ground and the visits she received at Buckden from her supporters, the Duke of Suffolk was deputed in December 1533 to remove the queen—or 'princess dowager', as she was officially called—to Somersham, a more discreet location. However, he found himself hitting a brick wall. He resorted to threats and strong language and insisted that her companions start referring to her by her new title. When one of her chaplains, Blessed Thomas Abel, refused to do this, he was locked up in the gatehouse at Buckden. He was eventually released but soon found himself in the Tower of London for supporting the treasonable prophecies of the 'Maid of Kent' regarding Henry's marriage. He was eventually hanged, drawn and quartered at Smithfield in 1540.

Despite the pressure, Catherine refused to move, fearing Somersham to be so damp that it would cause her death. She locked herself into her room and told the duke, 'if you wish to take me with you, you must break down the door'. Outside a threatening crowd of villagers had gathered, 'weeping and cursing to see such cruelty'. Suffolk realised that he was defeated, at least for now: 'we find her', he wrote, 'the most obstinate woman that may be'. In May 1534 Catherine was finally moved to nearby Kimbolton Castle, where she would die two years later.

The queen's courageous showdown with the duke is depicted on a stained-glass window at Buckden, along with scenes of her as 'Patron of Humanist scholars, talking to St Thomas More', a 'frequent pilgrim to Walsingham' and refusing to swear the Oath of Succession a second time, just before her departure from Buckden. She looked down on us as we celebrated Mass, in the modern chapel that stands on the site of the chapel that both she and St Hugh would have known.

In the sacristy, there is a copy of the last letter that Catherine wrote to Henry—a message of heroic forgiveness and enduring love: 'My most dear Lord, King and Husband, the hour of my death now drawing on, the tender love I owe you forceth me, my case being such, to commend myself to you, and to put you in remembrance with a few words of the health and safeguard of your soul which you ought to prefer before all worldly matters, and before the care and pampering of your body, for the which you have cast me into many calamities and yourself into many troubles. For my part, I pardon you everything, and I wish to devoutly pray God that He will pardon you also... Lastly, I make this vow, that mine eyes desire you above all things. Katharine the Quene.'

CLARE, SUFFOLK

A Priory Come Back to Life

The Suffolk village of Clare sits on the River Stour and provides the usual collection of tea shops, pubs and a large antiques centre. This makes for an excellent day trip but there is no immediate evidence of the place having been an important centre of power in the Middle Ages, except perhaps for the ruined castle and the splendid parish church.

The name 'Clare' may derive from the clear nature of the water running through one of its streams. William the Conqueror gave the land to Richard fitz Gilbert, one of his closest supporters, and the Clare family, as it became known, maintained its close links to the royal family. Two of Richard's sons were present when William Rufus was killed in the New Forest and some have accused them of staging an assassination; nevertheless, the family gained several prestigious titles and eventually gave their name to Clare College, Cambridge, founded in 1326 by Elizabeth de Burgh, heiress to the family's fortunes, who lived (as her forebears did) at the castle of Clare. It used to be thought that County Clare was also named after them though it probably derives from an Irish place name.

Medieval Clare was thus the seat of a powerful and wealthy family. It was also a religious centre, for the Clare family founded the first Augustinian house in England in 1248, just south of the castle on the road to London. It would be first of the thirty-four medieval houses established by the Augustinians in England.

The priory (as it was known) acquired a reputation for learning and holiness, and its prestige is shown by several of the high profile burials in the church. These include Joan of Acre, daughter of Edward I and Eleanor of Castile, who was born in Acre while her parents were crusading in the Holy Land. She married into the Clare family and died at Clare in 1307; it was said that her body remained incorrupt and miracles were claimed at her tomb. Another royal burial was Lionel of Antwerp, Duke of Clarence. He is hardly a household name but this prince, towering over his contemporaries at over seven feet tall, was the son of Edward III and the House of York later based their claim to the throne on his line of descent; he is a direct ancestor of the monarch.

Two friars of Clare took part in the Peasants' Revolt (1381). At the Reformation the community was divided. It is perhaps unsurprising that some were influenced by the writings of Martin Luther, a fellow Augustinian, while others were staunch opponents. One of these was John Stokes, who publicly challenged a local clergyman, Matthew Parker (later to become Archbishop of Canterbury), when he preached a sermon full of Protestant sentiment in the parish church at Clare. As a result, Stokes was imprisoned by order of Thomas Cromwell. The priory was duly suppressed and passed into private ownership. Remnants of this can still be seen today: many of the buildings are coloured pink, looking decidedly unmonastic, and there is an affectionate plaque to the house gardener of a hundred years ago, one William Lewis.

The memory of the friars never completely disappeared and, as so often happened, became mixed up with legend. At the beginning of the last century a story concerning one friar, Hugh of Bury, that had been passed down locally was finally written down. According to the tale, Hugh had pawned some of the priory's treasures but was desperate to repay his debts in case he was found out by the authorities. One evening a man, dressed as a friar, visited him and suggested a solution. Hugh, who worked as sacristan, should hide his candles and ask for new ones, saying that the old stock had been eaten by mice. He could then sell the surplus candles. The only catch was this: he should keep the very first candle and, if this was ever burnt down, the mysterious visitor would claim Hugh as his own for all eternity. The desperate friar agreed and for a time his situation improved. However, his various misdemeanours were gradually uncovered and he was put on a diet of bread and water as penance. One day he was searching for salt for the evening meal when he saw a cooked fowl sitting in the kitchen. He put his candle to one side—it was the one that he had carefully retained—and succumbed to temptation. As he enjoyed his forbidden meal the rest of the community arrived and Hugh fled, leaving the candle burning. The end is perhaps predictable. As the candle finally burnt out, the friars heard a ghastly scream and found Hugh dead at the foot of the stairs, with a look of horror on his face, his flesh seared and a smell of sulphur hanging in the air. The bloodstain at the bottom of the stairs was never successfully removed; some say it is still there.

Whatever we might think of the irremovable bloodstain, the religious nature of the place was equally firmly fixed. One of the last lay owners, Lady Helena May, told her daughter, who had recently become a Catholic: 'I depend upon you to bring about the return of the friars to Clare Priory'. She then took her medal of Our Lady and buried it at the door of the old Infirmary. After her death, the Augustinians returned to Clare in 1953. This was made possible when the property was unexpectedly vacated, as it happens, on the feast of Our Lady of Good Counsel. This is a devotion dear to the Augustinians, who run the original shrine at Genazzano near Rome, and a corner of Clare is set aside as a shrine to Our Lady under this title.

The friars remain to this day, running retreats and workshops, and providing pastoral care to local Catholics. A new church was consecrated in 2015, its contemporary design sympathetically using the medieval walls and, like so many East Anglian churches, making effective use of space and light. All around lie the old priory ruins, a silent witness to centuries of prayer and Christian life. Like Aylesford, Clare is a prime example of a medieval religious house that was dissolved and then came back to life.

ELY, CAMBRIDGESHIRE, AND THE FENS

The Holy Land of the English

Today it is fertile farmland, dotted with picturesque villages. Only a few centuries ago it was a watery wilderness of low-lying creeks, meres, mudflats and lakes, studded with uplands—so-called 'isles' and 'edges'. It was populated by a fiercely independent people, who made a living through wild fowling, reed cutting, fishing and eel catching. The topography was unforgiving—malaria was a common problem and locals sometimes used wooden stilts to move around through the liquid landscape. It was a land of mists and mystery; a place apart; and the final region to resist the Norman conquerors, under the leadership of Hereward the Wake. When plans were made to drain these wetlands from the seventeenth century, a similar tradition of defiance was exhibited by the 'Fen Tigers', desperate to cling on to their way of life.

The Fens cover well over a thousand square miles of Lincolnshire, Cambridgeshire, and Norfolk—once the largest inland area of water in western Europe. Despite its wildness, the area has long been populated, as shown by Flag Fen, a Bronze Age settlement near Peterborough, and the Roman road that was built through the region. In the Middle Ages the Fens became a centre of monasticism, leading some to call it the 'Holy Land of the English'. This monastic geography included the important foundations at Crowland, Ely, Peterborough, Ramsey and Thorney. The Fens were seen as an East Anglian desert, where those consecrated to God could find peace and solitude. Yet, there was also a more practical dimension: the potential for cultivation and wealth, from the rich peat and the life within the waters, supporting the monastic rhythm of 'prayer and work'.

Thus, Ramsey (Cambridgeshire) was an important centre of learning and manuscript production. It housed the shrine of St Felix and was briefly the home of St Abbo of Fleury, a French monastic reformer; all that now remains of this enormously wealthy abbey is the gatehouse. Thorney Abbey (Cambridgeshire) boasted a whole pantheon of shrines of the old English saints, including St Botolph and St Benedict Biscop. Crowland (Lincolnshire) was built around the reputation of another Saxon saint, Guthlac, who gave up the life of a noble warrior for that of a monk and lived the life of a hermit in an ancient barrow, which had partially been excavated by treasure-hunters. Here he lived for fifteen years, spending his time praying, giving counsel to visitors, and fighting demons. Indeed, the Fens were regarded into modern times as a place of ghosts, will-o'-the-wisps and bogeys: Marie Clothilde Balfour, a Scottish folklorist, moved to north Lincolnshire in 1887 and wrote 'I do not think that elsewhere in England one could nowadays find such a childlike certainty of unseen things or such an unquestioning belief in supernatural powers'.

The abbey at Peterborough (Cambridgeshire)—converted into a cathedral at the Reformation—is best known for its magnificent west front, with its three large arches. Such architectural glories perhaps made up for the lack of a saint's shrine, though it claimed an impressive collection of relics. Today pilgrims make their way there to pray at the tomb of a Tudor queen, undoubtedly a woman of virtue: Catherine of Aragon. Another tragic monarch, Mary, Queen of Scots, was initially buried at Peterborough before being moved to Westminster Abbey.

Most famous of all the Fenland sanctuaries, of course, is Ely, its cathedral—with its wondrous octagonal lantern—acting as the 'Ship of the Fens'. This is the city of St Etheldreda (or, more correctly, Æthelthryth). Her story is well-known: the daughter of King Anna of East Anglia—and therefore great niece of Rædwald, possibly the king buried at Sutton Hoo—she married twice and claimed to have preserved her virginity. After the death of her first husband, the ealdorman Tondberht, she inherited land around the Isle of Ely. Her second husband, King Ecgfrith of Northumbria, reluctantly granted her desire to withdraw from the court for the cloister. After a short time at Coldingham, the saint founded a double monastery—of both men and women—on her 'estate' at Ely in 663. She was supported in this intiative by the great St Wilfrid, who she had known in Northumbria. Seven years later she died as a result of a tumour on her throat, which she blamed on the decadent necklaces she wore in her youth. When her tomb was opened sixteen years later, the body was found to be incorrupt and her throat perfectly healed.

By this time, the abbess was her sister, St Sexburga. Indeed, the descendants of King Anna formed a remarkable saintly dynasty, many of them buried at Ely. There were the holy sisters Etheldreda, Sexburga, Withburga and Ethelburga. St Sexburga's daughter was St Erminilda, Ely's fourth abbess. And one should not forget King Anna's queen, St Hereswitha, who as a widow became a nun at Chelles, across the Channel, or St Wendreda, a probable relation, who lived a holy life and worked miracles at March (Cambridgeshire).

St Etheldreda herself was the most popular Anglo-Saxon female saint, partly because her life was included in Bede's famous *History* and partly because Ely became an important centre of monastic reform in the tenth century (by which time the saint's original monastery had been long-destroyed by Vikings). Devotion ended abruptly at the Reformation and the scars of this tumultuous time are clearly seen in the majestic Lady Chapel—the largest one of its kind in England—with its empty niches and headless statues.

Nevertheless, some treasures relating to the saint survived. In the eighteenth century some late medieval panels depicting the life of St Etheldreda were found in a cottage in Ely, having been adapted into cupboard doors. They may originally have been located in the cathedral and now are preserved in the collections of the Society of Antiquaries in London. Likewise, the relic of the saint's left hand was saved from destruction and preserved by a Catholic family who lived in a farmhouse near Arundel (West Sussex). It later passed to the Duke of Norfolk and then to the Dominican sisters at Stone (Staffordshire). In 1953 it was given to St Etheldreda's Catholic church in Ely, on Egremont Street; a portion was also given to St Etheldreda's church in London's Ely Place.

The visitor to Ely should certainly take a stroll to Egremont Street and the charming 1903 church. Built in the Decorated style, it feels much older and, as one venerates St Etheldreda's hand, there is a real connection with past pilgrims who journeyed across mere and creek to this Holy Land of the English.

GREAT DUNMOW, ESSEX

A Flitch of Bacon

I remember the first time I saw my maternal grandfather. Sadly it was not in the flesh, since he died in 1955, long before I was born, but by courtesy of YouTube. Here I unexpectedly found some grainy footage of an event he was involved in back in 1922. He played the part of 'Judge' in a recreation of the Dunmow Flitch organised by the Catholic parish in Ilford (Essex) and, so I am told, by playing this part he met his future wife, the daughter of one of the barristers in the mock trial. An eighteenth-century print of the Flitch, now presiding over the presbytery landing, has long been in the family.

What on earth was the Dunmow Flitch? Even to this day, at Great Dunmow in Essex, a gammon or flitch of bacon is awarded to married couples who could prove that in 'twelvemonth and a day' they have 'not wisht themselves unmarried again'.

The origins of this strange custom go back before the Reformation to the Augustinian priory at nearby Little Dunmow. The Victorians thought that a local worthy, Reginald FitzWalter, and his wife had disguised themselves as peasants and went to the prior to receive his blessing a year after their marriage. Impressed by the couple's devotion, the prior gave them a flitch of bacon that was sitting in the priory kitchen. Revealing his true identity, Reginald granted land to the Augustinian canons on condition that a bacon was given to couples who had not repented of their marriage for a whole year.

This charming legend probably owes more to the novelist, William Harrison Ainsworth, who did much to revive the custom in the 1850s, than it does to historical fact. The exact origins of the Flitch are unknown. It may have been a way of the Augustinian canons promoting the sanctity of matrimony, at a time when marriages could be entered into casually and often without the blessing of a priest. Perhaps, also, there was a link to the FitzWalters, the leading family in Dunmow, and a grant of land to the canons.

All that exists of the priory is the former Lady Chapel, now used as the parish church. There are several hints that this was once an important church, such as its medieval tombs with high quality alabaster effigies. Of particular interest is the tomb of Matilda FitzWalter, said to have been poisoned by 'Bad King John' after she refused his advances — and one of several candidates for the original 'Maid Marian' of Robin Hood fame! Although the great architectural historian, Nikolaus Pevsner, disappointingly describes the tomb as being of 'an unknown woman', Dunmow is clearly full of romantic associations.

The awarding of a flitch of bacon to faithful couples was not only found at Dunmow. A similar custom seems to have been observed at Whichnoure (Wychnor) in Staffordshire, where the manor had been granted to Sir Philip de Somerville in 1336 on condition that he hung a flitch of bacon in his hall 'to be given to every man or woman who demanded it a year and a day after the marriage, upon their swearing they would not have changed for none other'. It was awarded only occasionally up until the eighteenth century, although for many years an imitation flitch made of wood was kept in the hall.

Ancient rituals involving a flitch of bacon have also been discovered overseas, in places as far flung as Rennes (France) and Vienna (Austria). Some scholars have suggested that they go back to pre-Christian practices concerning Freyr, the Norse god of fertility, harmony and prosperity, who was often depicted riding a wild boar.

Whatever its origins, the Dunmow Flitch was mentioned by Chaucer's Wife of Bath and the first recorded winner was Richard Wright of Bawburgh, Norfolk in 1445. Two sharply pointed stones lying near the church door at Little Dunmow are thought to have been used in the ceremony, when the claimants knelt down and took an oath. Writing in the *Brentwood Diocesan Magazine* in 1921, Fr Field, the Catholic parish priest of Dunmow, noted that initially women were notably absent from the ceremony: 'the gammon was conferred as a reward for the patience of the enduring husband. It appears that the wife was not even present at the trial'! Fortunately, as the custom developed, both husband and wife came to be involved.

The Flitch disappeared at the Reformation and was revived in 1701 by Sir Richard May, who owned the former priory. The couples who presented themselves for the award were tried by a jury of six bachelors and six spinsters and, if successful, were carried in procession through the village, along with the flitch of bacon. The ceremony died out once again, to be revived at Great Dunmow in the 1850s, thanks partly to William Harrison Ainsworth, who wrote a novel entitled *The Flitch of Bacon, or the Custom of Dunmow, a Tale of English Home Life* (1854) and acted himself as judge. And so it has continued ever since; nowadays it takes place every leap year and is open to couples from across the world. Queen Elizabeth II and Prince Philip were awarded the flitch at their Golden Wedding in 1997. Having been presented to the Palace, it was returned to Great Dunmow so that it could be shared by seventeen local couples also celebrating this landmark anniversary.

There is a fascinating Catholic footnote to this custom. In the 1920s Canon Patrick Palmer, parish priest of Ilford and famously responsible for some 1,377 conversions to the Catholic Faith in fifty-two years of ministry, decided to introduce the Flitch as part of his Whitsun Fete. This caused consternation at Dunmow, one inhabitant saying 'You might as well take Barnet Fair to Southampton, or row the Varsity boat-race on the Clyde, as take the Flitch Trial to Ilford'. Another local is recorded as commenting: 'Oi down't reckon oi know where the ole Ilford plice is; oi count that must be somewhere out furrin. Ilford? Never he'erd tell on't'. Yet, the Flitch did not actually take place at Dunmow between 1913 and 1930 and the Ilford ceremony served to fill the gap.

It was a clever move by Canon Palmer: promoting marriage and family life in his parish, reclaiming the Flitch as a pre-Reformation Catholic custom and adding an enjoyable event to a day already marked by numerous sideshows and sporting competitions. It was the chief fundraising event of the parish year and received attention not only in the local but the national press. In fact, my grandfather only served as a judge several times. By 1925 the organisers managed to get a much bigger name in that role: one Gilbert Keith Chesterton. Other years saw the involvement of 'celebrities' such as the novelist Jeffrey Fernol (1924), Sir George Hamilton JP, later to become Baronet of Ilford (1929) and the comedian Will Hay (1932). The parish produced many vocations to the priesthood and it is interesting that the father of the future Cardinal Heenan sat on the jury at the Flitch.

There was much hilarity and banter. In 1932, my great-grandfather, Charles Edwin Grigsby, acting as counsel for the claimants, is reported as saying: 'Man has many faults, women only two: there's nothing right they say and nothing right they do!' I would, of course, like to publicly distance myself from these comments and trust that many readers might be deserving of a flitch of bacon this coming year.

INGATESTONE, ESSEX

Catholic Families: The Petres

Situated on the old Roman road between London and Colchester, Ingatestone is dominated by the Petre family. Their monuments can be found in the medieval parish church, their name appears on a picturesque row of almshouses and they also built the charming little Catholic church, dedicated to St John the Evangelist and St Erconwald. Even the railway station, linking commuters to London, echoes the style of the Petre's Tudor mansion a short walk away.

Ingatestone Hall was built by the founder of this Essex dynasty, Sir William Petre. He was the son of a Devon farmer who rose to become a trusted adviser and bureaucrat under the very different regimes of Henry VIII and his three children. This was a feat for any courtier but especially for one who remained loyal to the Catholic faith. His pragmatism, though, was shown by the fact that as a young lawyer he closely worked alongside Thomas Cromwell in the Dissolution of the Monasteries, efficiently transferring wealth and property from the monastic orders to private individuals. He himself enjoyed some of the fruits, building up an impressive property portfolio in his native Devon as well as in Essex, where in 1539 he bought the manor of Ingatestone, which had once belonged to the nuns of Barking. Later, under Mary I, he gained a papal dispensation to keep these former monastic properties.

Petre thought the old house at Ingatestone 'scarce mete for a fermor to dwell on' and so he built a modern, redbrick mansion, designed around a courtyard, much of which can still be seen today, though the west wing was destroyed in the nineteenth century. It was one of the first great houses to enjoy a piped water supply and flushing drains fed by local springs. In 1561 Ingatestone was visited by Elizabeth I, who stayed for three days and, together with her courtiers, feasted on five dozen chickens, twenty-seven geese, thirty herons, numerous types of fish, ten cygnets, a dozen gulls, and two dozen egrets.

Ingatestone not only received the queen as honoured guest but also many priests, who exercised their ministry here in secret. The most famous among them was the martyr, St John Payne, who acted as steward and chaplain to Sir William's wife, Lady Petre. He was finally arrested in 1581 and hanged, drawn and quartered the following year at Chelmsford. This secret ministry accounts for at least two hiding holes in the house, built by St Nicholas Owen: one was discovered when some rotten floorboards broke away while some children were playing. After investigation, a secret chamber was revealed, some fourteen feet long, ten feet high, and two feet wide. A twelve-step ladder led down into it and on the sandy floor there were the bones of a bird—perhaps the poor creature had got stuck there or it was food passed to a sheltering priest.

Ingatestone was also blessed to have the presence of one of England's greatest composers, William Byrd. From at least 1586 he was a frequent visitor to both Thorndon and Ingatestone. Seven years later he moved to nearby Stondon Massey, so that he could be near his neighbours. We know that the Petres, like many wealthy families, enjoyed music: in 1589 Lord Petre owned a virginal, lute and viol. Byrd was there that year for the Christmas and New Year celebrations and on his departure five musicians from London were paid for their services. His most famous works, the Masses for three, four and five voices, were written around this period and were probably 'premiered' at Ingatestone. Little could he have guessed that centuries later one of them would be used during a papal Mass at Westminster Cathedral! Byrd's Catholic beliefs were made possible not only by royal favour but also the patronage provided by the Petre family—posterity is thus in their debt.

Sir William is considered the second founder of Exeter College, Oxford, which he endowed with scholarships. It is no accident that in the early part of Elizabeth's reign it was known for its 'popery' and produced two future martyrs, St Ralph Sherwin (the proto-martyr of the Venerable English College, Rome) and Blessed John Cornelius.

As might be expected, several members of the Petre family served as priests or entered the religious life. Bishop Benjamin Petre was Vicar Apostolic of the London District from 1734 to 1758; in his youth he had served as chaplain to Lord Derwentwater and as bishop relied much on his assistant and coadjutor, Richard Challoner. He resided at Ingatestone and on one occasion, as he was in the garden, marching up and down Lime Walk with his breviary, was attacked by robbers. His life was saved by the heroic intervention of a trusty dog, whose ghostly form is said to still patrol Lime Walk. Curiously, although no portrait survives of the bishop, there is a painting at Ingatestone of the dog.

Another notable cleric was Mgr William Petre, 13th Baron Petre, who founded schools at Woburn Park, Surrey (1877–84) and Northwood Park on the Isle of Wight (1884–5). Both attempts were sadly short-lived and, tired out by his labours, he died at the early age of 46. A more lasting memorial, though, was the Petre Library at Downside Abbey, as well as the cloister which bears his name.

The Petres have lived at Ingatestone for fourteen generations. After Sir William left Ingatestone to his wife, John, his son and heir, needed a house of his own and bought nearby Thorndon Hall. This served as the family's principal seat until the house, which by now had been rebuilt in the Palladian style, was gutted by fire in 1878. It was later converted into apartments, while Ingatestone, which had always been used by junior branches of the family, enjoyed a renewal. After the death of the 16th Lord Petre during the First World War, his widow did much to restore the Tudor look and feel to the house.

Ingatestone is full of reminders of the Petre's colourful history. Perhaps most striking are the various family relics in the Long Gallery, including the clothes worn by James Radcliffe, 3rd Earl of Derwentwater, at his execution on Tower Hill in 1716. This staunch Catholic, directly descended from Charles II, had been caught up in the Jacobite Rising from 1715 and condemned to death; on the day of his death the Northern Lights were seen around his seat of Dilston Hall (Northumberland) and called 'Derwentwater's Lights'. His daughter, who married Robert 7th Baron Petre, brought with her these sad relics to Essex. Thankfully times change: her son, the 9th Baron Petre, was a prominent figure in the movement for Catholic Emancipation and was able to receive George III at Thorndon Hall.

Down the generations the Petres have sacrificed much for the Faith and tried to live out their family motto: *Sans Dieu Rien*, Nothing without God.

IPSWICH, SUFFOLK

Our Lady of Ipswich — and Nettuno

Ipswich was a major medieval port, full of churches and hostelries; by Henry VIII's reign it was the kingdom's fifth largest town. It seems a different world from Nettuno, a popular resort on the Tyrrhenian Sea, thirty-seven miles south of Rome, where Allied troops landed in 1944 to begin their advance on the capital. It is strange to see the neat lawns and rows of Portland gravestones so characteristic of the Commonwealth War Graves Commission in this quintessentially Italian setting.

Yet Ipswich and Nettuno are closely linked, thanks to the statue of Our Lady of Grace housed in the large modern basilica and shrine of St Maria Goretti, the twentieth-century 'martyr of chastity'. *Nostra Signora delle Grazie* can be found above the high altar and, according to tradition, was brought to Nettuno from a shipwreck in 1550. The statue, it is said, had been saved by English Catholics and was on its way from Ipswich to Naples.

Our Lady of Grace was originally venerated at All Saints' church, on what became known as Lady Lane in Ipswich. A clear sign of its prestige can be seen by the fact that Edward I's youngest daughter, Elizabeth, married John, Count of Holland, at the shrine on 8 January 1297. Ipswich was a natural location for such an occasion since it had good maritime links with Holland and the shrine was already prestigious. It was also linked to Walsingham many pilgrims passing through Ipswich on their way to 'England's Nazareth'.

Famous pilgrims included Henry VIII, Catherine of Aragon and St Thomas More. The fame of the shrine heightened after the so-called 'Miracle of the Maid of Ipswich' in 1516. Anne, the twelve-year-old daughter of Sir Roger Wentworth of Gosfield (who served as MP for Ipswich), had a vision of the Blessed Virgin. She was taken to the shrine, laid before the statue and cured of her seizures which were seen as demonic. She went on to become a nun. The decades leading up to the Reformation saw the shrine's heyday; the Salutation pub on Carr Street is a surviving hostelry from this time, its name honouring the Annunciation.

Ipswich's most famous son, Cardinal Wolsey, tried to establish a college there that would be the Eton of East Anglia and hoped to link it to the shrine, to heighten both its prestige and revenue. He organised an annual procession on the feast of the Birthday of the

Blessed Virgin; in 1528 it was curtailed by heavy rain. It seemed to be a portent of things to come: his downfall the following year meant these ambitious plans never came to pass. The shrine was suppressed, along with all others, in the spring of 1538. According to Sir Charles Wriothesley, the statues of Our Lady of Ipswich and of Walsingham were burnt at Chelsea 'with all the jewelles that hang about them, at the Kinge's commandment'. Thomas Cromwell's steward recorded that he had received the image with 'nothing about her but two half shoes of silver'—indeed, when the Duke of Norfolk visited Ipswich in August 1483 he left an offering 'to bow on Owr Ladys fote', which seems to have been an important part of the devotion. John Weever, writing a century later, added that the statues from Worcester and Willesden, as well as the Roods of Boxley and Bermondsey, also perished on this bonfire.

So, what are we to believe? Was Our Lady of Ipswich destroyed in the fire at Chelsea in 1538, as is made clear by one contemporary document? Or was it saved—either by loyal Catholics or, even, secretly sold by the agents of Cromwell? Both options are possible. Catholics did hide and rescue some of their treasures, while Cromwell would have been only too aware of the propaganda value of burning a well-known statue.

In 1938 the historian Martin Gillett confirmed that the Nettuno statue was most probably of English origin, although over time changes had been made to it. Interestingly it had two half shoes of English silver, which had been mentioned in the report of Cromwell's steward. During restoration in 1959 an old English inscription was uncovered below Our Lady's right foot: IU? ARET GRATIOSUS (thou art gracious). Once in Italy, SANCTA MARIA, ORA PRO NOBIS was written over it. The statue in Nettuno may indeed be the original statue. An alternative possibility, of course, is that it was one of many medieval English statues present on the continent. Over time and in the light of the Reformation, a narrative could have been created about its rescue from Protestant England, linking it to the country's Catholic past.

The truth, perhaps, will never be known for certain. Our Lady of Grace continues to be beloved by the people of Nettuno. More recently, the shrine of Our Lady of Grace has been restored in the Ipswich church of St Mary-at-Elms, famous for its Tudor tower that may have re-used bricks from Wolsey's ill-fated college. The statue was based on the one at Nettuno and carved by the Suffolk sculptor Robert Mellamphy. A memorial on Lady Lane also commemorates the site of the shrine. England was once full of shrines like this and truly was the 'Dowry of Mary'.

LITTLE WALSINGHAM, NORFOLK

England's Nazareth

The story of Walsingham is well known. The shrine was famous for a reconstruction of the Holy House, where Mary had said her 'yes' to the Archangel Gabriel. The 'original' in Nazareth was eventually transported to Loreto—according to tradition, through the agency of angels—and became a major shrine. Walsingham's copy was based on dimensions revealed to a local noblewoman, Richeldis de Faverches, in a vision or a dream in 1061—long before the sanctuary at Loreto was established. Two possible locations in Walsingham were indicated to Richeldis but attempts to construct the chapel on the first site proved unsuccessful. After praying to the Virgin, she discovered the next morning the completed Holy House, miraculously built in the second place.

To the medieval mind, a replica was no less holy than the original, and thousands of pilgrims flocked each year to 'England's Nazareth', joining their 'yes' to that of Our Lady. The village attracted royal patronage and almost every monarch from the third to the eighth Henry went there on pilgrimage. There were communities of Augustinians and Franciscans, and numerous hostelries such as The Bull (still happily open), The George, The Angel, The Saracen's Head and The Moon and Stars. Relics, such as St Peter's knuckle and a phial of the Blessed Virgin's milk, also attracted pious attention. It was said that pilgrims watching the night skies as they made their way to the shrine referred to the Milky Way as the 'Walsingham Way'—an expression that continued in use until at least the eighteenth century. In Spain, incidentally, it is called 'St James's Way'.

Richeldis herself remains obscured by the mists of time; unusually for a visionary, she was never the centre of a cult. The earliest surviving written version of the legend—the 'Pynson Ballad'—only dates from the fifteenth century. One recent writer, Bill Flint, has even deduced that 'Richeldis' was an honorary title, meaning 'rich and fair' and alluding to the wife of the last Saxon king, Harold Godwinson—Edith 'the Fair' or 'Swan-neck', who owned land in the area.

I once attended a meeting at which England's national shrine was discussed and the eccentric suggestion was made that it should be relocated to a more agreeable location. Perhaps closer to London or at least nearer a motorway. It raises the question, why does the Blessed Virgin choose certain spots as opposed to others. Why Walsingham?

North-west Norfolk may today seem like a remote hinterland, beloved by tourists and the royal family, but it was once one of the wealthiest corners of the country. Nearby King's Lynn was an important port and the gateway to much of Europe. Like Boston and Hull, it was a member of the Hanseatic League, bringing many trading privileges and a cosmopolitan society. It enabled pilgrims from abroad to visit Walsingham—and they came in substantial numbers each year. The village was four miles from the coast—Erasmus referred to the shrine as 'the Virgin by the sea'—and easily accessed by road from many parts of the kingdom.

Moreover, modern pilgrimages sometimes seem rather too easy, compared to the experiences of our forebears. They can be fitted into a day or a weekend, without any prolonged absence from home. Pilgrims sit comfortably in their coaches and cars, sheltered from inclement weather. Rarely is there any element of danger. A visit to Walsingham, though, at least still involves some effort and inconvenience. From London, the journey is a six hour round trip, much of it along country roads. For over a century there was a railway station there but, thanks to Mr Beeching, it was closed in 1964. Part of the old track forms the processional way from the Slipper Chapel into Little Walsingham, and the station buildings were converted into a Russian Orthodox church. In recent years, there has been an impressive revival of walking routes to the shrine, starting variously from London, Ely, Bury St Edmunds, Norwich and Cley-next-the-Sea, and ranging from 16 to 180 miles.

There is, then, an element of a real pilgrimage, of leaving behind the familiar. Even in 1896, a writer referred to Walsingham, with its 'narrow streets and red-roofed houses', as 'one of the most old-fashioned looking places in England'. Its picturesque appearance gives a sense of 'otherness' to modern pilgrims, so many of whom live in bustling cities.

Walsingham also has a long tradition of sanctity. Long before Christianity reached the area, there was a sanctuary dedicated to the Roman god Mercury—and, perhaps before that, an Iron Age shrine to a Celtic deity. Coins, rings, brooches and enamelled boxes have all been found in the area, attesting that this was a place of prayer and petition.

Mary has a tendency of being connected to out of the way places. The grotto at Lourdes, used as the town's rubbish heap. Fatima, a largely unknown backwater until the 1917 apparitions. Nazareth—can anything good come from there? Little Walsingham—without the pretensions of nearby 'Great' Walsingham—stands in this tradition. There are many reasons why Mary should have graced Walsingham with her presence!

The shrine was, of course, destroyed at the Reformation; the Augustinian priory closed in 1536 and the statue probably burnt, along with other Marian images, at Chelsea in 1538. A group of locals attempted to resist these draconian changes, which affected not only their souls but their livelihoods. Inspired by the Pilgrimage of Grace, the ringleaders were captured and executed before the uprising could be effected: Nicholas Mileham, the sub-prior at Walsingham, and George Guisborough, a yeoman, were hanged, drawn and quartered at a place still called the Martyrs' Field on 30 April 1537.

Walsingham continued to haunt the English imagination. St Philip Howard, the Earl of Arundel and a martyr, famously wrote:

> Weep, weep, O Walsingham, whose days are nights,
> Blessings turned to blasphemies, holy deeds to despites.
> Sin is where Our Lady sat, Heaven turned is to hell,
> Satan sits where our Lord did sway, Walsingham, oh farewell.

William Byrd and John Bull wrote variations on what was known as the 'Walsingham Air' and it is thought that Ophelia's song in Act IV of *Hamlet* refers to this ballad.

After several centuries of silence came restoration. Interest in the Middle Ages was awakened and the traditions of pilgrimage explored. Agnes Strickland, a popular historical writer, produced *The Pilgrims of Walsingham, or Tales of the Middle Ages: An Historical Romance* (1835), loosely based on Chaucer. Writers and pastors began to rediscover the Catholic roots of England and, at its heart, devotion to Our Lady. A shrine of Our Lady of Walsingham was erected in 1897, with papal permission, at the church of the Annunciation, King's Lynn, and the same year the Guild of Our Lady of Ransom organised the first pilgrimage to Little Walsingham. Around the same time, Charlotte Boyd, a local Catholic, purchased the medieval Slipper Chapel at Houghton St Giles. Most recently used as a cow shed, it had been the last of the wayside chapels for pilgrims and the place where they slipped off their shoes as they approached the holy shrine. It was restored to Catholic use and in 1934 officially became the Catholic shrine. Meanwhile, a magnificent Anglican shrine was built in the village, thanks to the vision of the redoubtable Fr Alfred Hope Patten.

Nearly a thousand years after its foundation, Walsingham goes from strength to strength. The statue was solemnly crowned in the Marian

Year of 1954 and taken to Wembley Stadium for the Mass celebrated by St John Paul II in 1982. In 2005 a new Catholic church was opened in Little Walsingham itself and ten years later the shrine was declared a minor basilica—joining a select list of English churches, including the cathedrals at Westminster and Birmingham, and Downside Abbey. Tens of thousands of pilgrims continue to travel there each year, despite any inconvenience, and such is the make-up of twenty-first-century English Catholicism that the most numerous groups come from the Tamil and Syro-Malabar communities. Richeldis—and Our Lady—must look down with much approval.

LONG MELFORD, SUFFOLK

The Glory of Long Melford

It is easy to see how the village of Long Melford got its name. We parked in the first available space on what looked like the High Street. We returned to the car shortly afterwards once we realised that the village stretched along an extremely long road and the church was still a mile away.

It is the church of the Holy Trinity that is the glory of Long Melford. Huge and lofty for a humble parish, its lay-out resembles that of a cathedral and its large windows fill the interior with East Anglian light. 'The slenderness of the piers of the arcades', wrote John Seymour in 1970, 'the delicacy of the moulding of the arches, the loftiness of the clerestories which they support, the high proportion of glass to stone: this is most skilful engineering—not just architecture ... Stone building can be carried no further than this'.

The magnificent building is evidence that the village was once one of the wealthiest places in England and, indeed, Europe, thanks to the thriving cloth trade. The church was rebuilt in the perpendicular style at the height of Long Melford's wealth, just forty years before Henry's break with Rome. Unlike many of our medieval churches, it was built in one go, though the tower is a later replacement. Much of the original decoration has disappeared, of course, but it takes only a little effort to imagine how it would have looked on the eve of the Reformation.

The church contains one of the finest collections of medieval stained glass in the country—one of the advantages of a large building is that the iconoclasts were unable to reach the higher windows. The glass has been moved to new positions since then, forming a veritable picture gallery of saints and local worthies. The depiction of Elizabeth Talbot, Duchess of Norfolk, is said to have been the inspiration for John Tenniel's Duchess in his illustrations for *Alice in Wonderland*.

One of the smallest pieces of stained glass is the most intriguing—the so-called 'Hare Window'. It is hard to make out due to its size and the damage inflicted by Cromwell's men but it is said to symbolise the Trinity: the hares are connected to each other by their ears so that there is a total of three ears between them. The origin of this symbol is unclear. It seems an obscure and rather irreverent way of explaining the most sublime of mysteries, but then St Patrick did use the humble shamrock (perhaps with greater effect?).

Walk down the north aisle and you find a large chantry chapel where Mass was once offered for the Cloptons, one of the great local families. It is one of several chantries that once existed here. Entrance is via a small vestibule, rather grandly called the 'priest's room', where there are the remains of a fireplace. I imagined the chantry priest warming himself as he prepared himself for the sacred mysteries.

The chantry would have originally been decorated with images and inscriptions, and the walls still show verses by John Lydgate, the poet-monk of Bury St Edmunds, peering through the whitewash. Above the altar, for example, you would have read:

> Behold O man lift up thine eye and see
> What mortal pain I suffered for your trespass
> With piteous voice I cry and say to thee
> Behold my wounds, behold my bloody face ...

The chantry's east window has a beautiful depiction of a 'Lily Crucifix' with Christ crucified not on the wood of the cross but on a lily. This is a reflection on the links between the Annunciation and the Crucifixion—Mary's *fiat* led ultimately to Calvary, something brought out from time to time when Good Friday falls on 25 March (feast of the Annunciation).

Another distinctive feature at Long Melford is the Lady Chapel, more common in abbeys and cathedrals than in parish churches. Here it is effectively a separate building and consists of a central chapel surrounded by an ambulatory that has the feel of a cloister. The Marian monogram can still be seen. For many years the chapel was used as a school room—albeit a very noble one—and a chart showing the multiplication tables can still be seen on the wall.

If you go to the edge of the churchyard, you will find the grave of the war poet Edmund Blunden. Unlike many of his contemporaries, he survived and became Professor of Poetry at Oxford, dying in Long Melford in 1974. He was haunted by the memories of war throughout his life. In 1937, twenty years after his experiences of Passchendaele, he wrote:

> Yes, I still remember
> The whole thing in a way;
> Edge and exactitude
> Depend on the day.
> ... And some are sparkling, laughing, singing,
> Young, heroic, mild;

And some incurable, twisted,
Shrieking, dumb, defiled.

The view from his grave is stunning: one of the country's most beautiful churches, framed by Elizabethan almshouses, a large green, the beginnings of the long High Street and Melton Hall (where Beatrix Potter was once a frequent visitor). It was for a view such as this that a whole generation went to 'Flanders fields' to die.

OXBURGH, NORFOLK

Catholic Families: The Bedingfields

Oxburgh Hall, situated nearly thirty miles from Walsingham, is a picture perfect fortified medieval house, with a wide, still moat and a crenelated gatehouse. Pugin judged it to be 'one of the noblest specimens of the domestic architecture of the fifteenth century'. All is not, however, quite as it seems: large parts of the hall were rebuilt and 'medievalised' from the 1770s onwards. Nevertheless, the Bedingfields have lived here for over five centuries, ducking and diving through shifting political and religious sands.

Around the house can be seen the distinctive motif of a fetterlock and falcon, symbols of the Yorkists during the Wars of the Roses. The Bedingfields gained Oxburgh through marriage from Sir Thomas Tuddenham, a staunch Lancastrian who had been executed in 1462 for plotting against Edward IV. The builder of Oxburgh — or at least of the gatehouse — was Sir Edmund Bedingfield, a keen Yorkist who was created a Knight of the Bath at the coronation of Richard III. Nevertheless, he was adroit enough to welcome Henry VII and his family several years later to Oxburgh, an occasion commemorated in both the King's and Queen's Rooms.

His son, another Edmund, was close to Henry VIII and acted as effective gaoler to Catherine of Aragon during her final months under house arrest at Kimbolton Castle. He treated her with dignity and it was his duty to arrange her burial at Peterborough Cathedral. Imprisoning queens seems to have been a family trait; the next Bedingfield knight, Sir Henry, a loyal supporter of Mary Tudor (Catherine's daughter), was responsible for the custody of the future Elizabeth I both at the Tower of London (where he was Lord Lieutenant) and Woodstock. On her accession, he prudently distanced himself from Court. Protestant authors such as John Foxe claimed that he had dealt with the princess severely; Elizabeth is even said to have discouraged his presence at Court, saying 'If we have any prisoner whom we would have sharply and straitly kept, we will send for you!' Nevertheless, Elizabeth treated him with respect, calling him 'Her Gaoler' as, perhaps, a sign of familiarity, and including Oxburgh on her progress in 1578. He died in 1583 and his monument describes his last years as such:

> Retir'd, old age to Christ, to himself, he gave,
> A pious man, and true Religion's friend.
> A generous Host, benign to needy Kin,
> He bore the toils of Sickness, firm till Death.

The Bedingfields remained staunch Catholics and faced fines and numerous restrictions. Evidence of these challenging times can be found in the priest hole, hidden beneath a brick-topped trap door off the King's Room—possibly the early work of St Nicholas Owen. Little is known, however, about who occupied it and how often it was used. Any priest sheltering there must have reflected with irony that the first Tudor sovereign had once slept on the other side of the thick wall.

One of the great treasures of the hall concerns another monarch of the period: Mary, Queen of Scots. She never visited Oxburgh but her presence can be felt in the 'Marian Hanging' she created during her long captivity, brought here from Cowdray Park in 1761 and now on loan from the Victoria and Albert Museum. It is a large piece, consisting of many separate panels which originally may have been served as cushion covers or stand-alone hangings. Embroidery was not only a lady-like pastime for the imprisoned queen but a form of communication. Alongside personal emblems and designs copied from books, there is a host of hidden meanings. The numerous birds—including even a toucan—suggest a desire to fly away to liberty. Likewise, the despair of the yellow rose eaten by canker (a funghal disease) says something about the queen's inner feelings as she awaited her fate.

The second Sir Henry was imprisoned in the Tower during the 1640s on account of his papist and royalist sympathies; he had fought with Charles I at Marston Moor. While sitting in his cell, he produced a series of meditations on Christ's Passion. The house, meanwhile, was ransacked and partly burnt down.

At the Restoration, the Bedingfields were created baronets. An unusual painting exists of the first Baronet and his family being protected under the mantle of Our Lady—such must have been their belief after the turbulent times of the Civil War. Yet, safety had not yet been reached. Successive Bedingfields lived for a time on the continent, displayed Jacobite sentiments or joined the English religious houses in exile there: two daughters of the first Baronet, for example, entered the English Carmelites at Lierre, where their great-uncle, Edmund, was chaplain. The portrait of one of these, Margaret, later prioress at Lierre, can be found near the North Bedroom. Moreover, between 1683 and 1795 Oxburgh had a resident Jesuit chaplain.

The subsequent history of the house is largely a narrative of rebuilding and attempts to save it for posterity. In 1830 the family was renamed 'Paston-Bedingfield' as they became heirs to another important East Anglian dynasty, formerly earls of Yarmouth. With mounting debts and taxes, however, Oxburgh was sold after the Second World War and then bought back by the family, who presented it to the National Trust, retaining a small section for their use.

Through all these changes the Faith has remained a constant and is represented by the splendid 1830s chapel in the grounds, dedicated to the Immaculate Conception and St Margaret and boasting a fine reredos. Nor is this Faith an abstract footnote of history. For much of the twentieth century Edith Bedingfield was a sister of the Society of the Holy Child Jesus. The tenth Baronet, a distinguished herald, is a Knight of Malta and his eldest son, like some of his forebears, was ordained a priest (for the Community of St John).

SOUTHEND-ON-SEA, ESSEX

Between Church and Sea

There is a faded photograph of members of my mother's family walking along Southend pier some time in the 1930s. As a boy I was fascinated by this pleasure pier, the longest in the world, jutting out into the Thames Estuary for well over a mile. How strange it must be, I thought, to be in the middle of the sea without being on a boat.

When I paid my first visit to the Essex town to fulfil my childhood ambition of standing at the end of the pier, it was shut. Perhaps this was just as well for the winds were strong that day. However, as so often happens in this country, I found plenty of historical interest.

The town's motto is *Per Mare per Ecclesiam*, 'By the sea, by the church', neatly summing up the town's position between the sea and a medieval priory. Southend only began to grow at the end of the eighteenth century, becoming popular as a 'watering place' after visits from Caroline of Brunswick, the Prince Regent's wife, in 1801 and 1803. It was even mentioned by Jane Austen in *Emma*.

Before it was a resort, Southend was a small fishing village, grouped around the manor and priory of Prittlewell. This had long been a site of political and religious importance. In 2003 an exceptional royal burial dating from the early seventh century was discovered nearby, complete with glass jars, a gold belt buckle and gold crosses. The identity of the person buried there will probably never be known for certain but scholarly opinion has suggested it was Sæberht, the first Christian king of the East Saxons, who died around 616. He was baptised by St Mellitus, one of St Augustine's band of monks, twelve years previously and allowed him to establish a diocese in London. Christians in the capital thus owe a great debt to this Saxon king buried by the Thames estuary.

The priory was founded around 1110 by Cluniac Benedictine monks from Lewes (East Sussex). It was never a large community and most of the buildings, including the church, disappeared at the Reformation, after which it became a private residence and now a museum. In the early fourteenth century there was a rather unedifying dispute between the priory and its Sussex mother house concerning the prior, William le Auvergnat. He had been accused of corruption and Lewes tried to remove him but he refused to go quietly. The result was two factions centred around rival claimants to the office. In August 1318 both were called before the king's council. William agreed to resign but then, on returning to Essex, forcibly occupied the priory. Appeals were made to Canterbury and Rome and decided in favour of William. Regrettably the matter was finally resolved when a group of armed monks from Lewes raided Prittlewell. William received a head wound while celebrating Mass in the church, which must have invited comparisons with St Thomas Becket (a great friend of the community), and taken as a virtual prisoner to Lewes. He died there shortly afterwards.

After the Reformation the focus of Southend's history drifted from the church to the sea. It does indeed have an enviable position. From the seafront there is an impressive panorama, with the Isles of Grain and Sheppey, the Kentish hills and, on a clear day, the distant Kentish coast stretching to Whitstable and beyond. The Estuary is the gateway to London and the constant procession of cargo ships is a reminder that our capital is a major port. Little wonder that in times of war this was very much the front line. There were Danish attacks in the Saxon period, Dutch offensives in the seventeenth century and Zeppelin raids during the First World War—Southend was, in fact, one of the first targets in May 1915. During the Second World War the Estuary saw constant attacks by the Luftwaffe, dropping bombs and mines into the murky waters and targeting docks and military bases. Among the defences erected were the Maunsell Forts, resembling oil platforms, that still eerily stand in the open sea.

It is no surprise that the Estuary is a place of shipwrecks—more than any other area of the United Kingdom. Some were brought down in battle, others through accident or some misfortune. They include the *London*, which mysteriously disappeared beneath the waves in March 1665 as it prepared to engage in the Second Anglo-Dutch War. Samuel Pepys recorded how 'she suddenly blew up' with the loss of 300—not only crew members but their wives and children, who were on board bidding their loved ones farewell. The ship had been launched only nine years earlier, during the Protectorate of Oliver Cromwell (which is why it was never 'HMS London'), and took part in the restoration of Charles II in 1660. While the new king boarded the appropriately named *Charles* at Scheveningen, his brother, James, Duke of York, embarked on the *London*. He eventually became the last Catholic king of England

I will have to return one day to make it to the end of the pier—not only to admire the view and stand in the middle of the sea but to pay my respects to the victims of these tragedies, who lie buried in the muddy bed beneath the waves, just off the pier.

SUTTON HOO, SUFFOLK

Sutton Hoo

When Edith and Frank Pretty moved to a modern eighteen-bedroom house at Sutton Hoo in 1926, they must have been delighted. There was a 1,200 acre estate, a large household staff and fine views of the River Deben. The couple led busy lives, with house parties, hunts and (for Edith) work as a local magistrate. A few years later, aged 47, she unexpectedly found herself pregnant and gave birth to a son, Robert. The home seemed complete.

Yet life is full of the unexpected. In 1935 Frank sadly died of cancer, aged 56, after only eight years of marriage. With a young child in a spacious house, Edith must have felt very alone, and it is little surprise that she pondered the great questions of life. She became involved in spiritualism, much at vogue at the time, and was influenced by William Parish, a well-known faith healer. It seems that he encouraged her interest in the curious mounds that lay in one of the fields of the estate, clearly visible from the house. There was talk, also, of strange sights in that area — dark figures seen at dusk and a warrior riding a white horse. What — or who — lay beneath those bracken-covered earthen humps?

Walking round the field today, it is easy to ask the same question. There are numerous rises and dips in the land. One is particularly large, a reconstruction by modern archaeologists both to give an idea of how large the mounds once were before the erosion of the centuries and to measure how quickly they change over time. Since being built in 1993 it has already lost a few inches in height. Added to the complex picture are execution burials from a slightly later period, medieval field boundaries, anti-glider ditches from the Second World War. There is a tremendous sense of past splendour and present mystery.

There was no real indication, though, that great treasures would lie beneath. In 1938 Mrs Pretty asked a local archaeologist, Basil Brown, to begin investigations. With only the minimum of equipment, he began carefully excavating three of the mounds, digging a trench to reveal differences in soil colour and identifying the location of the burial chamber, if it existed. There was evidence of impressive burials (one of which included a ship) but it seems that grave robbers had got there first in previous centuries — opening up the tantalising prospect that treasures from Sutton Hoo may lie unidentified somewhere in a museum or private collection.

Brown returned the following summer and began work on the largest mound. Here he was luckier. Farming and erosion had changed its shape, meaning that when grave robbers visited around the sixteenth century they looked in the wrong place and missed the buried treasures. As he dug, Brown found the ghost of a great ship—the wood had rotted but its shape and its rivets could be found in the sand. Word soon got around and experts were called in from Cambridge to continue exploring the site and discover what was in the burial chamber. Brown showed great humility in stepping aside, though Mrs Pretty was keen that he should still be involved.

The results of the dig are now among the highlights of the British Museum. It was considered the British equivalent of the discovery of Tutankhamun's tomb in Egypt seventeen years previously. Much had perished, of course, but there was enough to show the wealth of the burial—an armoury of weapons; a golden buckle once belonging to a purse; shoulder clasps, similar to those once worn by the Roman emperors, with garnets that may have come from Sri Lanka; silverware from Byzantium. The famous helmet, painstakingly reconstructed from over a hundred fragments, has become iconic, providing Anglo-Saxon England with a face.

It was the summer of 1939 and war clouds were looming. The dig needed to be concluded and secured as quickly as possible. Perhaps there was some embarrassment since, at the time of a feared Nazi invasion of England, the excavations spoke of a similar (and highly successful) Germanic enterprise many centuries previously. A Treasure Trove inquest held on 14 August ruled that the finds belonged to Mrs Pretty, who generously bequeathed them to the nation. War was declared a few weeks later and Basil Brown's final excavation at Sutton Hoo was the building of an air-raid shelter. The recently discovered treasures were taken off to London, to be stored in a disused Underground station, awaiting research in peacetime. By the time the war was over, Mrs Pretty had died of a blood clot and never saw 'her' treasures displayed to the public.

The big question, quite naturally, is: who was buried at Sutton Hoo? No trace of a body was found, though this was not surprising given the age of the tomb and the acidic nature of the soil. A buried ship, let it be remembered, would have trapped centuries of rainwater, meaning that the body effectively lay in an acid bath!

The prominent location, on a high piece of ground near the sea, the extent of the mounds and the richness of their contents all point towards a person of high status and wealth—most likely, a king of East Anglia. Although the original occupant of 'Mound 1' will never be known for certain, most scholars point towards King Rædwald, a seventh-century king who, according to St Bede, had 'overlordship' south of the Humber in the decade leading up to his death in *c.* 625. It is possible that some of his successors lie in surrounding mounds, making the field a royal mausoleum of the East Anglian Wuffing dynasty, a sort of open-air Westminster Abbey.

To some extent, Sutton Hoo can be seen as the last monument of the pagan Anglo-Saxons. Rædwald's personal faith was nuanced. Ship burials are unusual in England—in fact, only three have been found on the mainland and all of them in Suffolk: two at Sutton Hoo and one at nearby Snape—and are undeniably pagan. The symbolism was that the ship would somehow be involved in the transport of the deceased to the 'other side'.

According to St Bede, however, Rædwald travelled to Kent and was baptised, possibly by St Augustine himself. Once back in his kingdom he met opposition from his queen and other close advisers. He hedged his bets by setting up altars side-by-side to both Christ and the old gods. Despite the paganism of the ship burial, the treasures excavated included silver bowls with cross-shaped decoration and a pair of silver spoons, with the names 'Saulos' and 'Paulos'. Are there evidence of Rædwald's own conversion and baptism?

Eighty years on, Sutton Hoo continues to fascinate and attracts many visitors—the site is now in the hands of the National Trust and has an excellent new exhibition centre and viewing tower. The excavation unveiled the richness and cosmopolitan nature of early Saxon society. It also served as a reminder that the conversion of England was a process, the seventh century a time of transition with old and new practices standing alongside each other. Rædwald was buried in his ship, like his ancestors, yet he faced the East, the direction of the rising sun, awaiting his Messiah king.

WALTHAM, ESSEX

Waltham and its Holy Cross

Londoners love their open spaces—the famous parks and squares, the great expanse of Richmond Park or Hampstead Heath, and, largest of all, Epping Forest in the east. It is astonishing that such a huge expanse of woodland, comprising over 6,000 acres, can exist in Greater London and it gives an insight into what the landscape was like before mass urbanisation and industrialisation. There is a further link to 'Olde England' just north of the forest: the church of the Holy Cross and St Lawrence at Waltham Abbey, believed to be the final resting place of King Harold, who fell at the battle of Hastings. Pilgrims flocked there in times past not only to pay their respects to the last Saxon king but to honour a miraculous cross.

There seems to have been a church at Waltham from an early date but it was during the reign of Canute, in the early eleventh century, that a stone cross was brought there, which oozed blood and worked miracles. The details are recorded in the twelfth-century *De Inventione Sanctae Crucis* (Of the discovery of the holy cross). Medieval chroniclers often described foundation legends many centuries after their supposed happening. This one, though, is unusual since it deals with events within living memory. The author, a canon of the abbey, heard the story from the aged sacristan, Thorkell, who would have remembered the first members of the community.

The story begins in Somerset. Around the year 1035 the blacksmith at Montacute had a dream in which he was told about a stone cross buried in a nearby hill. Initially he was reluctant to act on this information but was eventually persuaded to see the local priest, who gathered witnesses together to dig for the cross. Among them was the great local landowner, Tovi 'the Proud', who acted as standard-bearer to the king. The cross was found, along with a smaller cross, a bell and a book (*Liber Niger*)—suggesting that these items had once been hidden by a Celtic missionary several centuries previously.

Tovi decided to donate the precious cross to a suitable sanctuary. He put it on a cart driven by twelve red oxen and mentioned the names of some suitable locations to which they could take their holy load. They refused to budge until he mentioned (perhaps out of desperation) the little church on his estate at Waltham in Essex, some 150 miles away.

The oxen immediately took off and Waltham Abbey quickly became famous for its miracle-working cross.

Harold himself is said to have been healed of an injury through the power of the cross. He owned land in the area and often stayed there to hunt and to rest from his labours in the capital. As a thanksgiving, Harold rebuilt the church and founded a community of secular canon, based, it seems, on similar communities he had visited on the continent. The church was consecrated on 3 May 1060, in the presence of St Edward the Confessor himself. It is clear that Harold had the support of the king. Not only did he attend the church's consecration but in 1062 presented the community with a golden-lettered confirmation of all the donations that Harold had made. This was kept, in later years, with the church's other relics. St Edward also gave a blue cloak to the community that was made into a chasuble.

Interestingly Harold's church was loosely based on the design of St Peter's in Rome. Harold may be remembered as briefly reigning as the last Saxon king, but this quintessential Englishman had travelled widely on the continent and had made a pilgrimage to Rome. It is said that he gathered together such a collection of relics to take back with him that the Romans begged him to leave some behind. Some of these ended up at Waltham, including hair from St Peter's beard and part of his chains. Harold made many other gifts: even at the time of the Dissolution the abbey still possessed two gospel books with rich decorations and covers which he had given. His foundation at Waltham was an attempt to emulate the magnificence of the Eternal City, heighten his own status and ensure prayers would be offered for him after death.

As we all know, this was just round the corner. Harold visited Waltham Abbey as he darted back from his victory over the Danes at Stamford Bridge to face the Normans on the Sussex coast. The author of *De Inventione* remembered speaking to Thorkell the sacristan, who had seen the king ride off to Hastings. Apparently, as he knelt in prayer before the great cross, the figure of Christ had bowed his head. Later this was interpreted as a gesture of sympathy, even sorrow, for his inevitable fate.

It is thought that Harold's body was brought back to Waltham by two canons, Osgod and Ailric. His corpse was so badly mutilated that it was only identified by his delightfully named sweetheart, Edith Swan-neck, who spotted several secret marks known only to her. Initially miracles were claimed at the tomb but William was anxious that no cult developed, which is why perhaps he treated the community with a degree of harshness. Although there are other sites where he is thought to be buried, and some even claimed that he survived Hastings and became a hermit, his tomb at Waltham Abbey is still marked out in the grounds of the existing church.

The canons were eventually replaced by Augustinians in 1177, as part of Henry II's penitential expiation for the murder of St Thomas Becket. Although the pope ordered him to found three monasteries, he chose to create one new one and refound two existing houses. The abbey continued to thrive until the Reformation, when it was the last great abbey to be dissolved. The monastic buildings were pulled down and only the nave of the church, which was traditionally the domain of parishioners, survived, becoming the parish church. A new tower was constructed, the only one in England to have been built in the reign of Mary Tudor.

Although the existing church is only a fraction of the size of the magnificent abbey, there are still traces of its previous splendour: part of a fourteenth-century screen, a medieval wall-painting of the Last Judgment showing St Michael weighing souls in a set of scales, and the massive Norman pillars. And Harold still rests in the churchyard, having lost his kingdom but, we pray, now wearing a heavenly crown.

THE MIDLANDS

BADDESLEY CLINTON, WARWICKSHIRE

Catholic Families: The Ferrers

A medieval church, a moated manor house with priest holes, and a nineteenth-century mission: Baddesley Clinton clearly demonstrates the changing fortunes of the English Catholic community over the centuries.

The historic church of St Michael, where Mass was celebrated for generations, is near the manor house and a little out of the village centre. There is an interesting, and not entirely edifying, story connected to Nicholas Brome, lord of the manor during the reign of Henry VII. Returning home one day, he caught his wife unawares in an embrace with another man. Enraged, Nicholas drew his sword and ran it through the lech, only to find it was the local priest. One can only wonder what explanations were offered by the good lady, but Nicholas came to regret his violent reaction and it is said that the permanent stain on the library floor is a reminder of the murder. In reparation, he built the tower at St Giles's church, in nearby Packwood, and extended the one at St Michael's. They stand to this day and are colloquially known as the 'Towers of Atonement'. In a further act of repentance, Nicholas asked to be buried in the church porch at Baddesley Clinton 'as the people may tread upon mee'. Perhaps this gesture also pointed to his father's own violent death, killed as a result of a feud in the porch of Whitefriars church, London.

Nicholas' daughter married Edward Ferrers, whose direct ancestor had fought alongside the Conqueror at Hastings. The house thus passed into the Ferrers family, who remained Catholic through the travails of the sixteenth century. Indeed, after the break with Rome, whenever Edward heard the bells of the parish church call the villagers to the worship of the official Church, he would retreat to his study and recite the Penitential Psalms. In time, Mass was celebrated secretly at the house and priests appeared and disappeared as guests.

This was especially the case during the 1590s, when the house was rented by two members of the Catholic Vaux family, Anne Vaux and Eleanor Brooksby. It was during this period that three priest holes were constructed by the master of such designs, St Nicholas Owen. When the house was used for a meeting of Jesuits in October 1591, there was an early-morning raid by pursuivants and seven priests hid for some four hours, their ankles deep in water. They escaped capture but others were less fortunate. Twelve years later, Blessed Robert Grissold, a yeoman from nearby Rowington, was captured after assisting the priest Blessed John Sugar, who had probably offered Mass at the house. They were both executed at Warwick on 16 July 1604. 'Bear witness, good people', Grissold said at the gallows, 'that I die here not for theft, nor for felony, but for my conscience'.

The owner of Baddesley at the time was Henry 'the Antiquary', whose long life spanned five reigns; well known for his studies of local history and genealogy, he was one of the first historians of Warwickshire and his manuscripts were extensively used, with little acknowledgement, by William Dugdale in his *Antiquities of Warwickshire* (1656). Despite his scholarly interests, Henry's Catholic sympathies led to serious financial problems and necessitated the selling of land and assets. It is largely because of this constant struggle to survive that the house was never rebuilt and remains a wonderful and picturesque survival from the end of the Middle Ages.

Baddesley long had connections with the Franciscans, stretching back to the seventeenth century; a friar was resident as chaplain at the house from the 1750s and in 1785 their Academy, originally based at Edgbaston, was moved there. Indeed, three daughters of Thomas Ferrers became Poor Clares. The chapel, built for the Academy in 1800, became the base for a mission that served the area and which passed into the hands of the secular clergy at the time of Catholic Emancipation.

In 1850 there was a new arrival: a community of Poor Clares of the Colletine reform, who travelled to England from Bruges, and used the former buildings of the Franciscan Academy. Initially, only one member of the community could speak English and they arrived wearing lay dress; they were glad of donations of potatoes from villagers and tea, sugar and soap from the ribbon-makers of Hinckley. In time, their community and their buildings grew, supported by the Ferrers and Clifford families. St John Henry Newman himself is recorded as sending hampers to the nuns at Christmas.

By the 1860s an unusual 'quartet' was living at the house. Marmion Edward Ferrers was the dutiful lord of the manor, highly popular with his tenants and villagers, but something of an eccentric: he wore black velvet knee breeches and doublet, cloak and hat. Attired as such, he could often be seen serving Mass at the church, which was rebuilt in 1870. His wife, Rebecca Dulcibella Orpen, was a prolific artist, who produced paintings both for the chapel they created at the house and the church. Also resident were her aunt, Lady Georgina Chatterton, a well-known author, and her husband, Edward Heneage Dering, also a novelist and an amateur neo-Thomist philosopher. Like Marmion, he adopted an antique mode of dress.

United by their Catholic Faith, they poured their resources into Baddesley and made many repairs and improvements. After Marmion and Georgina died, Edward and Rebecca married. According to some, this had been the original plan, for when Edward originally approached Georgina about marrying her niece, the good lady thought that the proposal was being made to her and Edward had not the heart to correct this impression. Rebecca lived on into the 1920s, continuing to paint in her studio by candlelight, for she refused the introduction of electricity.

In 1980 the house passed to the National Trust, who have maintained the buildings magnificently and kept alive the story of the Ferrers for the thousands who visit each year. Meanwhile, the Poor Clares continued to be a spiritual powerhouse for the locality and, despite their enclosure, were uniquely present to the outside world. Indeed, the brother of one abbess, himself a Franciscan, decided to drive his motor car into the nuns' garden so that his sister knew what such a vehicle looked like—for he often enthused about the new-fangled invention. Sadly, numbers dwindled in more recent times and the community moved to Hereford in 2011.

The church of St Francis of Assisi was radically reordered in the 1970s and the decoration in the sanctuary painted over. However, during the lockdown of 2020 a talented Catholic artist (and former parishioner of mine!), Martin Earle, painted a stunningly beautiful series of frescoes in the Byzantine and Romanesque styles and including the figures of St Nicholas Owen and the two Vaux sisters. Baddesley Clinton has been through many changes but the Catholic Faith, in all its beauty, remains a constant.

CHESTER, CHESHIRE

St Werburgh and her Goose

There is much of interest in Chester—the Roman remains, the medieval walls (preserved almost in their entirety), the distinctive shopping arcades and timber-framed buildings. The city was once the site of a Roman fort, perched on the edge of the known world, and, also, one of the last English towns to fall to the Normans.

In the heart of the city is the cathedral, which up until the time of the Reformation was a Benedictine abbey. Some of the monastic buildings survive, though the monks would have been amazed by twenty-first-century visitors tucking into Welsh rarebit and enjoying the benefits of WiFi in their thirteenth-century refectory. The cathedral also housed the shrine of the local saint: St Werburgh (or Werburga).

Born near Stone (Staffordshire) in the mid-seventh century, St Werburgh belonged to a blue-blooded family touched by God's grace, reminding us of the 'interconnectedness' of our Saxon saints. Indeed, when (as some sources suggest) St Werburgh became the fourth Abbess of Ely, she was following in succession to her mother (St Ermengild), her grandmother (St Sexburga) and her great-aunt (St Etheldreda). She was also a descendant of St Ethelbert of Kent, who had been converted by St Augustine in 597, and in her youth she was instructed by St Chad, Bishop of Lichfield. St Werburgh's father Wulfhere, on the other hand, though not venerated as a saint, was the first Christian King of Mercia and the most powerful Saxon leader of his generation. Her paternal grandfather was the dreaded pagan ruler Penda.

St Werburgh's life was more active than might be expected for a nun. Wulfhere's successor as King of Mercia is said to have made her abbess 'over all the nuns of every monastery within his realm'. Thus, she left Ely and travelled round her various communities, ensuring that they were observantly following the monastic rule. She also showed great compassion to the poor and was known for various miracles and portents.

Like so many of these early saints, we know more for certain about her 'afterlife', her cult, than her earthly life. St Werburgh died on 3 February 700 (or thereabouts) and was buried at Hanbury in Staffordshire, although at the time of her death there was an unseemly fight over her mortal remains. Relics could, of course, bring great prestige and wealth to their place of rest. By the tenth century her body had been moved to the church of SS Peter and Paul at Chester, which had been founded by her father. The reason normally given is that the fortified city seemed a safer place for the relics given the on-going threat of Viking raids. However, the clergy at Hanbury were less than pleased to lose the relics and claimed that the saint's body, which up until then had remained incorrupt, had dissolved into nothingness so that it would not fall into pagan hands. Such a story not only accounted for the absence of the relics but also reveals a hint of competition with the monks of Chester!

For over five centuries, pilgrims flocked to Chester to pray at the shrine of St Werburgh. Many miracles were attributed to her intercession and her cult was promoted by the Benedictines who formed a community at the church in 1093.

Around this Goscelin of Saint-Bertin wrote her life and further popularised her story. Painted as a beautiful princess who had rejected many suitors in order to consecrate herself to Christ, the most popular legend associated with her was surely that of the goose she raised from the dead—a creature that became her symbol in art and on medieval pilgrim badges. While she was living with the nuns at Weedon in Northamptonshire, a flock of geese arrived in the fields and destroyed many of the crops. The saint had them locked up overnight. Next morning one was missing, and it was discovered that a servant had killed the bird and eaten it. The bird was restored to life and flew away with its companions, never to trouble the fields of Weedon again—a charming tale of forgiveness and intimacy with nature.

The saint's shrine was dismantled at the Dissolution of the Monasteries. When the former abbey became Chester Cathedral in 1540, parts of the shrine were used in building a throne for the new bishop. With the Catholic revival in the Church of England in the second half of the nineteenth century, the shrine was recreated using surviving fragments and now stands in the Lady Chapel. Although the exact location of her relics is unknown, St Werburgh remains at the heart of the church founded by her father all those centuries ago, the much-loved patroness of a beautiful city.

COVENTRY, WARWICKSHIRE
Lully, lulla

It is not immediately apparent to those visiting modern Coventry that this was once one of England's best preserved medieval towns. That all changed, of course, when German bombers mounted an eleven hour raid on 14 November 1940. Twelve hundred were killed, 43,000 homes were damaged and the cathedral destroyed. Coventry no longer ranked as a medieval showcase, though some historians have pointed out that the steady march of modern town planning was inevitable and that several medieval buildings had already been torn down prior to the bombing. The tragedy of 1940 was, however, undeniable.

A link to this lost medieval past is provided every Christmas by the well-known 'Coventry Carol', one of the oldest to survive. It begins with the touching lines:

> Lully, lulla, thou little tiny child,
> By by, lully, lulla thou little tiny child,
> By by, lully, lullay!

It was not intended to stand alone but was part of *The Pageant of the Shearmen and Tailors*, a mystery play originally performed not at Christmas but Corpus Christi by one of the local guilds. There were ten such pageants performed at Coventry, though the text of only one of them, *The Weaver's Pageant*, survives. They were enormously popular. Indeed, Henry V, Henry VI, Richard III and Henry VIII are all known to have attended the Coventry plays and William Dugdale wrote in the seventeenth century that 'the yearly confluence of people to see that show was extraordinary great, and yielded no small advantage to this City'.

These mystery plays were normally based on Biblical subjects, such as Adam and Eve, Noah and the ark, Abraham and Isaac, the prophets, the life of Christ and the Last Judgment. In many places (including Chester and York) they were performed on special pageant wagons, which could be moved to various locations for different scenes. It is thought that this developed alongside the colourful Corpus Christi processions that brought the Eucharistic Lord through the streets, stopping at various 'stations' for prayers, adoration and benediction.

The plays themselves were sponsored, produced and (often) performed by the guilds, bringing them much prestige. They could be costly and ambitious affairs; at Chester the cycle of performances took three days to complete. The pageants were an effective mix of devotion, catechesis, entertainment and money-making.

The words of the 'Coventry Carol' were first recorded in 1534 by Robert Croo (or Crowe), who directed the *Pageant* for many years. It was sung by three women of Bethlehem to their infant children as a lullaby, just before Herod sent his men to massacre all male children under the age of two as he searched for the new-born king.

> Herod the King, in his raging,
> Charged he hath this day;
> His men of might, in his own sight,
> All children young to slay.

The scene was highly dramatic but also profoundly theological. The slaughtered children were witnesses to Christ, 'not by speaking but by dying'. They showed also that the Lord had come for everyone; as St Leo wrote, 'by His own early days He consecrated the beginnings of little ones, so that He might teach us that no man is incapable of the divine mystery'.

Despite being considered 'popish' by the Reformers, the Mystery Plays continued to be performed in many areas until the late sixteenth century — a sign of their enduring popularity. It seems also that what we now call the 'Coventry Carol' was remembered not only for its beautiful melody but its subject matter. The Massacre of the Innocents would have touched a chord in many families at a time when infant mortality was so common. One can imagine the mothers of Coventry singing it to their children generation by generation, until being written down by antiquarians in the early nineteenth century.

In the light of the 1940 bombings, the carol took on a new significance. It was broadcast from the ruins of the cathedral during the BBC's Empire Broadcast that Christmas — a cry for peace and goodwill in the face of hostility and war. The Coventry Carol brings us to the heart of Christmas.

DEENE PARK, NORTHAMPTONSHIRE

Recusant Cardigans

There was something quintessentially English as we left the car park at Deene Park. In the foreground there were neat rows of cars and helpful stewards in luminous vests. A worried father had hurried back to his vehicle to retrieve an essential item for the family picnic. In the distance the Sealed Knot was busy fighting a battle of the English Civil War. Hundreds of re-enactors, who no doubt spend the week unobtrusively as accountants, builders and teachers, were playing the part of Cavaliers and Roundheads. One had even introduced himself to me in character, painting a youth spent as a mercenary in the Low Countries. There was musket fire, long pikes, armoured cavalrymen in lobster-tail helmets and even several cannons (one of which had been spotted earlier, attached to a Range Rover). In the camp around the battlefield, demonstrations were being given about Stuart medicine, cooking and needlework. And, round a bend in the road, lay the magnificent house of Deene Park, which had once been besieged by Cromwell's men.

Like so many of our country homes, Deene Park was formerly a monastic property—a grange and 'shooting box' belonging to Westminster Abbey. Around the time of Magna Carta it was let to Sir Ivo de Deene for an annual rent of £18, with the condition that hospitality would be offered annually to the abbot and his household. Curiously, the rent of £18 was paid to the abbey until 1970, when the Church Commissioners abolished the practice in return for £200. The 'Monk's Well' can still be found on the grounds, testimony to this distant monastic past.

Various families have lived at this stately pile over the centuries but it is the Brudenells who have left the greatest mark. They acquired the estate in 1514 and the first Brudenells to live there were distinguished lawyers, grand enough to entertain Elizabeth I in 1566. In the words of Cecil Woodham-Smith, 'Brudenell had succeeded Brudenell since the fourteenth century, wealthy and strongly attached to the Crown. Indeed, it was from the Crown that they had derived their importance, rising in the world as courtiers and emerging from the respectable obscurity of county worthies through their ability to please a prince'.

It was Thomas Brudenell who allowed the family to emerge from this 'respectable obscurity' in the seventeenth century. In 1611 James I began the practice of granting baronetcies to gentlemen of good birth in return for their upkeep of thirty soldiers for three years. Thomas Brudenell was one of the first to take the opportunity. What is intriguing is that the family at this time openly professed their Catholic faith. Sir Thomas's wife was Mary Tresham, the daughter of Sir Thomas Tresham, who was frequently convicted as a Catholic and expressed his Faith in the plethora of secret symbols on the Triangular Lodge at Rushton (Northamptonshire), and Muriel Throckmorton, a member of the prominent Catholic family based at Coughton Court (Warwickshire).

Severe laws existed against those who did not attend Anglican services and who harboured 'Massing priests'. However, well-to-do Catholics were often saved from the full force of legal penalties by their sympathetic neighbours, who were often related by ties of blood, marriage, business and local interest. In 1613 the JPs of Northamptonshire remarked that only their esteem for Sir Thomas Brudenell had enabled him and fourteen of his family to escape a conviction for so many years. This is especially surprising since his brother-in-law, Francis Tresham, had died of natural causes while imprisoned in the Tower of London for his involvement in the Gunpowder Plot!

Thomas Brudenell was a keen book collector and acquired much of the library of his father-in-law, Thomas Tresham. These included not only standard Tridentine texts and works secretly printed for the English Catholic community but tomes by the likes of St Robert Bellarmine and other contemporary theologians, as well as volumes on heraldry, history and architecture. Brudenell clearly did not want to be cut off from developments in culture and scholarship overseas. The library was 'unjustly taken away from Deene' by Cromwell's troops but many were later re-purchased and now sit behind locked bookcases in the cosy Bow Room.

One treasure recently attracted much scholarly excitement. Found within the pages of a two volume 'home-made encyclopaedia' sold by the Tresham-Bridenell Library to the Bodleian in 1968 was a setting of the Latin antiphon *Adoramus te Christe*. It appeared next to an account of the 1606 execution of the Jesuit, Henry Garnet, who had uttered these words on the scaffold. The writing may be in the hand of Sir Thomas's wife, Mary Tresham, and the bottom part of the music is upside down, probably so that a small group could sing from the book while around a table. Perhaps it would have been sung at Masses secretly arranged by the family. Another relic from these times can be found in the nearby church of St Peter's, where the Brudenells await the Day of Reckoning in their family chapel. On one of the walls the visitor can just make out what is purportedly a reredos, part of a seventeenth-century Catholic altar.

Despite all this, Sir Thomas Brudenell's star continued to rise. In 1628 he became Baron Brudenell of Stonton (Leicestershire) and during the Civil Wars fought on the side of the king, ending up briefly in the Tower. Shortly before his execution, Charles I, by now a prisoner at Carisbrooke Castle, wrote asking him for £1,000 in return for an earldom. Events intervened but after the Restoration Charles II honoured his father's promise and raised Brudenell to the earldom of Cardigan.

Thomas's son, Robert, the second Earl, spent much of his life overseas, part of the English Catholic diaspora in France and the Low Countries. On one occasion he was captured by privateers and released only after a £3,000 ransom had been paid. He lived under every Stuart monarch, dying in 1703 aged 96, although after the Revolution of 1688 his sympathies remained with James II and his descendants. His son, Francis, spent four years in the Tower because of his Jacobite loyalties.

It was the third Earl, George, who put an end to this story of exile and secret Catholicism. He was enjoying what the guidebook describes as 'a life of merrymaking and dissipation' in Rome when he discovered that his grandfather had died and that he was now a peer of the realm. He returned to England, married well and, in January 1708, formally abjured his Catholicism. It was an astute move in worldly terms for this reformed Jacobite could now take his seat in the House of Lords and hold several prominent positions at Court, including Master of the Royal Buckhounds.

His great-grandson was perhaps the most celebrated (and one might say controversial) member of the clan: James, the seventh Earl. This bewhiskered Victorian led the Charge of the Light Brigade at the Battle of Balaclava (1854), as celebrated in Tennyson's poem and numerous pub names. There is a display of the earl's 'relics' at Deene, including the head, tail and hoof of his trusty horse, 'Ronald', also a Balaclava veteran. Few remember that this famous soldier was descended from some of our most prominent Catholic families.

DORCHESTER-ON-THAMES, OXFORDSHIRE

St Birinus

Cardinal Wiseman's famous prayer for the conversion of England includes the line: 'Be mindful of our fathers, Eleutherius, Celestine, and Gregory, bishops of the Holy City'. These popes are mentioned because they showed a great interest in the evangelisation of our islands—tradition asserts that St Eleutherius sent missionaries to King Lucius around 177 and we know that St Celestine I commissioned St Palladius to visit Ireland in 431 and St Gregory the Great sponsored St Augustine's mission to Kent in 597. If that list of pontiffs were to continue, then Honorius I would be a strong contender for inclusion. It is often forgotten that he sent St Birinus on a mission to the pagan Saxons in 634.

Perhaps one reason why Honorius is so often forgotten is that he is himself a controversial figure. Though he did much that was praiseworthy—including the building and decoration of churches in Rome (he is featured in a mosaic at Sant' Agnese fuori le mura)—he has the dubious distinction of having been condemned (after his death) by the Third Council of Constantinople. Though not guilty of formal heresy as such, Honorius showed much imprudence in his dealings with the Patriarch of Constantinople at a very sensitive time. He showed sympathy towards monothelitism (the theory that Christ has two natures but one will), hoping that this would help restore unity to the Church in the aftermath of the monophysite schism (the heresy that Christ has one nature). Honorius's condemnation became a *cause célèbre*, often mentioned in subsequent centuries by Protestant writers and those who opposed the definition of papal infallibility.

Another reason why Honorius is frequently neglected in this country is that little is known about St Birinus's mission; one of our chief sources is St Bede's *Ecclesiastical History* but this leaves many questions unanswered. St Birinus, we are told, had promised in the pope's presence 'that he would sow the seeds of our holy Faith in the most inland and remote regions of the English, where no other teacher had been before him'. He was consecrated bishop in Genoa by Asterius, Archbishop of Milan, and then began his journey towards the English Channel.

Why did Honorius send a mission to the English, barely four decades after the landing of St Augustine in Thanet? The conversion of the Anglo-Saxons was a slow and torturous process and there were numerous ups and downs. Kings were baptised, others reverted back to paganism and there were frequent military campaigns between them. Just before St Birinus' arrival, for example, St Edwin, King of Northumbria, was killed in battle. A convert of St Paulinus, he had exercised overlordship over the other kingdoms but following his death his territory was briefly divided between pagan rulers. The future must have looked bleak. Perhaps the pope felt that a 'Romish bishop' would strengthen the emergent English Church at this critical time and bolster its communion with Rome. That St Birinus was sent independently of the existing bishops and without reference to Canterbury implies the fragility of the situation.

St Birinus landed in the Southampton area and may have founded the church of St Mary, which many centuries later inspired the song, 'The Bells of St Mary's' (made famous in the 1945 film of the same name starring Bing Crosby and Ingrid Bergman). He then travelled northwards and passed through Wessex and the Thames Valley—the territory of the Gewisse. Although originally intending to find 'the most inland and remote regions of the English', he was so struck by the lack of faith among the people that he met that he 'decided that it would be better to begin to preach the word of God among them rather than seek more distant converts'.

Like St Augustine, he focused his attentions on the local ruler, King Cynegils, who was soon baptised. It is significant that his godfather was none other than St Oswald, the new King of Northumbria. The day of Cynegils's baptism was a momentous one, for not only was he born again in the waters of the font but he entered into an alliance with St Oswald against the pagan Mercians and was engaged to his daughter.

Moreover, now that he was a Christian king, Cynegils gave St Birinus the city of Dorchester-on-Thames as his seat. Like Canterbury, Dorchester was a Romano-British town of some strategic importance and for a time it became the only bishopric in Wessex and also the effective capital of that kingdom. St Birinus died in 650, having founded several churches around Wessex, and was succeeded by the Gaulish St Agilbert. However, things were changing and the see was moved to Winchester in the 660s (followed by St Birinus' body by the end of the century). It is interesting to speculate that Dorchester would probably have been the English capital in the early Middle Ages had it not been replaced by Winchester.

Dorchester would be a cathedral city twice again—briefly under the Mercians in the late seventh century, after political boundaries had been redrawn, and then again two hundred years later, in the aftermath of the Danish invasions. This third diocese of Dorchester was huge, being merged with the ancient see of Lindsey and stretching from the Thames to the Humber—the largest English diocese, though under the Normans the bishop's seat would be moved from Dorchester to Lincoln. The former cathedral at Dorchester passed into the hands of Arrouaisian canons, who followed the Augustinian rule and boasted twenty-four houses in England. During the thirteenth century relics identified as those of St Birinus were 'rediscovered' and with the support of another Pope Honorius, the third of that name, a shrine was built and Dorchester once again attracted pilgrims. Although destroyed at the Reformation, the shrine was reconstructed in more recent years.

Still remembered in Dorchester not only in the abbey but the beautiful Catholic church, St Birinus reminds us of the close involvement of the Holy See in the conversion of England.

EVESHAM, WORCESTERSHIRE

Evesham and its Abbey

There are enough remnants left to give an impression of the lost magnificence of Evesham Abbey — the two churches that stood in the shadow of the abbey church to serve the townspeople and pilgrims, the monastic fishponds and the impressive bell tower of Abbot Lichfield, which was left unfinished at the time of the Dissolution.

The monastery was established by St Egwin, Bishop of Worcester, at the beginning of the eighth century. This little-known Saxon saint was a member of the Mercian royal family and, such was his reforming zeal, he was denounced to both the king and the Archbishop of Canterbury and faced suspension. He travelled to Rome to answer his charges and went in the guise of a penitent pilgrim. According to tradition, he chained his legs with fetters and locked them, casting the key into the River Avon. Finally reaching the Eternal City, the bells of the churches began ringing by themselves. When the bishop sat down to a well-deserved meal, he discovered the key he had thrown into the Avon inside the fish: 'thus the Tiber restored what the Avon had swallowed'. He was sure that his sins were forgiven, and he returned to England vindicated.

Like many religious houses, Evesham Abbey was destroyed by the Vikings. One chieftain called Alchelm 'took over the abbey like a villainous wolf; drove out the monks and took their lands and properties'. However, destruction creates opportunities for rebuilding and Evesham could truly boast a majestic church by the time the Normans arrived. The abbey had been given many gifts of land and its wealthy patrons included the famous (or infamous?) Lady Godiva, who some think was buried at Evesham. There were precious relics too — not only St Egwin but St Credan (an eighth-century abbot), St Wigstan (a ninth-century Mercian prince) and St Odulph (whose bones had been stolen from Frisia by the Danes and had been acquired by one enterprising abbot).

With the arrival of the Normans, the church was rebuilt in the Romanesque style and a Norman became abbot. The new regime was suspicious of remnants of the Saxon Church and tried to downplay many of the old English saints. The validity of some of the shrines at Evesham was doubted and the relics tested by fire. Fortunately, we are told that the bones of St Credan shone like gold in a furnace and the head of St Wigstan sweated in the heat.

Evesham played a role in the monastic expansion of the times. In 1074 two monks from the abbey were involved in a mission to the north-east to revive the destroyed monasteries of Jarrow, Wearmouth and Whitby and, through them, the foundations at Durham, Fountains and St Mary's, York. Around the same time twelve monks went to Denmark to establish a daughter house at Odense. Amongst other things, they are credited with introducing apple trees to Denmark.

Closer to home, Evesham played an important role during the Second Baron's War of the mid-1260s—which essentially pitched Henry III against the powerful Earl of Leicester, Simon de Montfort. A decisive battle was fought at Evesham on 4 August 1265 and Simon killed in the fighting. His body was mutilated, and such remains as could be found were buried at the abbey. Soon his tomb was visited by pilgrims and miracles were claimed. Simon was indeed a charismatic leader and remembered today not only as a father of representative government but a man of great piety.

The monastery disappeared at the Dissolution under Henry VIII but, quite apart from the surviving buildings, an interesting relic of this lost world can be found in the Catholic church about ten minutes' walk away: the statue of Our Lady of Evesham, which still attracts its devotees 1,300 years on.

As bishop, St Egwin often retreated to a hermitage near what is now Evesham. In 700 a swineherd called Eoves was going about his business, near to the hermitage, when he noticed three beautiful maidens standing in a dense thicket, singing heavenly songs. Eoves sought the bishop and led him to the spot. After much prayer, St Egwin was also favoured with the same vision. One of the maidens held a book and a golden cross and St Egwin instinctively knew this to be the Mother of God. A church was built shortly afterwards—hence the origins of the town of Evesham that grew around the abbey, named after Eoves the swineherd ('Eoves-ham').

The shrine was lost at the Reformation but restored by the Catholics of Evesham in the twentieth century. The devotion provided much comfort during the difficult years of the Second World War and in June 1952 a large public procession was held, attended by over 4,000 Catholics. It was led by the Abbot of Douai, to whose house was given the privilege of electing the titular abbot of Evesham—the granting of such honorary titles connected to the pre-Reformation monasteries had been given to the English Benedictines by the Holy See.

FOTHERINGHAY, NORTHAMPTONSHIRE

The End of the Queen of Scots

Fotheringhay Castle today consists of little more than a mound, some earthworks and a small section of masonry. Until you find the commemorative plaques, there is little to suggest that this place saw not only the birth of the future Richard III (1452) but one of the defining events of the sixteenth century: the trial and execution of Mary, Queen of Scots (1587). It was a moment that had long been anticipated by the authorities and would continue to haunt Elizabeth, herself the daughter of a beheaded queen.

The circumstances of that tragic occasion in the Great Hall of Fotheringay on 8 February 1587 are etched into our historical memory. How Mary removed her black outer garment to reveal a striking bodice in red, the colour of martyrdom. How the headsman blundered, the first blow hitting the back of her head, near the knotted blindfold, and two further attempts being required to sever the head from the body. How the head fell from the executioner's hands as he held it up, since the queen wore a wig. How her favourite Skye terrier hid beneath her robes and, finally emerging onto the scaffold, refused to leave its mistress's body.

All the paraphernalia of the scaffold, along with the dead queen's clothes, were quickly burnt in the fireplace so that her followers could not collect relics. Mary was buried in Peterborough Cathedral and, once her son became King James of England, was moved to a triumphant tomb at Westminster Abbey, near that of Elizabeth. Fotheringay, meanwhile, was left to decay; it was already in a poor condition but, it seemed, no-one wanted to be associated with that dismal spot.

Mary's personal motto was 'In the end is my beginning'. As soon as her head left her body, she entered legend and, in a sense, became the success that she never had been in life. Since then, she has inspired paintings, operas, plays and films.

Mary's life was indeed marked by tragedy. Born in 1542, the only legitimate child of James V, she became queen at the age of six days when her father died after a short illness, having recently been defeated by the English at the battle of Solway Firth. It is curious that, in an age unaccustomed to female rule, Scotland not only gained a queen but also a powerful female regent, her French mother Mary of Guise.

Mary spent much of her youth at the French court and eventually married Francis II. And so the Queen of Scots for seventeen months was also Queen of France, just like Mary Tudor (the sister of Henry VIII); one of the great 'what ifs' of the sixteenth century is how things might have panned out had this Franco-Scottish empire survived. In the 2018 film, *Mary Queen of Scots*, Mary is red-headed and speaks with a Scottish accent; in reality, she had a French lilt, signed herself as 'Marie' and adapted her family name of 'Stewart' to the Frenchified 'Stuart'. Francis died at the end of 1560 and, on returning to Scotland, Mary found a kingdom divided among nobles, many of whom were anti-French and anti-Catholic, fuelled by militant churchmen such as John Knox.

Mary is so-often compared with her cousin, sister queen and nemesis, Elizabeth. The contrasts are immediately striking. Mary's effective reign was short while Elizabeth's was long. Mary is often presented as inexperienced, receiving poor advice, while Elizabeth became a skilled political operator, helped by the likes of her Machiavellian adviser, William Cecil, who was busy encouraging the factional in-fighting in Scotland and weakening Mary's hand. Mary had three husbands, who caused so many of her problems, while Elizabeth remained the 'Virgin Queen', married to her kingdom, her person hidden beneath the mask of office. Mary had a son, James, who ultimately united the English and Scottish thrones and solved the problem caused by Elizabeth's lack of issue.

Mary was not only ruler of one of England's traditional enemies; she had a viable claim to the English throne herself. This was only strengthened when she married her cousin, Henry Stewart, Lord Darnley, in 1565. Both were great-grandchildren of Henry VII, descended from Margaret Tudor (sister of Henry VIII) by different marriages. However, Darnley turned out to be a poor choice as a consort; he was an immature, inconsistent drunk and was involved in the gruesome murder of Mary's Italian secretary, David Rizzio—who, some say, was the real father of James. Indeed, it was pointed out in later years that the king always remained terrified of drawn swords, which was little wonder given his parentage.

Darnley himself was killed in 1567 after an explosion rocked the house where he was recovering from smallpox at Kirk o'Fields, just outside Edinburgh. Mary was suspected of complicity in his murder and rumours seemed to be confirmed when she married the principle suspect, the (Protestant) Earl of Bothwell, a few weeks later. It is unclear whether she entered her third marriage willingly and there are suggestions that the queen was the victim of rape. Whatever the

Fotheringhay, Northamptonshire • The End of the Queen of Scots

facts, her reign was visibly beginning to collapse. She was forced to abdicate while imprisoned by her enemies at Lochleven Castle and eventually fled to England, where she spent the last nineteen years of her life.

Although she was allowed the trappings of her royal position, Mary was kept under careful surveillance. Mary was, after all, considered the great hope of English Catholics. The fears of the authorities appeared justified when she was associated with several plots. The Northern Rising of 1569 was, in part, a reaction to unsuccessful attempts to arrange a marriage of Mary to the Duke of Norfolk. Then there followed the Ridolfi, Throckmorton and Babington plots, the last of which led to Mary's trial and execution, despite her protests that she was a queen and so incapable of committing treason. Mary's direct role in any of these plots remains open to question and it seems that the English were only too keen to find an excuse to send Mary to the block.

Mary remains a controversial figure. Catholics have long regarded her as a martyr, treasuring relics such as the rosary she carried to her execution, now at Arundel Castle. From 1887, the tercentenary of Mary's execution and the jubilee year of another British queen, there were attempts to push forward her beatification, inspired, no doubt, by the fifty-four English Martyrs raised to the altars the previous year. Pope Leo XIII and Cardinal Vaughan of Westminster both seemed in favour; others acknowledged the courage she showed in captivity and on the scaffold but raised the accusations of murder and adultery still being brought against her. The complexity of these issues has meant she has remained a national hero rather than a canonised saint.

It is curious, though, that two of the great Scottish icons, Mary, Queen of Scots, and 'Bonnie Prince Charlie', whose faces can be found on postcards and biscuit tins in every tourist shop, were both Catholic, both connected to foreign courts and both ultimately rejected by their own people.

GRACE DIEU & MOUNT ST BERNARDS, LEICESTERSHIRE

A Leicestershire Catholic Utopia

Craggy hills, buzzards, some of the country's oldest rocks, and a vibrant monastic heritage all characterise Charnwood Forest in Leicestershire. Before the Reformation the Cistercians had a house at nearby Garendon, and Augustinians at Ulverscroft and Grace Dieu. For one nineteenth-century grandee this monastic past became an inspiration for an ambitious project of evangelisation.

Ambrose Lisle March Phillipps belonged to a family based at Garendon Park, on the site of the Cistercian abbey; in later life he added the name 'de Lisle' and such was his prominence that Disraeli immortalised him in his novel *Coningsby*, in the character of 'Eustace Lyle'.

Ambrose converted to Catholicism in 1825, while still at school, inspired by his travels in France, his romantic sensibilities and the example of an old émigré priest, the Abbé Giraud, who had taught him French. Shortly afterwards he went to Cambridge, where he struck up a friendship with Kenelm Digby, a fellow convert and enthusiast of the chivalric ideals of the Middle Ages. Together they would ride each Sunday, still fasting, the twenty-five miles to the nearest Catholic church at St Edmund's College, Old Hall Green.

Friendship was Ambrose's gift: he numbered among his circle many of the pioneers of the nineteenth-century Catholic Revival, including John Talbot (16th Earl of Shrewsbury), the fiery architect Augustus Welby Pugin, and another convert, the Honourable George Spencer (son of Earl Spencer and an ancestor of Diana, Princess of Wales). Ambrose is chiefly remembered today for his dream of the conversion of England: 'Oh England', he wrote in 1831, 'if but once I could see the holy Catholick faith of Jesus Christ flourish again through thee, I could die contented!' With Spencer, he established the Association of Universal Prayer for the Conversion of England in 1838. He corresponded with many of the leading lights of the Oxford Movement and hoped for corporate reunion. Ambrose went on to set up the Association for Promoting the Unity of Christendom in 1857, though this was condemned by Rome, at Manning's instigation. Marrying into the recusant Clifford family, he also sired many children—including Eustace, one of the first posthumous winners of the Victoria Cross.

Ambrose's thoughts were also focused on his own corner of Leicestershire, where he built up a Catholic utopia. In 1833 he was given the manor of Grace Dieu by his father. He built a Tudor-style mansion, designed by William Railton (most famous for Nelson's Column in London), with a chapel later being added by Pugin, with the first rood screen erected since the Reformation. Here, Ambrose was able to indulge in another of his passions: the singing of Gregorian chant.

In 1835 he invited Trappist monks from Mount Melleray in Ireland to establish a monastery at Mount St Bernard—the first permanent monastery to be founded since the Reformation. Ambrose saw this, in part, as reparation for the dissolution of Garandon Abbey, where his family now resided. Communal life began in a half-derelict four-roomed cottage in Tynt Meadow. Fr Odilo Woolfrey, the superior, wrote: 'Here we are. I with my little company, already established in a little cottage on this land in Charnwood Forest which we have named "Mount Saint Bernard"'. Like their medieval forbears, the monks cultivated the wild and barren land. More fitting monastic buildings were opened in 1837, again produced by Railton, and were replaced eleven years later by the designs of Pugin, made possible by the generosity of the Earl of Shrewsbury.

All this was not without opposition. The local vicar wrote against the creeping 'Romanism' in his midst and there was talk of 'holding parties of pleasure upon the rock and of over looking the monks'. Ultimately, the monks were left in peace and in 1848 Mount Saint Bernards was raised to the dignity of an abbey. Dom Bernard Palmer thus became the first English abbot (on home soil) since the sixteenth century.

Ambrose did not stop there. Realising the shortage of English priests and the potential fruits of using foreign orders, he wrote to the likes of Blessed Antonio Rosmini (founder of the Institute of Charity) and the Passionist, Blessed Dominic Barberi. In 1840 Luigi Gentili, a Rosminian, arrived and used Grace Dieu as a base. His fellow missioner, William Lockhart, later wrote that 'from Grace Dieu as a centre, Father Gentili, with the zeal of a St Francis de Sales, in all weathers, on foot from the moment he had finished Mass till a very late hour at night, penetrated into all the villages for many miles round, and made acquaintance with the people'. Churches and schools followed at Loughborough, Shepshed and Whitwick. The first post-Reformation open air crosses or calvaries were erected on outcrops at Grace Dieu and Mount St Bernards.

Gentili had been shocked by the conditions of the poor. He wrote in January 1841: 'Not to be able to help these poor people is for me a great trial. Many cannot come to the chapel to be received or to receive the Sacraments or hear Mass, because they have no shoes, no hats, no decent clothing, as they are in rags and half-naked'. Gentili's missionary efforts were greatly helped by this compassion for the local population, who felt alienated from the 'respectable' Church of England—indeed, unlike the vicar, Gentili made a point of not charging for baptisms. His technique of evangelisation was based on house visiting and talking to people in the roads and lanes. By May 1841 he had succeeded in converting 320 people from Shepshed (out of a population of roughly 5,000), 100 from Belton (out of 2,000) and nearly 100 from Osgathorpe (out of 800).

Mount St Bernards still continues its work today. Members of the faithful, as well as tourists, come here to experience the peace, join the monks in prayer, visit the gift shop or enjoy the Tynt Meadow English Trappist Ale. One former member of the community, Cyprian Tansi, originally from Nigeria, was beatified in 1998. Though he died in Leicester Royal Infirmary in 1964, his body now rests in Onitsha, on the banks of the Niger river. Nevertheless, many pilgrims come to Mount St Bernards to seek his intercession.

The great actor, Alec Guiness, first visited Mount St Bernards in 1957 and witnessed the individual celebration of the monks' early-morning Masses around the church:

> For perhaps five minutes little bells sounded from all over and the sun grew whiter as it steadily rose. There was an awe-inspiring sense of God expanding, as if to fill every corner of the church and the whole world. The regularity of life at the abbey, the happy faces that shone through whatever they had suffered, the strong yet delicate singing, the early hours and hard work. All made a deep impression on me; the atmosphere was one of prayer without frills; it was easy to imagine oneself at the centre of some spiritual powerhouse, or at least being privileged to look over the rails, so to speak, at the working of a great turbine.

It was thanks to the vision of Ambrose Phillipps de Lisle that this great turbine was activated.

KENILWORTH, WARWICKSHIRE

The Romance of Kenilworth

The Warwickshire town of Kenilworth: for a Victorian it only meant one thing: Walter Scott's 1821 novel, firmly placing the romantic ruins of the castle on the tourist map. The book told of Robert Dudley, Earl of Leicester, who yearned for the favour (and love?) of Elizabeth I, and his secret marriage to Amy Robsart, who eventually died tragically and mysteriously. Liberties were taken with historical truth but there is no doubt of Leicester's ownership of the castle and the queen's sumptuous visits there, one of which, in 1575, lasted nineteen days. Murder, unrequited love and one of the England's most famous monarchs constituted an intoxicating cocktail for generations of readers and visitors.

The first castle was built in the twelfth century and in 1266 withstood a siege at the hands of Henry III, the longest in medieval England. After this bloody chapter, Kenilworth Castle settled down into becoming a favoured royal residence, especially under Henry V, who built 'the Pleasance in the Marsh' to retreat to in its grounds. It was apparently while staying at Kenilworth that he received an insulting gift from the French: 'because he was young, little balls to play with and soft pillows to sleep on to help him grow to manly strength'. He duly displayed his maturity and masculine qualities by defeating the French at Agincourt!

In the midst of the town is a large park, Abbey Fields, which calls to mind the Augustinian house that once stood there, as much a part of medieval Kenilworth as the castle. There are a few remnants to be seen—the gatehouse, sandstone barn, fish pond and snatches of walls. Other decorative elements, including an impressive Norman doorway, were incorporated into the nearby church of St Nicholas. The community of canons had been founded in 1119 by Geoffrey de Clinton, Henry I's chamberlain and treasurer, and the then occupant of the castle. Warwickshire was very much an Augustinian county, boasting six foundations, and the house at Kenilworth was one of the shire's leading landowners. It was elevated to the status of an abbey in 1447. By the 1520s, however, the canons complained that the abbot had too many servants and that discipline was too severe; there were financial strains too. In April 1538 it was the first Augustinian house to be dissolved, the abbot being generously pensioned off and granted the manor of Rudfyn.

There are few Catholic traces in the town until the 1830s, when the Amherst family arrived at Fieldgate House, at the eastern end of the High Street. They belonged to old Catholic stock and were cousins of the Earl of Shrewsbury. Of the six children who survived to adulthood, one (Francis) became Bishop of Nottingham, another (William) joined the Jesuits and two daughters entered the religious life. On their arrival at Kenilworth, however, there was only a handful of Catholics in the area. Nevertheless, the house became a hub of the 'Second Spring'; Nicholas Wiseman, then based at Oscott, later spoke of 'pleasant days' at the house. Mrs Amherst opened a day school and Sunday school and commissioned a little brick neo-gothic church nearby, on Hollis Lane.

The architect was none other than Augustus Welby Pugin, who Francis remembered as having 'an eye that took in everything, and with genius and enthusiasm in every line of his features'. His dress was decidedly eccentric, inclining to 'that of a dissenting minister of that day, with a touch of the sailor'. St Augustine's opened in 1842 but it is significant that seven years later further work was completed by another Catholic architect, Gilbert Blount. This was most likely because Pugin had fallen out with the Amhersts, for in 1845 he had proposed to Mary, the cleverest and prettiest of the daughters. Pugin had recently lost his second wife and looked for a new companion to help raise his six children; Mary seemed besotted and Pugin thought she would 'delight in everything I have' and was, indeed, 'an admirable sacristan' (a fine compliment from the neo-gothic master). However, Mrs Amherst was firmly against the plan, given Pugin's unstable character and humble social standing, as was the Earl of Shrewsbury, who threatened not to commission the architect again. Added to the mix was Mary's conflicting sense of being called to take the veil; in due course, and influenced by the charismatic Rosminian missioner, Fr Luigi Gentili, she entered the Sisters of Providence at Loughborough (Leicestershire). Sr Mary Agnes spent the rest of her life there, eventually becoming superior and helping to establish what is now the Loughborough Amherst School.

Pugin, meanwhile, was heart-broken; even Wiseman thought he had been badly treated and was worn almost to death. He would happily marry again—in 1848 to Jane Knill, known in the family as 'The Great Woman' and living into the twentieth century. Nevertheless, the story only adds to the romantic and at times melancholic atmosphere of Kenilworth.

LITTLEMORE, OXFORDSHIRE

In Newman's Footsteps

'Littlemore': the name has a hundred associations for the devotee of St John Henry Newman. The little village on the edge of Oxford was the focus of his apostolic labours for over fifteen years, the final resting place of his mother, the retreat where he prayed and studied and, ultimately, the location of his reception into the Catholic Church on 9 October 1845 (a date which is now his feast day).

On my last visit, the weather was so mild that I decided to walk to Littlemore from the city centre. After all, this was Newman's constant practice and if he could do it regularly, surely I could manage to make it down the Iffley Road just this once. Starting at the coach stop near the University Church of St Mary the Virgin, where Newman wowed Oxford with his profound sermons, it took me nearly an hour to reach my destination. Newman, I'm sure, was faster. One of his disciples, William Lockhart, remembered first seeing him in Oxford 'passing along in his characteristic way, walking fast, without any dignity of gait, but earnest, like one who had a purpose; yet so humble and self-forgetting in every portion of his external appearance, that you would not have thought him, at first sight, a man remarkable for anything'.

As I strolled along my daily pre-occupations seemed to disappear and my mind felt unusually clear. I wondered whether these walks had a similar effect on Newman; how many of his sermons were inspired, how many of his ideas were clarified as he passed along this way? The route is, of course, much more built up today, though the shape of the road and elevation of Rose Hill are obviously still the same. If you look carefully you can still see the one-time residence of Mrs Newman, where she moved in order to be near her son.

A bus rushed past on its way to 'Minchery Farm', reminding us that Littlemore was the site of a pre-Reformation Benedictine nunnery (or 'mynchery') dedicated to St Nicholas. Founded in the early thirteenth century by the head of the English Knights Templar, it seemed not to have had a very edifying reputation in its final years and was actually dissolved by Cardinal Wolsey in 1525—a reminder that monasteries could occasionally be dissolved for reasons of expediency before the Dissolution of the Monasteries. On this occasion the revenues raised were invested into the new Cardinal College (now known as Christ Church).

As I made my slow progress, there were eventually indications that the centre of Littlemore was near: clues such as 'Newman Road' and 'Cardinal Close', and then, after walking past a council estate and under the busy eastern bypass, a picturesque row of houses suddenly appeared, with the distant tower of the church. You could almost imagine Newman's slight figure hurriedly crossing the road in front of you.

As vicar of St Mary's, Newman had pastoral care for Littlemore from 1828 onwards. He quickly organised 'Evening Catechetical Lectures' and started visiting his flock, not something that was particularly common in the early nineteenth century. There was no church at Littlemore and so services were initially held in a cottage, until a new church building was ready in 1836—one of the first examples of the Gothic Revival in a village setting, which (in honour of the medieval 'mynchery') was jointly dedicated to St Mary and St Nicholas. A little school followed in 1838, which still can be seen.

Newman dreamed of founding a 'monastery' there, large enough for his extensive library, and bought land for this purpose in May 1840. However, his hurried retreat from Oxford following the controversial *Tract 90* forced him to set up home in the 'Cottages', a set of former stables in College Lane. His sister Harriet noted that it had 'a dozen windows—one storey. Inside it is very pretty and neat—just my fancy. I do not wonder at John's present enthusiasm. There are 4 or 5 sets of rooms—sitting and bedroom—all on the ground floor—the door opening into the verandah which runs all along, a length of the diagonal of Oriel quad. The kitchen is in the middle—a pretty little garden before the verandah. At right angles is the library, a large pretty room with a nice roof, the sides covered with books'.

Newman settled down to work on the Church Fathers and the lives of the English Saints. However, it would prove to be no rural idyll. Newman was, after all, a celebrity and his life was considered public property. The setting up of what appeared to be an Anglo-Catholic 'mynchery' led to varying rumours. In his *Apologia*, Newman complained that 'one day when I entered my house, I found a flight of Under-graduates inside. Heads of Houses, as mounted patrols, walked their horses round these poor cottages. Doctors of Divinity dived into the hidden recesses of that private tenement uninvited, and drew domestic conclusions from what they saw there. I had thought that an Englishman's house was his castle, but the newspapers thought otherwise'.

Littlemore is so often associated with Newman's subsequent conversion that it is often forgotten that the future Cardinal viewed it originally as a place of retreat, where he could lead a more regular life, spend more time working in the parish and, as he explained to the local bishop, help keep 'a certain class of minds firm in their allegiance to our Church'. He referred to Littlemore as 'my Torres Vedras', referring to the forts secretly built by Wellington to defend Lisbon during the Peninsular War. He soon gathered around him young disciples, who shared a common vision of the Church and wished to live a stricter life of prayer and study, initially at least firmly within the Church of England.

One of his disciples recalled that 'we spent our time at Littlemore in study, prayer and fasting. We rose at midnight to recite the Breviary Office, consoling ourselves with the thought that we were united in prayer with united Christendom, and were using the very words used by the Saints of all ages. We fasted according to the practice recommended in Holy Scripture, and practised in the most austere religious orders of Eastern and Western Christendom. We never broke our fast, except on Sundays and the Great Festivals, before twelve o'clock, and not until five o'clock in the Advent and Lenten seasons'.

As Newman continued his life at Littlemore, he became increasingly disillusioned with the Church of his birth. In 1843, following the conversion of one of the Littlemore men, the aforementioned William Lockhart, Newman resigned as vicar of St Mary's and preached his famous 'Parting of Friends' sermon in the village church. Then, on 9 October 1845, shortly after completing his *Development of Doctrine*, Newman was received into the Catholic Church at the hands of Blessed Dominic Barberi, who had arrived the previous night in the pouring rain. Newman received his First Communion at a Mass which the Passionist priest said on the writing desk that still can be seen at Littlemore.

The famous convert stayed on for a few more months, now attending the little chapel of St Ignatius in St Clement's High Street rather than his own foundation of St Mary and St Nicholas. In February 1846 Newman finally left Oxford and Littlemore behind him, taking the time to kiss his bed, the mantelpiece and other parts of the house: 'very happy times have I had here, (though in much doubt) — and I am loth to leave it'. Anyone who has had to leave behind a beloved home will understand such sentiments.

In 1951 Newman's former residence was purchased by the Birmingham Oratory and in 1987 entrusted to the care of the International Spiritual Family of the Work. The sisters welcome visitors, promote interest in Newman (especially through their extensive library) and pray throughout the day in the beautiful little Oratory. During my stay I attended Holy Hour and Compline there. As the sisters sung 'Lead Kindly Light' in four part harmony and then as I walked back to my room along the darkened 'cloister', I felt that St John Henry was still very much present in his former refuge.

MARYVALE, BIRMINGHAM

England's First Shrine to the Sacred Heart

It was Newman who first called the place 'Maryvale'—as a newly ordained Catholic priest he set up his first Oratorian community there and the name was a tribute to the Oratory church in Rome, Santa Maria in Vallicella (Our Lady in the Little Valley).

Maryvale's other name, Old Oscott, calls to mind another dimension of its Catholic history—the site of a college founded in 1794 which provided an education for the laity as well as a seminary formation for future priests. It was the first such institution to be founded from scratch on English soil, although its early years were plagued by financial problems and doubts over the orthodoxy of its teachers. In 1808 Bishop John Milner, the forthright Vicar Apostolic of the Midland District, was able to 'seize' control and inaugurate what came to be called the 'new government'. Such was the simplicity of Catholic ceremonial in those days that, at the grand opening, the Litany of Loreto was 'performed by the Jones family from Wolverhampton, accompanied by one of them on the pianoforte'.

Thirty years later the seminary moved to larger premises at New Oscott, with buildings designed by Pugin and others. By that time, Bishop Milner had put his college on the country's spiritual map. He had made his seminary the first shrine of the Sacred Heart in England.

Devotion to the Sacred Heart had, in its modern form, been preached in London as early as the 1670s by St Claude de la Colombiere, the Jesuit chaplain to Mary of Modena when she was Duchess of York. Before coming to London, St Claude was confessor to St Margaret Mary Alacoque at Paray le Monial, the first to hear of her famous Revelations. There is no evidence of the devotion surviving the Popish Plot of 1678, which forced the saint to return to France. But the ground was prepared for later developments. It is interesting that Old Oscott itself was closely associated with another victim of the Popish Plot, the priest Andrew Bromwich. He had been condemned to death in 1679 but the sentence was never carried out and, after being released, he was able to quietly minister as a priest in the Midlands. He founded a mission at Old Oscott and for many years the remains of an old oak tree that he had planted was admired in the garden.

Bishop Milner was a crusader against theological error and ecclesiastical compromise; Newman called him the 'English Athanasius'.

It is no surprise, then, that he was attracted to the devotion to the Sacred Heart, which in France had become a litmus test of loyalty to the Holy See and of proclaiming God's love and mercy against the general gloom and fatalism of the Jansenists.

During a visit to Rome in 1814, Bishop Milner obtained a plenary indulgence from Pius VII (recently returned from French captivity) for prayers said before an image of the Sacred Heart on First Fridays. On returning to his District, he established a special sodality and enshrined at Old Oscott an image of the Sacred Heart painted on glass. It is a simple image, in which Christ is holding His heart and pointing to it—as He does so, He not only reveals His love but invites us in to participate in His life.

The picture bears a crack which seems to have originated during the bishop's bumpy journey back from Rome. In front of the image a 'perpetual lamp' was lit for the conversion of England, in reparation for sins and for the intentions of the sodality's members. In 1820 Milner issued a pastoral letter to further promote the devotion.

Devotion to the Sacred Heart became one of the distinctive features of Second Spring Catholicism. Almost every church has an image or statue of the Sacred Heart and devotions like the First Fridays still prove to be popular. Next time we light a candle in front of the Sacred Heart at our local church, let us recall the work of Bishop Milner and his little shrine at Maryvale. As Newman later put it, the bishop 'set himself to soften and melt the frost which stiffened the Catholicism of his day, and to rear up, safe from our northern blasts, the tender and fervent aspirations of continental piety'. More importantly, he made English Catholics aware of the warmth and depth of God's love.

MILTON, OXFORDSHIRE

An Afternoon at the Manor

The first thing we saw on turning off the A34 and following the signs for Milton is the oppressive presence of Didcot Power Station, voted one of Britain's worse eyesores—and now no more. It does not bode well. Yet, a mile or so down the road, this is all forgotten. A sign advertises goose eggs and home-grown rhubarb in the 'serve yourself' farm shop. Nearby, an inviting pub faces the medieval church, dedicated to St Blaise. Then, down the shaded road and through the sturdy iron gates, we drive towards the manor house.

This is no sanitised National Trust residence, with large car parks, reception areas and gift shops. There are indeed signs that it has recently been open to the public: a small ticket kiosk, bunting hanging between the gates, tea shop tables glistening in the sunlight, a children's 'ferry' across the miniature 'Serpentine' lake and a tree house with the sign: 'No grown-ups or teenagers allowed'. This is no stuffy museum but rather a family home.

Our reception committee could not have been more welcoming: the lady of the house warmly greets us with a broad smile, along with an inquisitive dog, a strutting cock, two hens and a cat that had just disgraced itself by catching a baby mole. The family's two llamas, sadly, are elsewhere on the extensive grounds.

Milton Manor is part of a group of historic Catholic houses in the Thames Valley, which also includes Stonor, Mapledurham and East Hendred. Milton is not, however, the home of one of the old Catholic families. It has no secret priest holes or direct links with the martyrs, although the owners are certainly proud to be descended from St Thomas More. The house stands on land that once belonged to Abingdon Abbey. After the Dissolution, it eventually ended up in the hands of the Caltons, a prominent Berkshire family, who built what is now the central part of the house around 1663. In subsequent years two royal guests are reputed to have stayed at Milton: in December 1688, William of Orange, who heard while he was here of James II's flight from London, and in 1696 Peter the Great, who supposedly commented it was the coldest house he had ever slept in. It is a pity that the beds they (may have) used were sold, along with much else, in 1911.

In 1764 the house was purchased for £10,600 by Bryant Barrett, a wealthy merchant and lacemaker to George III, who represented the 'new money' of the eighteenth century. Having made his fortune in London he wanted to adopt the lifestyle of a grandee in the country. Unusually, he was a Catholic convert. Although he stood for much of what was new, he had to be prudent in the face of the old penal laws; it was his Protestant brother, Isaac, who bought the property on Bryant's behalf.

Barrett further augmented his position in society by marrying into the old Catholic gentry. His first wife, Mary Belson of Brill (Buckinghamshire), traced her lineage to the Elizabethan martyr, Blessed Thomas Belson. The marriage seems to have been happy but childless and, after her death, Barrett married Winifred Eyston, of the family based at East Hendred and descended from St Thomas More.

Barrett 'Georgianised' the house, building two wings, new kitchens and a brew house, and landscaping the garden. Most notably, he added Milton's two most spectacular rooms. On the ground floor is the gothic library, based on Horace Walpole's house at Strawberry Hill, Twickenham, although following the sale of so many of Barrett's books this room has become as much a showcase of the house's fine china as a repository of learning. Above, on the first floor, is the chapel, in a similar eighteenth-century gothic style, with white-painted wood panelling, and medieval glass placed in the windows. Barrett no doubt chose gothic because it was becoming fashionable but, for a Catholic, it also expressed continuity with pre-Reformation England and a hint of legitimacy. Milton has good claim to be one of the first Catholic chapels built in England after the Reformation and the first in the revived gothic style (Dr Milner's chapel at Winchester is of a later date).

The chapel was included on the first floor rather than in a separate building so as to avoid protests from non-Catholic neighbours. An internal window opens above the door, from which extra members of the congregation sitting in a gallery could follow the Mass—tradition records local Catholics using this facility.

On the windowsills are photos of more recent family weddings that have taken place here, along with that of Antony Andrews and Jane Seymour in the 1982 film *The Scarlet Pimpernel*, shot on location at Milton. Mass continues to be celebrated here occasionally and it was a great privilege to offer the sacred mysteries during my visit. I was shown into the nearby Dressing Room, adorned with precious eighteenth-century Chinese wallpaper, and allowed to use the chalice that once belonged to Bishop Richard Challoner. Around the chapel are various chasubles that he would have worn, along with his relic of the True Cross.

Milton may not boast martyrs but it takes pride in this great spiritual connection and I was asked to offer Mass for the cause of Challoner's beatification, which one day (we hope) may be reopened. This holy Vicar Apostolic of the London District and prolific author knew Milton well; indeed, it seems that Barrett was one of his converts. Challoner lived at various addresses in central London but seems to have been a regular guest at Milton, where he could enjoy the peace and solitude of the country. Little is known of his movements, however, and Barrett only receives three mentions in Edwin Burton's two-volume life of the bishop published in 1909.

Nevertheless, when the aged prelate died in 1781 he was buried in the Barrett vault below the church of St Blaise. It was perhaps deemed a discreet place of burial in the uncertain and violent aftermath of the Gordon Riots, which had destroyed several Catholic chapels around the country. The rector of Milton read the Anglican burial service—the Catholic rites seem already to have been observed in London—and recorded in the register: 'Anno Domini 1781, January 22. Buried the Reverend Richard Challoner, a Popish Priest and Titular Bishop of London and Salisbury [sic], a very pious and good man, of great learning and extensive abilities'. His body remained there until 1946, when it was translated to Westminster Cathedral.

After Mass we enjoyed a simple supper in the Breakfast Room. Even though it was June, the fire was lit, much to the delight of one of the cats—justifying Peter the Great's comments about the coldness of the place. What struck me was the warmth of the company and the sense of timelessness. There are only four generations standing between the current owner and Bryant Barrett and, as we sat there, I almost expected Bishop Challoner to walk in and join us at the table.

SEMPRINGHAM, LINCOLNSHIRE

St Gilbert of Sempringham

The Middle Ages are often remembered for the monasteries and religious houses that flourished around Britain and made a huge contribution to the Church and society at large. Their dramatic dissolution in the sixteenth century, together with the poignant ruins that remain in some places, makes their story endlessly fascinating. However, it is curious that this land of monasteries produced only one major home-grown Order: the Gilbertines.

Its founder, St Gilbert of Sempringham, was born in 1083, three years before the completion of the Domesday Book. His father was a Norman knight but a physical deformity (possibly of the spine) meant it was impossible for St Gilbert to folllow a military career. He was educated at Lincoln and (possibly) Paris and then, thanks to the patronage of his father, became rector of the Lincolnshire churches of Sempringham and West Torrington. Not yet ordained, he employed priests to celebrate the sacraments but did not neglect the pastoral duties of a rector: he tried to limit the local consumption of alcohol, for example, and founded a school for boys and girls.

He was eventually ordained a priest, having been spotted by the Bishop of Lincoln and appointed to his household. However, Sempringham remained in his thoughts and, despite being offered a prestigious archdeaconry, he asked to return to his rustic parish, selling his possessions and living henceforth a life of poverty. By this time, it should be noted, his father had died and he was effectively rector and 'lord of the manor'. He thus had the resources to do something quite extraordinary for God.

Around 1131 a group of 'maidens', probably old girls of the parish school, began living as a community of anchoresses under the rector's direction. They initially lived above the church entrance but then moved into a new building nearby. Since they were enclosed in order to lead the contemplative life, it was soon found necessary to have lay sisters and, later, lay brothers to look after their material needs — recruited from the poor of the area. At first it was very much a local affair, limited to Sempringham and funded largely by St Gilbert, who remained a secular priest, and his brother Roger. However, in 1139 the bishop placed another female community, founded at Haverholme, under St Gilbert's care. The seeds of the Gilbertine Order were sown.

The communities at Sempringham and Haverholme were nearly swallowed up by the Cistercians; indeed, St Gilbert travelled to the General Chapter of 1147, held at Cîteaux, with this hope in mind. However, the Cistercians showed no desire to oblige—they had just taken over control of two much larger reformed orders, those of Sauvigny and Obazine, and were not interested in a double community—but both Pope Eugenius III and St Bernard encouraged St Gilbert to carry on the good work.

In the years that followed, the Gilbertines became more structured, the different elements following a variety of rules—the nuns followed that of St Benedict, the lay brothers that of the Cistercians and the canons regular, who were introduced in the 1150s to act as chaplains to the nuns, followed an adaptation of the Augustinian Rule. In many of the houses there were male and female communities gathered round the same church but with separate sets of monastic buildings. A wall or barrier cut down the church, so that both could attend Mass but not see each other. In many ways, a Gilbertine house was not merely double but quadruple, with nuns, canons, lay sisters and brothers living on the same site. However, single sex foundations were also made.

With the growth of the Gilbertine Order came the inevitable series of growing pains and crises. An infamous scandal involving a pregnant nun at Watton, Yorkshire, revealed that the two communities were perhaps not as separate as they should be and also that the Order could be firm in its discipline. The nun was imprisoned and eventually reconciled, while the lay brother (or canon) was castrated—not an unusual punishment for the twelfth century.

St Gilbert was attacked by the king for his support of St Thomas Becket, who stayed at several Gilbertine houses on his way to exile—although Henry II also proved to be a valuable patron, founding the priory at Newstead, Lincolnshire. Moreover, like many a Founder, St Gilbert later faced a rebellion from his own Order, centred around lay brothers who claimed they were overworked and underfed. Even the pope was involved and eventually the Rule was moderated.

St Gilbert comes down to us as an austere figure, following a penitential life although also warm and playful in his personality. He lived for much of his life as a secular priest and master of the Order, only formally taking the habit in his dotage. He reached a venerable age—some say 106—and remained active to the last though he suffered much from blindness and physical weakness. It was at Newstead that he received Extreme Unction at Christmas 1188 and was quickly moved to Sempringham to die—dying at the mother house ensured his burial there. Having said his farewells to the Gilbertine priors, the saint died on 4 February 1189.

St Gilbert was buried at Sempringham, his tomb being situated in the dividing wall so that both communities could have access to it. Miracles were quickly reported and finally he was canonised in 1202 — the first process to follow the new guidelines set down by Innocent III. Soon afterwards the saint's body was translated to a new shrine; indeed, the lengthy ceremonies were nearly ended prematurely when the Archbishop of Canterbury was taken ill but, fortunately, he was quickly cured through St Gilbert's intercession. The shrine continued to attract pilgrims up until the Reformation and the Order continued its good work, though it was never very large or wealthy; the lack of resources meant, for example, that they had to give up the church that they were given in Rome (San Sisto). At the Dissolution there were a total of twenty-trhee communities, only three of which had a net income of over £200 (Sempringham, Watton and Chicksands in Bedfordshire). The fact that the Order had never survived beyond the Channel (despite an attempted foundation in Normandy) meant that by 1538 the Gilbertines were extinct; their last master, Robert Holgate, a protégé of Thomas Cromwell, became Archbishop of York.

There was nothing showy about the Gilbertines. Their churches were Cistercian in their simplicity, their chant was unadorned and often sung on a monotone, their houses were poor and modest. Truly English in their understatedness, it is perhaps appropriate that today they are an impressive but largely forgotten footnote to our monastic history.

SHREWSBURY, SHROPSHIRE

The Churches of Shrewsbury

Shrewsbury rises gently from a loop in the River Severn. For England, it is not an ancient town: first mentioned in 901, it is five miles distant from Wroxeter, which was the fourth largest city in Roman Britannia (Viroconium Cornoviorum). The locations of both these conurbations can be explained not only by the river but the proximity of the Welsh border: this was frontier territory. And the Welsh were not the only threat: an important battle was fought just outside the city walls in 1403 between Henry IV and his one-time ally Henry Percy, known to posterity as 'Hotspur'. The king won but not before a storm of arrows that 'fell like leaves in autumn'. A village on the probable site actually bears the name 'Battlefield' and the collegiate church of St Mary Magdalene was founded there to pray for the fallen.

Shrewsbury is itself a town of churches, four of which boast Saxon origins. One, at the town's highest point, is named after the obscure St Alkmund and was founded by Alfred the Great's daughter, Æthelflæd, the famous 'Lady of the Mercians' and a ruler in her own right. But perhaps the grandest is the Abbey of SS Peter and Paul, which stood on the site of a Saxon chapel and became a Benedictine house in 1083, thanks to the patronage of the powerful Roger of Montgomery (who also built Arundel Castle in West Sussex).

Situated in the medieval suburb of the Foregate, to the east of the river, the Abbey's most famous resident is actually fictional: Ellis Peter's monastic detective, Brother Cadfael. Yet the monastery's history is full of memorable moments: twice Parliament sat there, in the days when it followed the monarch; the Royal Exchequer was briefly located there; and in 1137 the body of St Winefride was enshrined there. Her body rested *en route* at the hamlet of Woolston and a miraculous spring welled up, mirroring the more famous Holywell in Flintshire. The Abbey came to also house the shrines of other saints linked to the Welsh virgin martyr: her uncle, St Beuno, and her companion, the abbot St Elerius. Pilgrims flocked to these holy sites and it seems that in 1416 Henry V went on foot from Shrewsbury to Holywell to give thanks for the victory of Agincourt. As he passed through, he no doubt thought of his father's victory over Hotspur that secured him the throne.

The monastery's final days were marred by decaying buildings and financial irregularities. It was dissolved in 1540; the buildings gradually disappeared and the church reduced in size. The abbey's most poignant relic is perhaps the fourteenth-century pulpit from the monk's refectory, now standing in isolated splendour in its own garden. The figures of SS Peter, Paul, Winefride and Beuno gaze out from this peaceful spot at the hustle and bustle of the twenty-first century.

One of the most interesting of Shrewsbury's churches, though, only opened in 1856. Located near the medieval walls, Our Lady Help of Christians and St Peter Alcantara is unique among our Catholic cathedrals for housing the only cathedra in the county. Its construction was marked by death. Commissioned by the 16th Earl of Shrewsbury for the genius of Augustus Welby Pugin, the project was completed posthumously by their sons, the 17th Earl and Edward Pugin. Even then, the new earl died three months before the church's opening, and plans for a 300-foot spire had to be discarded due to the sandy soil.

A walk inside introduces us to a notable local Catholic family and a talented artist of the Arts and Crafts Movement, who is finally getting the recognition she deserves. The cathedral's jewels are the seven windows designed by Margaret Agnes Rope: the great West Window was her first major commission and shows scenes of the English and Welsh Martyrs, both ancient (St Alban) and more modern (More and Fisher); the Soldier Window is a memorial to an Irish Guardsman killed in 1917; and the Seminary Martyrs Window, which includes a scene of the Tyburn Walk, once organised annually by the Guild of Our Lady of Ransom, and must be one of the few church windows to feature a 1920s London bus!.

The daughter of a popular Shrewsbury doctor, 'Marga' converted to Catholicism, along with her mother and most of her siblings. Like other members of the family, she had a strong artistic bent and studied stained glass in Birmingham under (the appropriately named) Henry Payne. She soon gained a reputation for her art, working first from home in Shrewsbury and then from London (Glass House in Fulham). She was a lively young lady who smoked and rode a motorbike, but she felt the call of the cloister and joined the Carmel at Woodbridge (Suffolk). Despite her enclosed life, she continued her craft and sent her glass by train to London to be fired up. Sadly, the difficulties of wartime and declining health meant that by the time the community moved to Quidenham in 1948, she had fewer opportunities to exercise her creativity.

Her brother, Henry Edward George Rope, was a well-known and somewhat eccentric priest and writer, who served for over two decades as Archivist of the Venerable English College, Rome. An opponent of many aspects of modernity and mechanisation, he was proud never to have used a motorcar, and when he finally left the Eternal City in December 1957 insisted on taking a horse-drawn *carrozza* to the station. On his death in 1978, he was described as 'a collector of the minutiae of the past, an antiquary of the character of Leland, a fascinating man for his company and his conversation... For him to have lived on into the age of the atom bomb, the supermarket and the computer was a penance'.

Fr Rope would have been delighted that in 2019 the 1980s reordering of his cathedral was itself reordered and the nineteenth-century wall-paintings in the sanctuary and original tiling uncovered once again—a fine complement to his sister's magnificent windows.

STRATFORD-UPON-AVON, WARWICKSHIRE

Shakespeare's Guild Chapel

Stratford-upon-Avon is Shakespeare's town. Its modern heart is the Royal Shakespeare Theatre, situated on the River Avon and a short walk away from Holy Trinity church, where the playwright is buried. On the eve of the Protestant Reformation, however, the town's centre was surely the complex of guild buildings, most of which still stand on Church Street and Chapel Lane. There was a chapel, guild hall, almshouses and a school, where Shakespeare was educated, along with (possibly) Blessed Robert Dibdale, martyred at Tyburn in 1586. What is remarkable is not only how many of these buildings still survive but also that they are still in use: chapel, school and almshouses continue to make their contribution to town life today.

The Guild of the Holy Cross, the Blessed Virgin Mary and St John the Baptist is first mentioned in 1296, when the Bishop of Worcester, Godfrey Giffard, gave it permission to open a 'hospital' both for its members and poor priests of the diocese. By 1389 members paid a penny four times a year, on the feasts of St Michael, St Hilary, Easter and St John the Baptist. One benefit of membership was a candle lit at every Mass, 'so that God and the Blessed Virgin and the venerated Cross, may keep and guard all the brethren and sisters of the guild from every ill'. There was a great celebration each year on the feast of the Holy Cross with Masses, processions and a banquet. In 1410, for instance, 108 of the 245 members attended.

Guilds were a common feature of medieval society both in England and overseas. Their purpose was primarily religious. For an annual subscription and participation in the guild's activities, members benefited from its Masses, its prayers (especially for the dead) and the burning of its candles in front of an image. The spiritual life of a guild was often based around a particular altar in the local church or, in some cases, its own chapel. Indeed, in Stratford there were complaints that members never attended the nearby parish church!

According to the information boards that greet the visitor today, the chapel at Stratford is 'one of the finest examples in Europe of a purpose-built medieval guild chapel, as well as a fascinating example of mercantile arts patronage in late medieval England'. Dating back to the guild's early years, the chapel was remodelled in the late fifteenth century and a series of wall-paintings added thanks to the generosity of a wealthy local: Sir Hugh Clopton. This merchant had risen to become Lord Mayor of London and erected a large house, New Place, opposite the guild buildings, which later became Shakespeare's final home.

The new paintings covered the chapel interior: there was an impressive 'Doom' (Last Judgment) over the chancel arch, with the Lord sitting on a rainbow and dispensing justice to the saved and the damned, as well as depictions of the Finding of the True Cross, the Dance of Death, the life of Adam, the story of St George and the murder of St Thomas Becket. There were also more obscure subjects: a wild boar hunt and an allegorical representation of the popular poem 'Earth upon Earth', which ends with the words: *Mors solvit omnia*, 'Death dissolves all things'.

Guilds often had their own chaplains. By the fifteenth century, Stratford had four of them, who celebrated daily Masses on the hour from six to nine in the morning. They lived together in the guild complex, following strict regulations; they were appointed by the guild and only allowed to celebrate Mass elsewhere with its permission.

The guild was not solely a religious organisation. Open to both men and women, it was an important way of fostering fraternity and support within a community. It took on many socio-economic roles: charity, bank, landowner, funeral director, trade union, and organ of local government. Indeed, at Stratford one room in the guild complex was known as the 'Draper's Chamber' and in time the guild effectively became the town's governing body.

Given their stress on the Mass and prayer for the dead, it is little surprise that guilds took a direct hit at the Reformation—although historians have argued that their suppression in the mid-sixteenth century was also a move towards centralisation and the elimination of a local power base that could prove to be subversive. In Stratford, though, the good work of the guild did not completely disappear. The chapel, school and almshouses were granted by the Crown to the Mayor and Corporation of Stratford, which had replaced the guild as the town's governing body. Funds originally intended for the lighting of candles and the celebration of Mass were redirected to the school (now known as the 'King Edward VI School') and the maintenance of the bridge over the Avon that had also been built by Clopton.

In 1563 many of the wall-paintings in the chapel were whitewashed, under the authority of the Chamberlain of the Corporation, one John Shakespeare (father of the playwright). On the surface this seems to be evidence of the town's Protestant spirit. However, the reality is more nuanced. Whitewash removed 'offensive' Catholic subjects, such as the saints, and placated the authorities, but it also had the advantage of easily being removed should religious policies change once again.

John Shakespeare, it should be remembered, was a Catholic at heart. This is clear from his spiritual testament, discovered hidden in Shakespeare's birthplace in 1757. It expressed his desire to die a Catholic and regretted his past 'mumurations against God, or the Catholic Faith'—suggesting his regret in whitewashing the images in the chapel. He wrote that 'since it is uncertain what lot will befall me, for fear notwithstanding lest by reason of my sins I be to pass and stay a long while in Purgatory, they will vouchsafe to assist and succour me with their holy prayers and satisfactory works, especially with the holy sacrifice of the mass, as being the most effectual means to deliver souls from their torments and pains'. The language is unmistakably Catholic and follows St Charles Borromeo's *Last Will of the Soul*, popularised in England by Jesuits such as St Edmund Campion.

The chapel entered a period of decline: in 1620 the clergyman in charge of the chapel had to answer the Corporation for allowing 'his children to play at ball and other sports therein, his servants to hang clothes to dry in it, his pigs and poultry and dog to lie and feed in it and the pictures defaced and windows broken'. The paintings seem to have been subsequently painted over several times, only being uncovered during renovation work in 1804. Since then, there has been much conservation and the chapel recognised for its historical and artistic merit, giving a glimpse of the Catholic roots that coloured the imagination and fed the heart of our famous bard.

WATERPERRY, OXFORDSHIRE

Waterperry

Sandwiched between a shopping centre and a dual carriageway, my presbytery stands on the Oxford Road, a reminder of the time when Uxbridge was an important stopping point on one of the chief routes going out of London. One day I decided to trace the old road leading from London to the 'dreaming spires' — not the dreary, anodyne motorway but the far more interesting A40 which winds its way through market towns and the countryside of the Chilterns.

For those with eyes to see, there was plenty of interesting associations. As we entered the centre of Beaconsfield, the cemetery in which G. K. Chesterton is buried was just a stone's throw away. At West Wycombe the Palladian home of the Dashwoods lay to the left and the church with its distinctive golden ball sat high up the hill to the right. As we drove over the high Chiltern ridge close to Stokenchurch, we could see Beacon Hill. According to legend, a battle was fought here around 914 between the Saxons and the Danes. A local saying has it that 'juniper only grows where blood has been spilled' and the area is indeed covered in juniper. Before long we were in Oxfordshire and found ourselves at Waterperry, eight miles from Oxford. Since rush hour was approaching, we decided to make this our final destination.

Waterperry is today best known for its gardens, with seasonal displays of snowdrops and Michaelmas Daisies. These stand in the grounds of a stately Queen Anne house, beside which, now tucked away behind the garden shop and tea rooms, is a small, atmospheric medieval church. The door still has the notice that was there in 1942 when Arthur Mee was writing his guide to Oxfordshire:

> Of your charity latch this door
> Lest a bird enter and die of thirst.
> He prayeth best, who loveth best
> All things both great and small:
> For the dear God who loveth us,
> He made and loveth all.

The church, dedicated to the Blessed Virgin, has a little bit of everything: the traces of a Saxon arch, early-medieval glass, splendid funerary monuments and brasses, a three-decker pulpit and boxed pews (including a particularly large one for the manor family). The interior was full of flowers and the Parochial Church Council had kindly left a note explaining that, although it was customary not to have flowers during Lent, there was a forthcoming wedding. It was therefore felt that everyone should be able to enjoy the arrangements.

Like most country manors, Waterperry was held by several families down the centuries. From just before the Reformation onwards it became the home of the Cursons, originally from Derbyshire, who made Waterperry an important centre of Catholicism for the area. The first Waterperry Curson, Walter, was initially buried at the church of the Augustinian friars in Oxford, where he was well-known as a benefactor. After the Dissolution the brass depicting Walter and his wife Isabel was piously removed to the safety of Waterperry, where it remains to this day under a carpet in the nave. Curiously, the large brass was originally laid at the Augustinian church on Leadenhall Street, London around 1440 for a different couple. When the priory was voluntarily surrendered to the Crown in 1532 due to its huge debts, the brass was sold and refashioned to serve as a monument to the Cursons. The figures gained new heads and the shoes rounded to meet modern fashions, though the pointed toes can still be seen. Such a reused brass is referred to as a 'palimpsest'.

Like most Catholic families of the time, the Cursons went through ups and downs. Sir John Curson faced financial difficulties due to the heavy fines for non-attendance at church and sided with the king during the Civil War, causing a brief confinement in the Tower in 1642. There is a tablet in Waterperry church commemorating his wife, Magdalen Dormer, of the noted Catholic family, describing her as 'a Magdalen by name, a Saint by grace'. Other Cursons seem to have conformed to the Church of England. Sir Thomas, who was respectable enough to have been created a baronet in 1661, seems to have been an Anglican, as was his son Sir John, who is described as only becoming a Catholic after marrying Penelope Child. It was he who, in 1713, built the fine house that we see today.

Waterperry was an important Mass centre for the area. During the seventeenth century, the Jesuits had established a mission in Oxford. In more tolerant periods, away from political crisis, Mass was celebrated in hotels and even (during the reign of James II) some colleges. However, this ended after the 'Glorious Revolution' of 1688 and by 1715 there were only two 'reputed papists' in the city. Mass was only celebrated in houses such as Waterperry, which became particularly associated with the Jesuits. When Sir Francis Curson died in 1750, he left £200 'for the maintenance of a priest of the Society of Jesus ... for ever amongst the Catholics of Waterperry ... whether the said Priest live in the Family of Waterperry at the Mansion House, or do not live in the said Family'.

On the south side of the chancel arch there is an interesting detail that might easily be missed. There are several groups of letters, in seventeenth-century script, including an 'L', 'V' and 'EL' and then below a 'Q' and 'SCA'. The church's antiquarian vicar between 1925 and 1952, Rev. John Todd, suggested that the letters spelt out the words 'Luvel' and 'Requiescat', possibly commemorating the Jesuit priest Fr Lovell, who died in 1683 and was known at Waterperry. Perhaps he was buried nearby? The intriguing letters on the arch are a visible reminder that while the Book of Common Prayer was followed in this charming church, the Catholic Mass was more or less openly being celebrated in the house next door.

The situation continued until 1790, when the family living at Waterperry asked the priest to leave. Conditions were changing for Catholics and the next year the great Catholic Relief Act passed. The Jesuit chaplain, Fr Charles Leslie, bought a house in the poor Oxford suburb of St Clement's in 1791, just across Magdalen Bridge. Catholicism had at last made a return to the university town. Many other churches and institutions would follow.

As we made our way back to the car park, we bumped into a man who knew Waterperry well. He pointed out that this was close to the dividing line between the Cavaliers and Roundheads during the Civil War. He identified himself as a Parliamentarian from Berkshire. On asking my persuasion, I revealed myself as a Royalist from Middlesex. As I headed to the car with a wry smile, I realised that the ebbs and flows of history are never far away.

WOBURN ABBEY, BEDFORDSHIRE

Abbey Ghosts

Make a list of the grandest stately homes in England and Woburn Abbey would surely make the Top Ten. This magnificent house, largely rebuilt in the eighteenth century, is the home of the Duke of Bedford and sees thousands of visitors each year, many of whom head for the famous Safari Park. As the name suggests, Woburn Abbey stands on the site of a Cistercian house, founded in 1145 from the more famous Yorkshire abbey of Fountains. Few traces remain of the monastery, save a few stones and a downstairs corridor in the house known as 'Paternoster Row', which follows the side of one of the cloisters.

The abbey had once been wealthy but by the time of Henry's break with Rome the community had dwindled to an abbot and about thirteen monks. It seems to have been in good order and there is no evidence of any scandals. The last abbot, Robert Hobbes, was noteworthy for his resistance to the religious changes. The community dutifully complied with Dr Petre when he arrived to administer the oath of supremacy, remove all papal bulls and erase the pope's name from the liturgical books. The abbot later confessed, though, that he had the bulls secretly copied and expressed his wish that the pontiff's name should merely be struck out rather than completely erased. When news reached him of More's and Fisher's executions and the first wave of monastic dissolutions, Hobbes ordered fasting and penance in reparation for the outrage.

The abbot grew increasingly distressed at his own cowardice in taking the oath of supremacy, especially in the light of the examples set by these contemporary martyrs. When he was struck down with sickness, he confessed that he wished he had died alongside them. Little did he know that his wish was soon to be granted. Some of the secretly copied bulls were found and delivered to the authorities in London by a former religious who had been rebuked by the abbot for his 'new learning'. The regime acted swiftly. On 8 May 1538 Woburn Abbey was surrendered to the Crown. The abbot and several others were questioned. It was clear that Hobbes was in grave danger, admitting that he had failed to preach the royal supremacy and was critical of the changes. The sub-prior, Ralph Barnes, had also failed to address this topic and prayed publicly for the pope when taking his degree at Oxford, while another monk, Dom Laurence Blunham, boasted that he would never take the oath.

These three were tried at Bedford and executed at the end of June 1538. They appealed for mercy but to no avail, the abbot writing that it was 'out of a scrupulous conscience that he then had, considering the long continuance of the Bishop of Rome in that trade being, and the sudden mutation thereof'. It is perhaps because they showed human weakness as they faced death and even seemed open to admitting their errors that they were never included among the official list of Catholic martyrs. But no matter how reluctantly, they paid the ultimate price.

According to tradition, they were hanged on an oak tree that stood near the abbey gate and to this day is referred to as the 'Abbot's Oak'. It is possible that they were executed elsewhere, at a more populous location, but that one of the abbot's quarters was displayed at Woburn, giving the tree its name.

Woburn was subsequently given to the Russell family, who became earls and then dukes of Bedford. They owned estates across the country, many of which had formerly been monastic land. These included the Benedictine house at Tavistock (Devon) and the garden of the monks at Westminster, better known as Convent or Covent Garden. In time they added Bloomsbury to their impressive portfolio, hence the well-known London squares bearing the names of 'Bedford' and 'Russell'. Their family motto calls to mind a popular song: *Che sara sara*, 'whatever will be, will be'.

The family were staunchly Protestant, as can be seen in the poem that was later placed on the 'Abbot's Oak', proclaiming:

> Yes, old memorial of the mitred monk
> Thou liv'st to flourish in a brighter day,
> And seem'st to smile, that pure and potent vows
> Are breath'd where superstition reigned: thy trunk
> Its glad green garland wears, though in decay
> And years hang heavy on thy time-stained boughs.

One of the family's heroes was Lord William Russell, the heir to the 5th Earl, who appears on numerous paintings throughout the house. He was beheaded after being implicated in the Rye House Plot (1683), an attempt to assassinate Charles II and his brother James in order to avoid a Catholic succeeding to the throne. Once James had been deposed and William and Mary safely wore their crowns, he was posthumously pardoned, and his grieving father raised to the dignity of a duke by way of compensation.

It is interesting, though, that despite this strong pedigree, not only does Woburn still call itself an 'abbey' but one of its present glories bears the name of a French Catholic priest. The extensive parkland around the house, dotted with august oaks, is famous for its deer and among the rare species found there is 'Pére David's Deer'. The animal's Chinese name, *Milu*, means 'four not alike' because it was said that it had the hooves of a cow, the head of a horse, the antlers of a deer and the body of a donkey. The breed is now extinct in the wild but its survival in captivity is largely the result of the efforts of the 11th Duke. Pére David was a remarkable Lazarist missionary, who was sent to China shortly after his ordination in 1862 and managed to combine pastoral work with the collection and identification of species, many of which were hitherto unknown in the Europe. These included the giant panda and the deer, rat snake and bird (tit) that bear his name.

If the ghost of Abbot Hobbes still walks near his oak, as some say he does, he no doubt admires the majestic antlers of these deer and perhaps ponders on the twists and turns of Woburn's history. *Che sara sara.*

THE NORTH

DURHAM (COUNTY DURHAM) & LINDISFARNE (NORTHUMBERLAND)

St Cuthbert's Resting Place

Ask a group of people what their favourite English cathedral is, and Durham will almost certainly be in pole position. This is easy to see why: the picturesque position high above a bend on the River Wear, the pristine Norman architecture, the large number of surviving monastic buildings and the nearby castle (long incorporated into the prestigious university). Dr Johnson was struck by its 'rocky solidity and indeterminate duration'. In more recent times, it is briefly enjoyed by train passengers whizzing between London and Edinburgh: indeed, the East Coast mainline is the most ecclesiastical of routes, with glimpses also of the cathedrals at Peterborough and York.

Durham Cathedral has been compared to a great liner sitting in a dry dock. The maritime analogy is appropriate for the origins of Durham lie in the sea, or, to be more precise, the 'Holy Island' of Lindisfarne, separated from the Northumberland coast by a tidal causeway and also observable from East Coast trains. St Aidan founded a community of Irish monks there in 634 and it became the hub of the evangelisation of much of northern England and the seat of a bishopric. It's most famous monk, abbot and bishop was St Cuthbert, in whose honour the Lindisfarne Gospels, one of the treasures of the British Library, were created shortly after his death.

St Cuthbert, despite his Saxon origins, fully embraced the traditions of Celtic Christianity, as can be seen in his love of solitude and closeness to nature—seen as a mark of his holiness and return to humanity's original harmony with creation, lost through original sin. Reluctantly appointed a bishop and resigning after eighteen months, he was happiest living as a hermit on Inner Farne, five miles out to sea. It was a hard life; the surrounding waters could be perilous (as witnessed today by the two lighthouses and heroic stories of Grace Darling) and a constant soundtrack provided by the many species of birds: including gulls, shags, razorbills, and puffins (whose genus name, *Fratercula*, denotes the similarities between the bird's plumage and a monk's habit). St Cuthbert had a special affinity with the eider duck; he offered them protection and to this day they are known locally as 'Cuddy's ducks'. Such were his links to the very soil of

Northumberland that the fossilised crinoids that often turn up were known as 'Cuthbert's beads'. A similar connection was made between ammonites and St Hilda at Whitby.

In death, St Cuthbert's fame spread far and wide, especially when his body was found to be incorrupt. Lindisfarne became a pilgrimage site. However, the island proved to be no oasis of peace: it was raided by 'Vikings' in 793, causing shock around Christendom. 'Never before', wrote Alcuin, 'has such terror appeared in Britain ... The heathens poured out the blood of saints around the altar, and trampled on the bodies of saints in the temple of God, like dung in the streets'. Initially there were hopes this raid would be a one-off, but as the situation became more dangerous it was decided to move St Cuthbert's body to a place of safety. And so, he left his beloved island in 875 and his body began an odyssey of over a century, wandering from place to place, rather like the Israelites in the desert. Chester-le-Street proved to be one such base and in 995, as the relics were being moved to Ripon, the cart got stuck at what is now Durham. Refusing to move forward, it was taken as a divine sign and a church was built—around which a settlement soon developed. Construction of the present cathedral began under the Normans in 1093.

Durham owes its existence to the need for a secure sanctuary for its precious relics. Yet the cathedral itself, next to the castle, was also a powerful display of Norman power. Sir Walter Scott's words, which can be found on Prebends Bridge, testify to this:

> Grey towers of Durham
> Yet well I love thy mixed and massive piles
> Half Church of God, half castle 'gainst the Scot
> And long to roam these venerable aisles.

The Scots were only part of the problem. Norman control was achieved through much violence and bloodshed; the massacre of a Norman Earl of Northumbria along with his men at Durham in January 1069 led to the 'Harrying of the North' and the building of fortifications, including a 'New Castle' on the Tyne. As William's troops headed towards Durham that autumn, they were confused by a fog that, it was believed, had been instigated miraculously by St Cuthbert himself. Nevertheless, the saint soon shifted allegiance—though not before his body was temporarily taken back to Lindisfarne, far away from the turmoil. For subsequent centuries the great Norman cathedral was the spectacular setting of his shrine; pilgrims flocked to ask his intercession. Such were their numbers that in the thirteenth century one of the few substantial additions to the original fabric, the Chapel of the Nine Altars, was built to provide extra devotional space and light.

The nearby location of the castle is a reminder that the cathedral was a centre of secular as well as spiritual power. In 1071 the bishop, Walcher, was (unusually) made Earl of Northumbria—and the first of Durham's prince bishops. This position, which seems more akin to the powerful prelates of the Holy Roman Empire, was unique in England. Nevertheless, Durham was frontier territory and the local leader, whether he be secular or ecclesiastical, needed to be strong and effective. Palatinate powers were given to the bishop on behalf of the monarch, including the raising of taxes, issuing of charters, licensing of fairs and appointment of judges. The concept of the 'prince bishop' survived into the nineteenth century.

The final chapter of the story of St Cuthbert's is sadly familiar and inconclusive. The tomb was opened and demolished in 1538 and the body still found to be intact. It was placed in a revestry until 1542, when it was reburied. Further excavations in 1827 revealed a skeleton along with other items, which were removed for display: an ivory comb, portable altar, jewelled cross, a book of Gospels, various silks and fragments of an ornately carved wooden coffin.

An alternative tradition holds that the saint's body was buried secretly and substituted with another (which was found in 1827). The location of the grave is apparently known only to three monks of the English Benedictine Congregation. Whatever the truth of his final resting place, St Cuthbert's presence still imbues the city of Durham and the Holy Island nearly eighty miles to its north.

FURNESS AND SHAP, CUMBRIA

Cumbrian Abbeys

Motorways can be fairly monotonous affairs, with banks and trees obscuring most interesting local features. There are, of course, exceptions and one of them must be the M6 as it carves its route through the hills between Kendal and Carlisle. To the west, are the Cumbrian fells; to the east, the Pennines.

Before the construction of the M6, an older road (the A6) formed one of the key routes between England and Scotland. It ascended to an altitude of well over a thousand feet as it crossed Shap Fell and, as a result, became known as one of the wildest, coldest and most hazardous stretches of road in Britain. Coaches and (later) trucks were often stranded there in poor conditions. A modern memorial 'pays tribute to the drivers and crews of vehicles that made possible the social and commercial links between north and south on this old and difficult route over Shap Fell before the opening of the M6' and also remembers 'those who built and maintained the road and the generations of local people who gave freely of food and shelter to stranded travellers in bad weather'.

Bonnie Prince Charlie spent the night at the village of Shap as he made his retreat at the end of 1745 to the relative safety of Scotland and eventual defeat at Culloden. Conditions were atrocious and some of his baggage and ammunition had to be left behind—cannon balls are said to have been used by farmers as ornaments on their land. One tradition depicts the prince complaining of being over-charged for his room and this seems at one time to have been a fairly common complaint made against the local innkeepers. Of more certain veracity is the skirmish fought at nearby Clifton Moor on 18 December 1745 between the Jacobite rearguard and Hanoverian troops. This clash is often described as the last 'battle' on English soil.

Given its remoteness, Shap has a surprisingly rich history. The name derives from 'Hepp' or 'Heap', referring to the megalithic monuments that can be found in the area. Below the village, in the secluded valley of the River Lowther, are the ruins of Shap Abbey, the only medieval monastery in the old county of Westmorland. To reach the abbey we had to drive down narrow country lanes before heading across a field. There were no other vehicles, only cattle, grazing unobtrusively and watching us with considerable disinterest. There was a small space to park, near a deserted house and a picturesque bridge crossing the Lowther. Farm buildings stood at the other side of the ruins and we joined a flock of chickens as we walked around the site. Refreshments were available: a battered plastic box bore the label 'Coast to Coast Walkers and Visitors Please Grab a Drink, Price List Inside'. This continued an ancient tradition, for the abbey must once have been a welcome haven of hospitality in these harsh surroundings.

The Abbey of St Mary Magdalene dates from the twelfth century. A community of Premonstratensian (or Norbertine) canons was originally founded at Preston Patrick, near Kendal, in 1191 by a local grandee, Thomas de Workington. Ten years later the house was moved to Shap.

The history of the abbey is, to a large extent, uneventful, made up of the unceasing round of prayer and the living out of the Norbertine charism. The care with which the Sacred Liturgy was celebrated, even in this forlorn location, can be seen by the circular markings found on the paving of the nave, indicating where the canons should stand during the procession after High Mass.

The house was never very wealthy and the Black Death reduced the community to six. Nevertheless, it owned land across the county and ran a hospital for lepers at Appleby. The abbey church saw the burials of pillars of the local community, such as members of the Clifford family—including the first Baron de Clifford, killed at Bannockburn in 1314, and the tenth Baron, who took an important part in another battle against the Scots, at Flodden in 1513. He was known as the 'Shepherd Lord' since, such was political instability of his childhood, he was apparently hidden by his mother among the Lakeland shepherds.

Shap's greatest abbot was Richard Redman, the son of a local landowner. Elected in 1459, he went on to Bishop of Ely in 1501. Under his direction, parts of the abbey were rebuilt and extended. The most impressive monument to his ambitious vision is the great tower at the west end of the church, which still stands remarkably complete. Similar towers were built at the Cistercian abbeys of Furness and Fountains and the same masons were probably used.

The last abbot, Richard Evanwood (or Baggot) surrendered the house to Henry VIII on 14 January 1540 and the lands were given to the Governor of Carlisle. The abbot himself received a generous annual pension of £40 and seems to have served as the priest at Kirby Thore, where one of the old abbey bells (it is said) can be found in the church tower. The monastic buildings at Shap were either incorporated into the farm that now stood near the site or gradually dismantled. Some of the stonework was recycled at Lowther Castle.

Not far away at Keld there is a stone building owned by the National Trust and normally described as a chantry chapel. There is some controversy about its purpose, sparked off in 1917 when Lord Lonsdale wanted to demolish the building in order to broaden the road and make his shooting lodge more accessible. Supporters of the structure claimed it was a late medieval chantry chapel, once served by the Norbertine canons, while Lonsdale claimed it was merely a barn. A local antiquary put forward a third option. No document mentioned the erection of a chantry at Keld but the building may date from the reign of Mary I, when chapels were sometimes built near former monasteries, using stone from the ruins. Perhaps Mass was celebrated here in those confusing times, continuing the work of the abbey and healing the wounds caused by its sudden dissolution?

Indeed, the presence of Shap Abbey can never be completely obliterated. Even today the ruins stand in isolated splendour, on sunny summer days and in howling winter winds alike, its splendid tower glorifying the Lord as much today as when it was first built.

Another great abbey can be found on the other side of the county on the Furness Peninsula, sandwiched between Morecambe Bay and the Lakeland Fells. Once one of the wealthiest in England and distinctive with its red sandstone, Furness Abbey is set in the Vale of Nightshade, as picturesque in reality as it is in name. William Wordsworth loved the place and described it as 'a mouldering Pile, with fractured Arch, Belfry, and Images, and living Trees'.

The abbey was founded in 1124 by the future King Stephen. Originally situated at Tulketh (near Preston), it was moved to Furness a few years later—a better site since it was near the sea, surrounded by forest and with good mining potential. At first it belonged to the little-known Congregation of Savigny, one of the monastic reform movements that originated in twelfth-century France and strictly interpreted the Rule of St Benedict. It quickly spread to England; Savigniac houses included those at Byland (Yorkshire) and Buckfast (Devon). In 1147, however, the Congregation was merged with the Cistercians, despite the initial protests of the Furness monks.

Furness Abbey grew to become powerful and wealthy, with a close connection to the Crown. It produced scholars such as Jocelyn of Furness, who wrote lives of St Patrick, St Kentigern, St Helen and others. The abbot was an important figure in the north-west. Acting as a semi-independent 'border baron', his influence spread beyond that of the monastery to the running of businesses, the collecting of taxes and the administration of land and justice.

With easy access to the Irish Sea, the abbey founded daughter houses not only in England (including nearby Calder) but in Ireland, Scotland and the Isle of Man. It was as easy to get to such places than to traverse mountains and travel inland. Furness was granted the right to elect to the see of Man and several bishops were buried at the abbey church. During repair work in 2010 archaeologists uncovered the burial of a middle-aged man wearing a gilded silver ring set with a precious stone and bearing a crozier depicting St Michael the Archangel. It was a significant discovery, though the identity of the man remains unknown—either an abbot or one of the bishops of Man.

Being located near the Irish Sea had its definite disadvantages. This was Border territory and there were on-going raids from the Scots. In 1322 Robert the Bruce himself headed one such incursion. The ghost of a headless monk, riding a horse through the abbey gateway, is supposed to originate in one of these fourteenth-century skirmishes.

Nevertheless, by the sixteenth century Furness was the second richest Cistercian abbey in England after Fountains (Yorkshire). But time was nearly running out. The abbey was implicated in the Pilgrimage of Grace of 1536–7 and had questioned the king's supremacy over the Church. It was thus one of the first major abbeys to be dissolved: invited to surrender to the king as a 'voluntary discharge of conscience'. The monks left in 1537, the abbot was pensioned off and the demolition work begun almost immediately. The roofs were stripped of lead, the tracery broken in the windows and the stones re-used elsewhere. The abbey passed into private ownership.

The ruins are now in the care of English Heritage and there are many glimpses of its pre-Dissolution splendour: the round arches in the east range, the magnificent sedilia where the ministers sat during Mass, the vaulting of the infirmary. As the Lakes opened up as a tourist venue in the nineteenth century, a visit to Furness was seen as an essential part of the itinerary. Wordsworth himself included it in his *Guide to the Lakes*.

In one of his poems, he summed up the atmosphere of the ruined abbey in writing of visitors who

>with fixed eyes admire
>That wide-spanned arch, wondering how it was raised,
>To keep, so high in air, its strength and grace:
>All seem to feel the spirit of the place,
>And by the general reverence God is praised.

HAZLEWOOD, NORTH YORKSHIRE
Catholic Families: The Vavasours

Like many great medieval houses, Hazlewood Castle's origins are largely hidden beneath an eighteenth-century Palladian mansion. Set in stunning countryside, both Lincoln and York cathedrals can be seen from the tower, for they are only sixty miles apart. Indeed, much of the magnesium limestone used to build the minster came from a local quarry.

The castle was the home of the Vavasour family between the reigns of William the Conqueror and Edward VII. As might be expected, there were periods of prosperity and crisis during these long centuries. Maud le Vavasour is thought to be the inspiration for Maid Marian after her husband, Fulk Fitzwarren, fell out with King John and the couple sought refuge in the woods. During the baronial struggles of the reign of Henry III, the house was sacked, and two centuries later the congregation celebrating the liturgy of Palm Sunday 1461 in the chapel of St Leonard could hear the cries and shouts (it is said) from the nearby battlefield of Towton. Nearly 30,000 lost their lives that day.

At the Reformation the Vavasours remained staunchly Catholic and it was their boast that only the Catholic Mass had ever been celebrated there. Some protection was received from their connections locally and at court—one member of the family, Thomas, equipped vessels to fight the Armada and Anne Vavasour was a favourite maid of honour to Elizabeth I (despite her affairs with the Earl of Oxford and Sir Henry Lee). Nevertheless, in Elizabethan York Thomas and Dorothy Vavasour, no doubt related to the Hazlewood family, were well-known recusants and protectors of priests; Dorothy seems to have converted the future martyr, St Margaret Clitherow, to the Faith.

Charles I made the Vavasours baronets in 1628 and a younger son was killed at the battle of Marston Moor. The family had many sons and daughters who were called to the priesthood and cloister. The siblings of Sir Thomas, the first Baronet, included a Franciscan, a Jesuit, a secular priest, a Poor Clare and three Benedictine nuns—one of whom became abbess at the English Benedictine house in Brussels. The fifth Baronet, Sir Walter, was himself a Jesuit priest in the eighteenth century and his successor, another Walter, offered the estate to Bishop Gibson in 1801 for the modest sum of £12,000 so that it could become a seminary and school for the Northern District, a successor of war-torn Douai. However, he died in 1802 and his successor, Sir Thomas, was not as enthusiastic about parting with his inheritance. Negotiations collapsed and the college was eventually established further north, at Ushaw.

The baronetcy expired with him in 1826 but a new line of baronets was created with his cousin, Edward Stourton, who then assumed the name Vavasour. He became one of the first Catholic magistrates after the Emancipation Act of 1829 and as well as being a man of business and sporting interests, lived a extremely devout life: daily Mass and family prayers in the chapel; during Lent the seven Penitential Psalms and Litanies were recited each evening. Little wonder that one of his children, Philip, became a priest and founded the missions at Tadcaster and Ripon. In his old age, Sir Edward considered entering the religious life himself but died suddenly in 1847 as he was travelling to Rome to receive the blessing of Pius IX.

In the 1860s two sons of Hazlewood, William and Oswald Vavasour, joined the Pontifical Zouaves to defend the pope's temporal power in Rome. Hazlewood continued to be a centre of Catholicism in the area. Those buried in the little cemetery included Bishop John Briggs, first Bishop of Beverley and before that Vicar Apostolic of the Northern and (from 1840) Yorkshire District. William, the former Zouave, inherited the castle in 1885 but difficult finances forced him to sell in 1908. It passed to several different owners throughout the twentieth century, serving time as a maternity home (many mothers named their daughters 'Hazel' as a result) and Carmelite retreat centre.

Today it is a hotel and wedding venue, complete with spa and restaurant. Portraits of the family hang from the walls and their monuments still stand in the chapel. Guests can even enjoy Vavasour wines from the New Zealand vineyard established by a member of the family in 1986.

HOWDEN, EAST RIDING OF YORKSHIRE

Howden and its Minster

Howden is an elegant market town in the Vale of York, which, between the reigns of King John and Queen Victoria, was the location of a famous horse fair. Many horses were bought here for the British Army and so one could say that Waterloo was partly won on the fields of Howden. The connection is kept alive in the Wellington Hotel on Bridgegate.

What most strikes the visitor is the huge medieval church, of cathedral proportions. The tower of Howden Minster dominates the landscape, though the choir and chapter house itself lies in ruins. The nave and transepts form what is now the parish church. An open door at the west end led us to hurriedly park the car and step inside.

The church exudes medieval charm with its dusky gloom and many interesting remnants of sculpture and glass. The statue of Our Lady, shown holding a dove (the Holy Spirit) whispering into her ear, is fourteenth century. One fragment of glass in the South Porch shows the coat of arms of Anthony de Bek, Bishop of Durham, who not only fought at the battle of Falkirk and celebrated Edward I's funeral but, in the early years of the fourteenth century, became the only Englishman to hold the office of Latin Patriarch of Jerusalem (though the title was nominal by this stage).

There was a Saxon church at Howden, which for a time came under the monks of Peterborough. Tradition suggests that an obscure Northumbrian princess, St Osana, the sister of King Osred and a nun, was buried at the minster. The shrine probably still existed in the thirteenth century, when Gerard of Wales records an unedifying story of the saint reprimanding and beating an immoral woman who had sat on her tomb. It is the sort of moral tale much beloved by medieval authors.

William the Conqueror gave the manor and church to the bishops and monks of Durham. Despite being situated in the diocese of York, the area became an enclave of Durham with certain privileges and liberties: until 1846 it was known as Howdenshire and the term is still sometimes proudly used today. The prince bishops often used the manor as they travelled to York and beyond. A gateway built by one of them, Cardinal Thomas Langley, can still be seen in the rectory garden; another prelate, Walter de Kirkham, died at the manor in 1260 and his entrails were buried in the minster while the rest of him was taken back to his cathedral.

In 1264 a college of secular canons was established: there were five, later six, canons and the same number of vicars to act as substitutes. Chantry priests also said Mass at the various altars. The canons founded a grammar and song school—the Tudor schoolrooms were in use until the 1920s—and their presence is perhaps most vivid in the ruins of the octagonal chapter house.

One of the first canons, 'St' John of Howden, won fame for sanctity and after his death in 1275 many pilgrims flocked to his tomb in the choir. It is said that during his Requiem Mass the corpse raised its arms at the elevation of the Host. Revenue from the cult allowed the canons to extend and embellish the church. Near the west door is a large fourteenth-century chest, which once received the contributions of pilgrims. Today a contactless card reader stands next to it.

The college initially survived the Dissolution, since it was not a monastic foundation, but when Edward VI turned his attention to collegiate churches and chantries in 1548 the minster lost much of its revenue and purpose. It was vandalised by Parliamentarian troops in the 1640s and in 1696 the choir roof collapsed during a thunderstorm. The ruins at the eastern end remain as they are, though the chapter house roof was restored in the 1980s.

The Victorian Catholic church of the Sacred Heart, at the junction of Buttfield and Knedlington Roads, is smaller but, in its own humble way, no less impressive. It was designed by Joseph Aloysius Hansom, the noted Catholic architect and inventor of the eponymous cab, and opened in 1851. It stands as a reminder of those locals who upheld the Catholic Faith in penal times, sometimes at great personal cost.

The area was much involved in the Pilgrimage of Grace of 1536, the uprising that combined local and economic grievances with opposition to Henry VIII's religious changes and the Dissolution of the Monasteries. Its leader, Robert Aske, came from Aughton, seven miles to the north-west. The relic of the True Cross kept by the Howden canons was carried at the head of the rebels. The protest failed and Aske was hanged in York.

The 'Howdenshire Martyrs' also include a number of the seminary priests who ministered under Elizabeth I and the early Stuarts. Blessed John Finley, a graduate of Cambridge and Douai, came from nearby Barnaby and suffered in 1586. Blessed Alexander Crowe, from Howden itself, was captured while baptising a baby at South Duffield and hanged, drawn and quarter at York the following year. On the morning of his execution he freshly shaved a tonsure on his head to show pride in his priestly vocation. Blessed Thomas Atkinson was another Howdenshire native, executed in 1616 after rosary beads and the text of an indulgence were found on his person.

A side altar was brought to the church of the Sacred Heart from nearby Everingham Park, the home of a well-known Catholic family who by that time were known as the Constable-Maxwells — and held the title Lord Herries of Terregles. Among their ancestors was the fifth Earl of Nithsdale, a Jacobite supporter who daringly escaped from the Tower of London dressed as a maid on the eve of his execution. The figures on the altar relief depict members of the family. In the 1860s Lord Herries was prominent in helping those volunteers who took up arms to defend the pope against Italian nationalists. It is interesting that both a Constable-Maxwell and Hansom the architect's son joined the Papal Zouaves, that glamourous, transnational unit of the final days of the pontifical army.

Back at the minster, all is quiet. The shadows cast long over the nave and the church clock ticks the passing of the minutes. Past and present merge into one in this corner of the East Riding.

KENDAL, CUMBRIA

A Lakeland Jesuit

Much of the current interest in the Lake District is thanks to the quirky handwritten walking guides produced by Alfred Wainwright, whose day job was for many years in Kendal. But it is often forgotten that the first guide to the Lakes was written by a Catholic priest, a Jesuit, who is buried in Kendal's historic parish church—Fr Thomas West.

'Thomas West' was the name he used, though he seems to have been born as 'Thomas Daniel' in Inverness. He studied at several Catholic colleges overseas and joined the Jesuits. Early on he developed an interest in ancient monuments and while still in his thirties was elected Fellow of the Society of Antiquaries in London. He worked quietly as a priest and tutor at Swynnerton (Staffordshire), Holywell (Flintshire), Dalton in Furness, Ulverston and Sizergh Castle (all now in Cumbria). His first major work was *The Antiquities of Furness* (1774), principally concerned with the famous abbey of St Mary which had once dominated the area. Visiting the lakes, valleys and fells that were on his doorstep, and, we are told, accompanying 'genteel parties on the tour of the Lakes', he then produced his popular *Guide to the Lakes* (1778).

Watching the tourists and walkers crowd on the little train from Oxenholme to Windermere, it is hard to believe that two and a half centuries ago the Lakes were largely undiscovered, regarded as remote, rough and dangerous. Even Daniel Defoe dismissed the region as 'wild and barren' and thought the mountains had 'a kind of unhospitable terror in them'.

By the second half of the eighteenth century, however, attitudes were changing. The Grand Tour had popularised travel and engendered a growing appreciation of the scenery of the Alps and Apennines. Mountains began to be regarded not so much as places of terror but of picturesque beauty, worth seeing in themselves. People started exploring the countryside and early writers such as Thomas Gray (famous for his *Elegy Written in a Country Churchyard*) and Thomas Pennant (a Fellow of the Royal Society) began to make favourable comments about the Lakes.

West noted, also, the influence of landscape painters, such as Nicolas Poussin and Claude Lorrain, who 'induces many to visit the lakes of Cumberland, Westmorland and Lancashire, there to contemplate in Alpine scenery, finished in nature's highest tints, the pastoral and rural landscape, exhibited in all their styles, the soft, the rude, the romantic, and the sublime'. The Lakes were, in truth, the English Alps, 'not inferior in beauty of line, or variety of summit, number of lakes, and transparency of water; not in colouring of rock or softness of turf; but in height and extent only'.

The author does not allude to the fact that he was a clergyman, let alone a Jesuit—the title page merely says, 'By the Author of *The Antiquities of Furness*'—nor did he highlight the Catholic aspects of Lakeland history but there are hints of his background if you look hard enough. Firstly, he stresses the spiritual dimension of a visit to the Lakes. 'The contemplative traveller will be charmed by the sight of the sweet retreats that he will observe in these enchanting regions of calm repose' and those who 'spend their lives in cities, and their time in crowds, will here meet with objects that will enlarge the mind, by contemplation and raise it from nature to nature's first cause. Whoever takes a walk into these scenes, must return penetrated with a sense of the Creator's power in heaping mountains upon mountains, and enthroning rocks upon rocks'. That certainly applies equally to us today.

Secondly, West's unique selling point was the suggestion of 'stations' from which the best views could be enjoyed. Rather like the Way of the Cross, they provided an opportunity to pause and contemplate, in this case with the help of a Claude glass, a portable tinted convex mirror which created an image resembling a painting. As West explained, 'the person using it ought always to turn his back to the object that he views. It should be suspended by the upper part of the case...holding it a little to the right or the left (as the position of the parts to be viewed require) and the face screened from the sun'. It was an amusing gimmick, of course, but thanks to it, West established an itinerary of beautiful scenic views which would encourage 'rapture and reverence'.

West did not simply stay on ground level. He ascended into the hills and included among his 'stations' summits of at least the lesser fells. In one passage, he praises the locals for being 'hospitable, civil and communicative, and readily and cheerfully give assistance to strangers who visit their regions'. The priest remembered that on missing a track 'I have been surprised by the dale-lander from the top of a rock, waving me back, and offering me a safe conduct through all the difficult parts, and who blushed at mention of a reward'.

West did not survive his *magnum opus* very long. He died on 10 July 1779 at Sizergh Castle, the home of the Catholic Strickland family, and was buried near their chapel at Kendal parish church. His book went through several editions, up until the 1820s, and was widely read and followed. The Lakes became increasingly popular, especially with the effects of the French Revolution and Napoleonic Wars (which made the Grand Tour almost impossible to make) and the influence of poets such as Wordsworth. Then there was the coming of the railways and of improved accommodation. Writing just over a century after West's book. Richard Ferguson could write that 'visitors are countless. To stand, during the Lake season, on the steps of that admirable hostelry, the Prince of Wales, at Grasmere, is to witness an everlasting procession of four-horse coaches, *char-à-bancs*, cyclists, and pedestrians'.

Visitors to the Lakes should be grateful to this adventurous Jesuit, who could once be seen following little-known paths with his notebook and Claude glass, and who did much to popularise the beautiful scenery that millions enjoy today.

KESWICK, CUMBRIA

The Saints of Derwentwater

The Lake District is full of beauty spots but one of the most celebrated must be Friar's Crag, a short walk from Keswick. The promontory juts out into Derwentwater and gives fine views of the lake and the surrounding fells, including the ever-popular Catbells. John Ruskin numbered it among the three most beautiful spots in the whole of Europe and wrote of his feelings of 'intense joy, mingled with awe' when he first visited it as a boy.

The lake's islands each tell a story. The owner of Derwent Island at the end of the eighteenth century not only built a house but a fort, boathouse and fake stone circle. He held an annual regatta and encouraged the locals to attack his property, so that he could make use of his cannon. Nearby Lord's Island was once home to the earls of Derwentwater, one of whom was a hero of the Jacobite Rebellion of 1715, beheaded for treason on Tower Hill. A narrow cleft in Walla Crag, one of the fells on the edge of the lake, is known as 'Lady's Rake', supposedly marking the escape route of the Countess in the aftermath of the rising.

The largest island, St Herbert's, was the setting for Owl Island in Beatrix Potter's *Tale of Squirrel Nutkins*. Remember how the protoganist made a raft out of twigs and crossed the lake with his brother Twinkleberry and their cousins, ingeniously using their tails as sails?

It is doubtful that Squirrel Nutkins knew much of the island's past. As the name suggests, this was once the abode of a seventh-century hermit and, in later centuries, a place of pilgrimage. Indeed, it is believed that boats were launched from Friar's Crag so that pilgrims could reach the island, where there was a small chapel.

The Christian Faith had reached these remote parts by the sixth century. The Celtic missionary, St Kentigern (or Mungo), founded several churches in Cumbria, including that of Crosthwaite, on the edge of Keswick. Perhaps it was here that the saint planted a cross in a clearing or 'thwaite'.

In the seventh century St Herbert moved to the island 'to avoid the intercourse of man, and that nothing might withdraw his attention from unceasing mortification and prayer'. The lake not only cut him off from worldly temptations but provided him with his meagre diet of fish, as well as vegetables that he grew himself.

St Herbert was remembered for his close friendship with St Cuthbert. The two men met each year to pray together and speak of the eternal truths; the only time that the hermit left the solitude of his island. According to the story recorded by St Bede, at their last meeting in Carlisle around 687 the bishop spoke of his approaching death. On hearing of this, St Herbert fell at his feet, saying 'I beg you not to leave me! Remember that I am your most devoted friend and ask God of His mercy to grant that as we have served Him together on earth, so may we pass away to the heavenly vision together'. And so it came to pass that on 19 March 'their souls departed from their bodies, and were straight in union in the beatific sight and vision; and were transported hence to the kingdom of heaven, by the service and hands of angels'.

St Herbert's cell became a place of pilgrimage; as recently as 1984 a mould was found that had once produced pilgrim badges in the middle ages. In 1374 Bishop Thomas Appleby of Carlisle granted an indulgence of forty days to any inhabitant of the parish of Crosthwaite who went to the island for Mass on his feast day. Pilgrimages have resumed in more recent times, made by the Catholic parishioners of Keswick as well as the church dedicated to the saint in Chadderton, Greater Manchester.

The beauty of St Herbert's Island inspired Wordsworth to write his poem *For the Spot where the Hermitage Stood on St Herbert's*. Since 1920 Friar's Crag has been in the care of the National Trust (established 125 years ago this year) and there is a memorial to one of its founders, Canon Hardwicke Rawnsley, sometime vicar of Crosthwaite. It is inscribed with words that St Herbert would surely approve of:

> The Spirit of God is around you in the air that you breathe, His glory in the light that you see, and in the fruitfulness of the earth and the joy of its creatures. He has written for you day by day His revelation as He granted you day by day your daily bread.

LADYEWELL, LANCASHIRE

Forgotten Lancashire Shrines

When I venerate the altar at the beginning of Mass, I like to think that I am uniting myself to all the Masses offered down the ages. The presence of relics in the altar stone, of course, calls to mind those early Masses in the catacombs, celebrated on the tombs of the martyrs. I recall the Masses said by millions of priests all over the world across the centuries, in very different situations to my own but essentially the same mystery. I remember also some of the more memorable Masses that I myself have celebrated. Of course, every Mass is memorable, but some particularly stand out — my ordination, for instance, or Masses offered on pilgrimage, or those said at home while on holiday, which were served by my late father. This sea of Masses, whether offered in magnificent cathedrals or wayside chapels, in prisons or in the trenches, in homes or on mountaintops all find their root in Christ's Sacrifice on Calvary, represented in an unbloody way at every Mass.

I once had the privilege of celebrating Mass on the Burgess Altar at the shrine of Our Lady at Ladyewell, near Preston, and as I did so it seemed as if the centuries disappeared. The altar was made by one Thomas Burgess for the Catholic Towneley family in 1560, at a time when the Mass was being pushed underground. The altar was constructed so as not to attract attention. It would have stood discreetly in a room, looking like a typical Tudor wardrobe, without any ecclesiastical decoration. However, when the doors were opened and the candles, crucifix, Missal, altar cards and cloths put out, it very clearly resembled an altar, a worthy setting for the celebration of Mass. It was moved around different locations in Lancashire during the days of persecution and has quite a history.

As I kissed the altar at the beginning of Mass I thought of those who had gone before me. St Edmund Campion offered Mass on the altar in April 1581. Just a few months later he would be captured and executed. Fr Abbot, a descendant of the Burgess family and one time guardian of the altar, wrote of how the Lancashire faithful eagerly 'received the blessing from those consecrated hands, so soon to be torn and crippled into a useless burden by the cruel rack in the Tower of London'.

Blessed John Woodcock, a Franciscan martyr, also celebrated Mass on this 'Old Missionary Altar' in the 1640s, at which point it was kept at 'Woodend', near Brindle. On one occasion he stood in front of the altar beginning Mass (as I was doing in a very different context) when word reached the congregation that the pursuivants were on their way. The priest hurried into the nearest hiding hole, while the altar was closed and the liturgical vessels and cloths put away. By the time the search party entered the room, the altar looked like an ordinary cupboard and Mrs Burgess was sitting in her rocking chair, complaining that a sick woman should be disturbed in such a way. When asked why there were so many people in the house, she replied that 'they are some neighbours come kindly to sit up with me'. Catholics had, of course, to be very careful about gathering in suspiciously large numbers. Sometimes they met at the nearby St Helen's Well and observed the custom of throwing in pins for good luck, before adjourning for Mass—hoping that they would not be noticed. Woodcock managed to escape on that occasion but shortly afterwards was apprehended and martyred.

Another martyr connected to the altar was St Edmund Arrowsmith, who is remembered particularly vividly in the area around Brindle. He was born at Haydock in 1585 to a family of confessors—his parents were imprisoned for their Faith—and it is reported that he recited the Little Office of Our Lady back and forth from school. He went on to the seminary at Douai and spent most of his priesthood in his native Lancashire, becoming a Jesuit four years before his martyrdom.

His final arrest in 1628 (the second time he was apprehended) must have caused a local trauma for the details of his final journey were carefully handed down. The place where he offered Mass just before his arrest is today known as 'Arrowsmith House' or the 'House of the Last Mass'—and Mass is still celebrated there today. When Dom Bede Camm visited the house at the turn of the last century, he reported that 'it is said that a cross of light appears at intervals on the wall of the room in which the last Mass was said, and remains visible for a little time. My informants, including a Catholic doctor of the neighbourhood, tell me that there is no possible natural explanation of this phenomenon'. The spot where Arrowsmith was captured on Brindle Moss was long remembered. His horse refused to jump over a ditch, at which point his tiny statue of Our Lady, which he always carried with him, was dropped to the ground (giving away his identity). This is still treasured at the Catholic church in Brindle.

Arrowsmith was a much loved figure in the area and the fact that he had been betrayed by an 'insider' must have torn the local community apart. A local tradition has it that one of the pursuivants gave the priest's cloak to a farmer, who had given some helpful information. He made his child a suit out of the cloak and, when the boy wore it the first time, went for a ride with his father. The horse unexpectedly bolted and the poor boy was killed—the rock on which he had hit his head was still being pointed out in the mid-nineteenth century. Moreover (and here perhaps an element of folklore has been introduced into proceedings) the descendants of the family, hitherto admired for their fine looks, were in some way deformed or stunted in growth.

St Edmund Arrowsmith was finally executed at Lancaster on 28 August 1628. What is particularly interesting, as we look back on his life, is that he was betrayed not by a government spy or Protestant informer but by a member of his own flock with an axe to grind. Two first cousins by the name of Holden had married in the presence of an Anglican minister and Arrowsmith was arranging a dispensation to validate the marriage in the eyes of the Church. He asked the couple to separate until the process was completed—but this caused such offence that the Holdens gave intelligence of the priest's whereabouts to the local JP.

Marriage was indeed a central issue at the Reformation. Henry VIII's violation of the sanctity of marriage led to his break with Rome; St Edmund Arrowsmith was captured because of his zeal for the sacrament; and others also suffered because of it—for example, the layman Venerable Roger Ashton was convicted partly because he had obtained a papal dispensation so that he could marry his second cousin.

RIEVAULX, NORTH YORKSHIRE

'Bare Ruined Choirs'

There is something very atmospheric about the ruined abbeys dotted about our countryside and it is interesting how our attitude towards them has changed over the centuries. In the years after the Dissolution of the Monasteries they were seen simply as ruins which, more often or not, were a useful source of stone and other materials. Supporters of the Reformation, of course, would have perceived in them a sign of triumph of Bible truth over 'popish' falsehood, an end to old corrupt ways. Catholics, meanwhile, continued to treat them with respect and even made pilgrimages to them as tangible memorials of an England that was no more.

In the seventeenth century ruined abbeys were increasingly of interest to antiquarians and historians and then, by the 1700s, they were seen as picturesque—romantic if slightly melancholic relics of 'merry old England'. They were part of the landscape, a tourist destination and a beloved subject for artists and poets. As the clergyman William Gilpin put it in 1786, 'a ruin is a sacred thing. Rooted for ages in the soil; assimilated to it; and become, as it were, a part of it; we consider it as a work of nature, rather than of art'.

One of the most celebrated of these ruins, Rievaulx Abbey, is situated near the other great Cistercian houses of Fountains and Byland (also with impressive remains). It was founded in 1132 by 'Blessed' William, a Yorkshireman who was one of St Bernard's right-hand men. Indeed, the English had a close connection with the great monastic movement based around Clairvaux for one of its co-founders was St Stephen Harding, originally from Dorset.

Many of the buildings at Rievaulx whose ruins we see today were actually built by the third abbot, St Aelred, known as the 'Bernard of the North'. If St Bernard was noted for his single-mindedness and sometimes sharp wit, whether he was meditating on Scripture or preaching a crusade, St Aelred comes across as a warm, conciliatory figure. Amidst the busy life of a medieval abbot, with all its domestic administration, visitations of daughter houses and trips to Court, Clairvaux or even Rome, St Aelred found time to compose some spiritual classics, including his celebrated treatise on *Spiritual Friendship*. 'God Himself is friendship', he wrote, 'he who dwells in friendship, dwells in God and God in him'.

It was moving to stand on the site of his abbatial cell, where he put his teachings into action. According to his biographer, the saint's room was often crowded with monks 'for every day they came to it and sat in it, twenty or thirty at a time, to talk together of the spiritual delights of the Scriptures and of the observance of the Order ... they walked and lay about his bed and talked with him as a little child prattles with its mother'. He continued to delight in the company of his monks even in his last years, when he was plagued by illness and kidney stones limited his physical activities. He died on 12 January 1167 and his relics were later translated to the abbey church. A simple plaque marks the spot of this once magnificent shrine.

The medieval monasteries were important centres not only of prayer, liturgy and scholarship but social and medical care, agriculture and technology. Although the number of monks at Rievaulx declined in the years after its plunder by the Scots following the battle at nearby Shaws Moor (1322) and the Black Death (1348–50), it still managed to have a huge sheep farm and even boast an nascent iron industry. At the eve of the Reformation it seems the monks were on the verge of developing a blast furnace and, according to one historian, the Dissolution of the Monasteries may have delayed the Industrial Revolution by two hundred years! The closure of Rievaulx Abbey did not completely end these early attempts at iron production for they were continued by the new owners, the earls of Rutland. In the 1570s Rutland built on the work of the monks by constructing a blast furnace with bellows driven by a waterwheel — the first of its kind in northern England.

When I visited Rievaulx, it was early in the morning and I was allowed to walk around the still deserted ruins and the large shell that had formerly been the abbey church. The soundtrack to all this was an impressive rendition of the dawn chorus coming from the woods around the valley, the birds singing in the 'bared ruined choirs' where once the monks sang. It was a most 'picturesque' sight and little surprise that an eighteenth-century landowner, Thomas Duncombe, created an extensive landscape garden nearby (Rievaulx Terrace) designed so that there were stunning views of the ruined abbey and surrounding landscape.

Ruined abbeys continue to haunt the English imagination. Perhaps this national fascination derives partly from a guilty conscience over the effects of the Dissolution and a now long-vanished England. The abbeys may have been closed, the monks scattered, their good works halted and precious treasures looted but the memory and achievements of these once vibrant institutions could never be lost.

USHAW, COUNTY DURHAM

Treasures on the Moors

Working as an archivist, you can become easily blasé about the treasures of the past. Dealing so closely with historical manuscripts and artefacts, they can soon become overly familiar and lose some of their magic. That's why it's so important to take a step back and rediscover the wonder and awe that the past inspires.

One place that does this for me is Ushaw College, near Durham. I first visited when it was still a working seminary, and I remember going round with my mouth open as I was shown the numerous gothic chapels, the long corridors, the spacious halls and the many priceless items contained within.

Ushaw was founded in 1808 as the final location for the 'northern' continuation of the great English College at Douai, which had been closed as a result of the French Revolution. The 'southern' descendant was set up at St Edmund's, Ware. Like Douai, Ushaw taught both schoolboys and seminarians; it also became a major focus of northern Catholic identity. During the nineteenth century, the original buildings were lavishly expanded. A complex of chapels was designed by Augustus Welby Pugin, with paintings by the Nazarene painter Franz von Rohden and sculptures by Karl Hoffman. Just as the medieval monks used the best artists of the day, so too the newly confident Victorian Catholics. The magnificent library at Ushaw was also a conscious emulation of the medieval monastic past and an attempt to ensure educational excellence. It contains many early printed books and items not available even in the British Library. Several Ushaw Presidents made it their mission to linger round bookshops and auction rooms both at home and in Europe and so restore some of the artistic and literary inheritance lost at the Reformation and the French Revolution. In more recent times, Ushaw has received further collections of books and papers, such as those that once belonged to the English College, Lisbon.

There are a number of items dating from before the Reformation, including liturgical books and vestments. One of these, a red chasuble which probably belonged to the royal wardrobe of Richard III, was worn by Cardinal Nichols at the king's obsequies at Leicester. What is particularly interesting is how these items were saved for posterity. The fifty or so books at Ushaw which once belonged to Durham

Cathedral Priory came through two former monks who belonged to the local Tempest family.

Another remarkable piece is a medieval Missal once used at Esh—a parish which no longer exists but which Ushaw would have fallen under. It claims to be 'the only pre-Reformation parish liturgical book which has never left the parish for which it was first brought'. The book was rescued by a Catholic family who lived for many years at Esh Hall. Such relics formed a valuable link with the Catholic medieval past and also chronicled the violent changes of the sixteenth century. Thus, the pope's name has been erased from the Roman Canon and a prayer to St Thomas of Canterbury has been scored through.

Unsurprisingly Ushaw contains many memorials of those who suffered for the Faith during the sixteenth and seventeenth centuries. There are relics of the martyrs, as might be expected, items used for secret recusant Masses, and souvenirs of the Jacobites. Most surprising, perhaps, is a copy of William Allen's *A True, sincere and modest defence of English Catholics* (1584) signed and annotated by Richard Topcliffe, Elizabeth I's notorious torturer-general. He calls Allen 'that monsterous trator' and reveals that the book was 'lent for the service of God, Queen Elizabeth and England' in 1599. Who would have thought that the book would end up once again in Catholic hands? And who would have thought, also, that Ushaw would possess a Lutheran work once owned by Thomas Cranmer—particularly rare since many of his Protestant books were confiscated and destroyed at the time of his arrest and execution.

On leaving the college, the eye of the visitor is drawn not only to the elegant buildings but a strange series of arched structures that look like the start of a city wall. The area was known as the 'Bounds' and here a unique ball game was played: 'cat'. It had been played in Douai from at least the eighteenth century, and college lore even went as far to say it had been brought over from Oxford by Cardinal Allen himself! The game, which had some similarities with rounders, baseball and cricket, featured seven players on each side and a large ashen bat. Cat was also played elsewhere, at Stonyhurst and Ushaw's sister college of Old Hall Green in Hertfordshire, though the point was forcibly made to me that the wimpish southerners preferred a much lighter ball. As a writer in *The Month* explained in 1893, this traditional sport is 'the object of a fond and reverential love to all Ushaw men, but to the profane outside world a dark and unintelligible mystery'.

Ushaw closed as a seminary in 2011 but it still keeps its religious identity and houses the Centre for Catholic Studies, part of Durham

University. The College will hopefully continue to be a focus of Catholic identity and learning for many generations to come.

WARDLEY HALL, LANCASHIRE
The Skull of Wardley Hall

It is not often that you come face-to-face with a saint but such is the opportunity if you visit Wardley Hall, now the residence of the Bishop of Salford. Here, the skull of the 'Martyr Monk of Manchester', St Ambrose Barlow, is respectfully preserved in a niche on the main staircase. It must be unique among English episcopal residences for being known colloquially as 'The Skull House'.

There are many extraordinary stories about this skull. One relates how a maid accidentally threw the skull into the moat, whereupon a violent storm erupted. It was thought that the maid's action had displeased the skull (or rather its original owner) and the moat was drained so that the relic could be quickly returned to its rightful place. About eighty years ago the skull was stolen but the thieves were so disturbed by the consequences of their actions that they quickly returned it. The Wardley relic is sometimes included in rather sensationalist lists of 'screaming skulls'.

Another tradition claims that the skull belonged not to the 'Martyr Monk' but Roger Downes, a member of the family that acquired the hall in 1601. It seems that he had been buried in the family vault in Wigan after being decapitated in a drunken brawl, variously located at Epsom Wells or London Bridge. The skull was allegedly sent to Roger's sister, although the macabre legend was disproved when his tomb was opened a century later and his skeleton found to be intact.

Returning to objective fact, the skull is generally thought to be that of St Ambrose Barlow. It was presumably brought to Wardley Hall shortly after his death and its being displayed either at Lancaster or Manchester. It was venerated as a precious relic for many years but, at some stage, was hidden in a wooden box, only being rediscovered in the mid-eighteenth century. Wardley had been ransacked by the army of 'Bonnie Prince Charlie' in 1745 and the tenants, falling on hard times, decided to turn to hand-loom weaving in a bid to raise money. This necessitated the adaption of the existing buildings and the resulting work led to the skull's discovery in a part of the house that had served as a secret Catholic chapel. Forensic research carried out in 1960 confirmed that the head had been violently severed from the body and that it belonged to a man of similar age and height to that of St Ambrose. Moreover the 'Martyr Monk' often celebrated

Mass at Wardley and was a kinsman of the Downes family. It seemed that science had confirmed what local tradition had long proclaimed.

Edward Barlow (to use the saint's baptismal name) was one of fourteen children and his father, Sir Alexander Barlow of Barlow Hall (near Manchester), was a faithful Catholic. The future martyr studied at the English College, Douai, where he presumably got to know the English Benedictines at St Gregory's (now at Downside Abbey). It was there that he eventually received the monastic habit and took the name 'Ambrose'. After his ordination in 1617, Barlow returned to his native Lancashire and became particularly associated with Morleys Hall, the home of Sir Thomas Tyldesley, a Catholic and (during the Civil War) a Royalist.

The saint lived simply and preferred to walk from place to place 'with a long staff on his back like a countryman' in order to celebrate Mass. Sometimes there were several Masses in a day and, unsurprisingly, he 'found himself very weary at night'. His was an attractive personality: 'our martyr was so mild, witty and cheerful in his conversation', wrote one contemporary, 'that, of all men, that ever I knew, he seemed to me the most lively to represent the spirit of Sir Thomas More'.

The threat of persecution always loomed over him. In 1628 Barlow visited St Edmund Arrowsmith on the eve of his execution and offered him the consolation of the sacraments. Shortly afterwards the monk had a dream in which Arrowsmith told him: 'I have suffered and now you will be made to suffer. Say little, for they will endeavour to take hold of you by your words'. Barlow knew that his own arrest and execution was highly likely, especially when, in 1641, Parliament (increasingly dominated by puritans) decreed that all priests should leave the country or else face the punishment for treason.

His hour finally came on Easter Sunday 1641, as he was celebrating Mass at Morleys. A local clergyman, described as an 'ardent Protestant', led a mob of some 400 people to the house. Barlow's friends offered him the chance to hide and escape but he refused to abandon his flock and so he was taken in chains to Lancaster. He languished in the castle for several months and found much comfort in reading Boethius (the sixth-century philosopher). When the jailer took this away from his, Barlow said: 'if you take this little book away, I will betake myself to that great book from which Boethius learned his wholesome doctrine, and that book you can never take away from me' — meaning the 'book' of mental prayer. By the time of his arrest, his health was failing and just a few months before he had suffered a stroke resulting in some paralysis on one side

Several months later he was put on trial and Barlow admitted that he was a 'Romish priest' who had been working in the Manchester area for over two decades. This effectively tied the judge's hands, for it seems he had some sympathy towards the ailing monk. On being condemned, Barlow was granted a private cell where he could properly prepare for his death. Interestingly, at the time of the trial, the English Benedictines met in General Chapter and elected Barlow as (titular) Cathedral Prior of Coventry—for Urban VIII had granted them the rights and privileges of their pre-Reformation confreres. It seems that Barlow was never given intelligence of this decision.

St Ambrose Barlow was hanged, drawn and quartered at Lancaster on 10 September 1641. He took a wooden cross that he had made to his death and before ascending the ladder walked round the gallows three times reciting the *Miserere*. He faced his barbaric death, we are told, with great constancy.

It is appropriate that his skull is such a visible presence at the very heart of the present-day diocese of Salford, watching the comings and goings at the bishop's house, inspiring those who now minister in his beloved Manchester and reminding them that the blood of the martyrs is the seed of the Church.

WHITBY, NORTH YORKSHIRE

St Hilda and her Abbey

'This is a lovely place', wrote Lucy Westenra in her diary. 'The little river, the Esk, runs through a deep valley, which broadens out as it comes near the harbour. A great viaduct runs across, with high piers, through which the view seems somehow further away than it really is . . . The houses of the old town . . . are all red-roofed, and seem piled up one over the other anyhow, like pictures we see of Nuremberg. Right over the town is the ruin of Whitby Abbey'. Little did she know that a mysterious and menacing presence would soon arrive in the Yorkshire fishing town from Transylvania and turn her life, and the lives of her nearest and dearest, upside down.

Ever since the Russian schooner, *The Demeter*, ran aground after a violent storm on Tate Hill Sands, Whitby has been intertwined with the Dracula legend. Modern visitors can indulge in night-time walking tours or the 'Dracula Experience', and see the house in the fashionable Crescent where Bram Stoker was inspired to write his novel. The town is a noted mecca for goths. Even the local gemstone, Whitby Jet, brought to especial popularity by the widowed Queen Victoria, confirms that this is a place associated with darkness.

Yet, Whitby is remembered in Christian history as a town of saints and the location of the great synod that decided on the dating of Easter, the quintessential festival of light. Those who visited Whitby in former days are likely to have headed to the great abbey, which still dominates the town and the surrounding countryside. It is an iconic location; Montalembert, in his great history of *The Monks of the West*, thought that 'of all the sites chosen by monastic architects, after that of Monte Cassino, I know none grander or more picturesque than that of Whitby', especially with 'the distant horizon of azure sea, viewed through the great hollow eyes of the ruinous arches'.

It was King Oswiu of Northumbria who founded the minster in 657, in thanksgiving for a decisive victory two years previously over the pagan Penda, King of Mercia. It was entrusted to the care of St Hilda (or Hild), a member of the royal family and, up until then, abbess of Hartlepool. Situated on the coast, it was one of a series of seventh-century communities founded by the seafaring Angles near river mouths. It soon became an important ecclesiastical centre.

The conversion of England was the result of indigenous Christians and the work of Celtic, Frankish and Roman missionaries. As a result, though one Church, there were differences in such matters as customs and calendars: so much so that, whereas King Oswiu celebrated Easter (and therefore observed Lent) according to the Celtic usage, his Kentish queen followed the Roman way. And so, a synod was called—by royal authority—at Whitby in 663, sometimes presented as a clash of cultures and a turning point when the 'English' Church was subjugated to the 'despotism' of Rome. It is true that the discussions were, at times, fiery. The Roman viewpoint was represented by the Frankish Bishop of Dorchester, St Agilbert, and St Wilfrid, then abbot of Ripon; St Colman of Lindisfarne put the arguments forward for the Celtic ways. It was claimed that 'the only people who stupidly contend against the whole world are those Irishmen and their partners in obstinancy, the Picts and the Scots, who inhabit only a portion of these, the two uttermost islands of the ocean'. The 'obstinate' Irish argued they followed in the tradition of St John, the Beloved Disciple, while the Romans cited the authority of St Peter; 'Peter is guardian of the gates of heaven', Oswiu surmised, 'and I shall not contradict him. I shall obey his commands in everything to the best of my ability; otherwise, when I come to the gates of heaven, there may be no one to open them, because he who holds the keys has turned away'. A simplistic argument, perhaps, as reported by Bede, but the result was increased unity in the English Church.

St Hilda was clearly a remarkable woman, presiding over a mixed community of both sexes, building bridges between conflicting factions, and promoting the work of one of England's first poets. According to tradition, St Cædmon was an aged and illiterate cowherd, with no aptitude for verse and song which were so essential in a pre-literate society. Out of embarrassment, he avoided the beer hall when people came together and the great epics were recited and sung. Then one night he had a dream and a mysterious man said: 'Cædmon, sing to me of the first creation'. His tongue was loosened and, after the abbess heard of his miraculous new gift, he joined the abbey community and, as he progressed in the study of Scripture, produced beautiful poetry in the English tongue. Thanks to St Hilda, it could be said, English literature was born, and the pagan tradition of heroic poetry Christianised.

St Hilda left a further legacy. The shops at Whitby are full not only of jet but fossils found in the local rocks, especially the ubiquitous ammonites—prehistoric ancestors of squid and octopus. In the absence of modern science, folklore tried to explain the presence of these strange forms: ammonite shells looked like coiled snakes, giving them the name 'snakestones'. Walter Scott explained the legend connecting the fossils with the Saxon saint in his poem *Marmion*:

> When Whitby's nuns exalting told,
> Of thousand snakes, each one
> Was changed into a coil of stone,
> When Holy Hilda pray'd:
> Themselves, without their holy ground,
> Their stony folds had often found.

Ammonites have become her heraldic symbol—as seen in the coat of arms of Whitby and her Oxford college—and a type of the fossil even bears her name, *Hildoceras bifrons*. To validate the tradition, Victorian tourists could buy specimens on which an enterprising local had carved a snake's head!

St Hilda's monastery was almost certainly destroyed by Viking raiders, and it is at this time that the Anglian settlement of Streaneshalh (literally 'Streane's headland') gained the Danish name of Whitby. It was re-established by the powerful Percy family (later earls of Northumberland) around 1090, the community being centred around Reinfrid, a former companion of the Conqueror who had entered the monastic life. The monks built the parish church of St Mary's close to the abbey, which is, in itself, well-worth climbing the famous 199 Steps to visit—a wonderful example of what Anglican interiors used to look like, with boxed pews, three-decker pulpit and little emphasis put on the altar table.

Modern tourists seem more concerned with finding Dracula's tomb in the graveyard or finding the spot where the vampire claimed his first victims: 'It seemed to me as though something dark stood behind the seat where the white figure shone, and bent over it. What it was, whether man or beast, I could not tell'. Nevertheless, Whitby is a place of light not darkness—the birthplace of English literature and, thanks to the synod and the witness of St Hilda, transfigured by the light of the Resurrection.

YORK, NORTH YORKSHIRE

The Many Pearls of York

The centre of York has never been completely touched by modernity: it is a city of medieval houses and alleys, of numerous churches and ecclesiastical foundations, all still encircled by its ancient walls. At its heart is the great Minster. There is much more besides: cats and chocolate, trains and tea (at Betty's, of course), pubs that proudly list their resident ghosts, and picturesque street names such as 'Whip-ma-wop-ma-gate' (apparently meaning 'neither one thing or the other').

The past is always present — the pilgrim only has to look around and, indeed, below. This is particularly apparent in the Minster undercroft, where Saxon and Norman stones mix with Roman remains. York owes its existence to a fort built around AD 70 by the famous ninth legion — whose mysterious disappearance from recorded history half a century later has led to many colourful theories and Rosemary Sutcliffe's popular novel, *The Eagle of the Ninth* (1954).

At the time Eboracum was founded, the legionaries were chiefly concerned with the threat posed by the rebellious Brigantes, the tribe or collection of tribes that dominated northern England at the time. Initially, relations had been cordial and their leader, Cartimandua, Britain's first-known queen, had been happy to co-operate. However, domestic politics soon intervened. Cartimandua divorced her husband, Venutius, who was replaced in her affections by his armour-bearer, Vellocatus. The furious Venutius responded by rebelling against his former lover and her imperial allies; the resulting upheaval lasted for well over a decade and York was born out of military necessity, a useful headquarters and depot for the emperor's troops, with links to the sea via the rivers Foss and Ouse.

The Minster itself is built upon the Roman basilica, the large public building at the heart of the fortress and probably at one time the grandest and tallest building in the north. An excavated Roman pillar stands in Minster Yard, giving a sense of its scale. Nearby is a modern statue of the Emperor Constantine, sitting on a throne and holding his sword. It takes us to the end of the Roman period and one of the great moments in the city's history. Constantine's father, Emperor Constantius, died in York in 306, after campaigning against the Picts, and it was here that Constantine was declared Emperor. After finishing some of his father's work in Britannia, he left for Trier. Few could have predicted what would happen next: how Constantine had a vision at the Milvian Bridge and introduced a policy of tolerance for the long-persecuted Christians; how he convoked the Council of Nicaea and built the churches of the Holy Sepulchre in Jerusalem and St John Lateran and St Peter's in Rome; and how he founded a new Rome on the Bosphorus, which bore his name—Constantinople. Here he ended his days, far away from Eboracum.

Christians were undoubtedly present in Roman York but they left little behind them, beyond a stone marked by the Chi-Rho (the symbol seen by Constantine in his vision) and an ivory plaque with what seems to be a Christian inscription. However, it would not be until the seventh century that York became an important ecclesiastical centre, by which time Romans had been replaced by Angles. St Paulinus, one of the disciples of St Augustine of Canterbury, arrived to preach the gospel, spurred on by St Gregory the Great, who had remembered the importance of Roman York and decided it should be an episcopal see. King Edwin of Northumbria was duly baptised in 627 and the first minster built, though exactly where is not known for certain. Over subsequent centuries it was rebuilt several times. From 866 the Norsemen arrived and Jorvik, as the city was now known, became the centre of Viking England. They seem quickly to have adopted the Christian Faith and their way of life is brought vividly alive at the Jorvik Viking Centre.

York has had several saintly archbishops: Paulinus, Chad, Bosa, John of Beverley, Wilfrid, and Oswald. But it was William Fitzherbert who won the most fame, even though he is now perhaps one of the least known of our medieval saints and hardly competes with Thomas Becket or Hugh of Lincoln. Born into the high echelons of Norman society, he served as treasurer at the Minster and Archdeacon of the East Riding, before being elected as archbishop. However, despite his reputation for holiness, his final years were overshadowed by a long-standing dispute over the validity of his appointment. The Cistercians in particular railed against him, led by St Bernard himself and Pope Eugenius II, who was one of their number. St William was deposed, moved to Winchester 'in exile' and then returned triumphantly to York; as he crossed the River Ouse the bridge collapsed but (miraculously) no-one was hurt. The story ends sordidly: in 1154, while celebrating Mass, this two-times archbishop drank the Precious Blood into which poison had been placed. He was canonised in 1226 and his remains moved successively to ever-more ornate shrines within the Minster. At the Reformation the shrine was carefully dismantled and hidden, hoping for better times: much of it can now be seen at the Yorkshire

Museum, while the saint's bones rest quietly where they once were venerated by medieval pilgrims.

York experienced the highs and lows of the Reformation period and in particular bears testament to the courage of Catholic women during these turbulent times. In households across the country it was the women who provided visiting priests with hospitality, arranged for the celebration of feasts, and instructed the children. Most celebrated is St Margaret Clitherow, whose little shrine can be found on the Shambles, where she once lived. A butcher's wife and mother of three, she was well-connected in the city and was imprisoned several times for her Catholicism. Refusing to plead in response to a charge of harbouring priests, she was pressed to death on 25 March 1586 (which happened to be Good Friday) on the Toll Booth at Ouse Bridge. This turned out to be a barbarous way of death, though it was hoped that a plea would be forced by the torture. Her 'ghostly father', John Mush, left a detailed account of her life and martyrdom, which was a key source for her eventual canonisation in 1970. It was part of a wider polemic, at the time, encouraging recusancy among Catholics—complete separation from the Church of England, whatever the consequences, rather than any sort of compromise. Clitherow made the ultimate sacrifice not only as a witness to the Faith but also to prevent her family and friends from having to testify against her.

The hand of this 'Pearl of York' is kept at the Bar Convent, where another remarkable lady is remembered—Mary Ward, a Yorkshire lady born the year before Clitherow's death. Her family were closely involved in the Gunpowder Plot—which led to the execution of two uncles—and she went overseas to join the Poor Clares. However, the contemplative life did not suit her and she refused to adhere to the norms expected of religious women of the time. She founded her own institute, dedicated to the education of girls; inspired by the work of the Jesuits, some called the sisters the 'galloping girls' or 'Jesuitesses'. She wrote: 'There is no such difference between men and women that women, may they not do great things? And I hope in God that it may be seen in time to come that women will do much'. The Institute of the Blessed Virgin Mary (now the Congregation of Jesus) still runs many schools and colleges around the world, including many in Germany. Ward died at Heworth Manor in 1645, at the time of the English Civil War, and was buried at Osbaldwick; her tombstone can be seen inside the church but no-one knows exactly where her body rests. She is present, however, at the Bar Convent, established for her Institute in 1686, England's oldest surviving convent and the location of an excellent museum.

The Minster is not the only cathedral in the city: standing almost opposite is St Wilfrid's, now the York Oratory. At the time of its opening in 1864, it was the pro-cathedral of the diocese of Beverley, inheriting this dignity from the church of St George's, which had only been built fourteen years before. In 1878, however, the diocese was split into two and the episcopal seats moved to Leeds and Middlesbrough.

Eyebrows must have been raised given the church's close proximity to the Minster, yet relations seem to have been respectful in this pre-ecumenical age. At the funeral at St Wilfrid's of its longstanding rector, Dr Joseph Render, in 1881, the minute bell of the Minster was rung in tribute. The same honour had been given to another Catholic missioner, Fr Thomas Billington, Vicar General to what was then the Yorkshire District, who died of typhus 'caught in the discharge of his ministerial duties' in 1847. More recently St Wilfrid's itself has become noted for its peal of ten bells, rung by an enthusiastic team of ringers. Along with the Minster, they bear witness to the city's long Christian history, stretching back to Constantine.

EPILOGUE

Our Final Pilgrimage

I decided to include these words as an epilogue. They were written after the death of my mother, Clare, on 26 February 2016 and are an attempt to reflect on the ultimate journey that we all will make.

There are many sacred places: shrines and sanctuaries, great basilicas and wayside chapels, tombs of saints and sites of apparitions. Pilgrims flock to these locations coach load by coach load, hoping to catch a glimpse of the divine, to touch the untouchable.

There are other places that are also holy but have no pilgrim's bureau, no souvenir shop and no schedule of processions and Masses. As I sat by my mother's death bed, I realised that our local hospital is one of these.

There was nothing very beautiful about the ward she was on. Out of the window there were stunning views of London in one direction and Heathrow and Windsor in the other, but all my mother could see, if she was aware of anything, was the blue curtain around her bed, the tape covering cracks on the window frames, and the white ceiling tiles. Nurses and consultants kept passing, looking sadly at the little family group huddled around her bed. The lady next to her kept talking to a non-existent man called 'Harry', telling him how her money had been taken. It was hard not to feel anger towards her for disturbing our peace, though I tried to recognise that her dementia deserved patience and compassion.

Despite all this, there was the sense of a great drama unfolding—a drama that we will all one day have to face. For most of us, it is in a ward like this that we will hesitantly approach the gates of God's Kingdom and meet our Maker. Clare was unconscious for most of her last day, her eyes three quarters closed, her mouth open, her breathing shallow. It seemed she already had one foot in eternity.

Books of Christian spirituality make much of the moment of death. Old prints show the death bed as a battlefield between good and bad angels, with all the paraphernalia of weighing scales and red forks, and with a priest sent into the front line with his sacramental weaponry. In my mother's case, death seemed to be a gradual process, a slipping away, a transition from one world to another. She was anointed and absolved several times and the sisters from her nursing home prayed by her side. This is what made her stuffy sixth floor ward into a holy place, an ante camera to everlasting life. Mum was reaching the end of her eighty-three year-long pilgrimage and she was coming into the presence of God. What holier, more solemn moment could there be?

I wondered how many people were preparing for the same divine encounter that day in the hospital. As I looked out of the window, I imagined sudden shafts of light illuminating the sky as people were gathered up, one by one, into the Father's arms. The veil between this world and the next was indeed very thin.

The moment of death came as I was having my dinner. It was probably easier for mum to make her final journey without me standing by, for what mother wants to leave her child behind? She was with a friend, who told me that she had suddenly opened her eyes and looked up. After a few minutes the breathing stopped. I saw her shortly afterwards. All the pain of the pneumonia and the effects of the devastating stroke she had suffered four and a half years ago had disappeared. She looked so much at peace, with a faint smile on her lips. The scene in that ward was as beautiful as any ornate chapel.

At times like these there is a strange interplay between time and eternity. We turn to the Lord in the present with our prayers, knowing that—in a way we don't fully understand—they will ease the passage into eternity. I held on to the belief that my mother had now entered a new stage in her existence; that where she is now is even more real than the life we lead in this world. We may no longer see her or hear her but we believe she has come into God's loving and merciful presence, and that she is now closer to us than ever before.

Our pilgrimages on earth are but reflections of a greater one that we have to make into eternity. Having traversed the highways and byways of this world, changing directions and retracing our steps many a time, enjoying beautiful vistas and climbing exhausting gradients, we reach the gateway to our final destination, to peace, light and love. This transition may linger over many years or come suddenly and without much warning. Our Faith allows us to approach these great mysteries with hope rather than fear. As we find God's presence in a thousand ways around us and keep focused on our journey, let us always strive for Heaven.

www.ingramcontent.com/pod-product-compliance
Lightning Source LLC
Chambersburg PA
CBHW022104150426
43195CB00008B/261